COSMOLOGIES OF MENTAL HEALTH

Bloomsbury Advances in Religious Studies

Series Editors: Amy L. Allocco, Bettina E. Schmidt, and Steven Sutcliffe

Founding Editors: James Cox and Peggy Morgan

Bloomsbury Advances in Religious Studies publishes cutting-edge research with a particular focus on new and emerging scholars and approaches. The series draws on anthropological, ethnographic, historical, sociological and textual methods, amongst others. Topics are diverse, but each publication is designed to integrate theoretical analysis with empirical data. In this way, the series refreshes the interdisciplinary agenda in new evidence-based studies of 'religion'.

A New Paradigm of Spirituality and Religion, Mary Catherine Burgess
A Phenomenology of Indigenous Religions, James L. Cox
A Sense of Belonging, Stephen Friend
Acute Religious Experiences, Richard Saville-Smith
American Evangelicals, Ashlee Quosigk
Becoming Buddhist, Glenys Eddy
Charismatic Healers in Contemporary Africa, edited by Sandra Fancello and Alessandro Gusman
Community and Worldview among Paraiyars of South India, Anderson H. M. Jeremiah
Conceptions of the Afterlife in Early Civilizations, Gregory Shushan
Contemporary Western Ethnography and the Definition of Religion, Martin D. Stringer
Cultural Blending in Korean Death Rites, Chang-Won Park
Free Zone Scientology, Aled Thomas
Individualized Religion, Claire Wanless
Levinas, Messianism and Parody, Terence Holden
Neo-Spiritual Aesthetics, Lina Aschenbrenner
One Nation, Many Faiths, Liam T. Sutherland
Orthodox Christianity, New Age Spirituality and Vernacular Religion, Eugenia Roussou
Post-Materialist Religion, Mika T. Lassander
Redefining Shamanisms, David Gordon Wilson
Reform, Identity and Narratives of Belonging, Arkotong Longkumer
Religion and the Discourse on Modernity, Paul-François Tremlett
Religion and the Inculturation of Human Rights in Ghana, Abamfo Ofori Atiemo
Religion as a Conversation Starter, Ina Merdjanova and Patrice Brodeur
Religion, Material Culture and Archaeology, Julian Droogan

Rethinking 'Classical Yoga' and Buddhism, Karen O'Brien-Kop
Secular Assemblages, Marek Sullivan
Spirits and Trance in Brazil, Bettina E. Schmidt
Spirit Possession and Trance, edited by Bettina E. Schmidt and Lucy Huskinson
Spiritual Tourism, Alex Norman
Spirituality and Alternativity in Contemporary Japan, Ioannis Gaitanidis
The Appropriation of Native American Spirituality, Suzanne Owen
The Critical Study of Non-Religion, Christopher R. Cotter
The Dynamic Cosmos, edited by Diana Espírito Santo and Matan Shapiro
The Globalization of Hesychasm and the Jesus Prayer, Christopher D. L. Johnson
The Innateness of Myth, Ritske Rensma
The Problem with Interreligious Dialogue, Muthuraj Swamy
Theology and Religious Studies in Higher Education, edited by D. L. Bird and Simon G. Smith
UFOs, Conspiracy Theories and the New Age, David G. Robertson

COSMOLOGIES OF MENTAL HEALTH

Pentecostal Prayer Camps and Indigenous Knowledge of Healing Mental Illness in Ghana

Francis Ethelbert Kwabena Benyah

BLOOMSBURY ACADEMIC
LONDON • NEW YORK • OXFORD • NEW DELHI • SYDNEY

BLOOMSBURY ACADEMIC
Bloomsbury Publishing Plc, 50 Bedford Square, London, WC1B 3DP, UK
Bloomsbury Publishing Inc, 1359 Broadway, New York, NY 10018, USA
Bloomsbury Publishing Ireland, 29 Earlsfort Terrace, Dublin 2, D02 AY28, Ireland

First published in Great Britain 2026

Cover design: Jade Barnett

Library of Congress Control Number: 2025950167

ISBN: HB: 978-1-3504-6347-9
ePDF: 978-1-3504-6348-6
eBook: 978-1-3504-6349-3

Series: Bloomsbury Advances in Religious Studies

Typeset by Newgen KnowledgeWorks Pvt. Ltd., Chennai, India

In memory of my late grandmother, Elizabeth Afful, affectionately known as Aunty Aba Donkor of Lower Dixcove, I wish to express my profound gratitude for the time we shared and for her pivotal role in introducing me to the healing camps of the Twelve Apostles Church during the formative years of my life.

CONTENTS

FIGURE

TABLE

LIST OF ABBREVIATIONS

WHO – World Health Organizations
MHA – Mental Health Authority of Ghana
CoP – Church of Pentecost
IPA – Interpretative Phenomenological Analysis
TFHs – Traditional and Faith Healers
AICs – African Indigenous/Independent Churches
GPTHA – Ghana Psychic and Traditional Healing Association
GHS – Ghana Health Service
CHAG – Christian Health Association of Ghana
PCG – Presbyterian Church of Ghana

PREFACE

Growing up as a young boy in Dixcove, a rural town situated within the Ahanta West Municipality of the Western Region of Ghana during the late 1990s, I became acquainted with various religious groups. These groups encompassed Western historic mission-established churches, African Independent Churches such as the Twelve Apostles Church – commonly referred to as Nackabah – alongside Akan traditional worship and its associated practices. My maternal grandmother was an active member of the Twelve Apostles Church in Dixcove before later joining the Christ Apostolic Church. She made significant contributions by assisting the prophets in the healing of individuals who were sent to the healing camps commonly referred to as the 'gardens'. Although my grandmother was qualified to establish her own healing camp after spending a considerable number of years in the ministry of the Twelve Apostles Church, she declined the opportunity for familial reasons. As a young boy and as part of the social fabric of the community, I accompanied my grandmother to several of her meetings at the healing camp. Despite my young age, attending the camp familiarized me with its operations and allowed me to witness aspects of the healing process. Furthermore, my family's involvement in the activities of the Twelve Apostles Church extends beyond my grandmother. One of my uncles, Mr Henry Gladstone Nerbah Nathan, was a prominent member of the Twelve Apostles Church in the Western Region. Nathan was interviewed by Baëta for his classic work on spiritual churches in Ghana and is credited with the statement, 'We are here to heal', when asked about the mission of the church (Baëta 1962: 15).

Dixcove is renowned for its artisan fishing economy, attracting many fishermen and individuals involved in fishing from neighbouring villages and towns, as well as beyond. Some fisherfolk also travel with their canoes to the neighbouring country of Côte d'Ivoire for artisanal fishing on a seasonal basis. School-age children who drop out of school due to poverty, poor academic performance or various other reasons are sometimes drawn to the fishing industry and consequently become fishermen. This was the case for Joe Adams (pseudonym), who was my childhood friend while growing up in Dixcove. Adams, my cousins and I lived in the same neighbourhood and attended the same primary school. He became so close to my family that he occasionally spent days or weeks at our house. After I left for the city to continue my education, Adams remained in Dixcove and completed junior high school. For reasons unknown to me, Adams was unable to further his education and subsequently became a fisherman. Upon my return to Dixcove, I later inquired about him, only to be informed that he had travelled to Côte d'Ivoire with the canoe he had been working on for their seasonal fishing harvest.

A few months later, upon his return to Dixcove, Adams began to exhibit unconventional behavioural traits that led those around him to believe that something was amiss. As time passed, his condition deteriorated, and he began displaying mild symptoms of what is locally referred to as 'abodam' (madness). Concerned about his situation, Adams's family sought medical assistance to restore his health. It is noteworthy that Dixcove is home to the largest district hospital in the Ahanta West Municipality, thereby providing individuals living in the area with substantial exposure to, and familiarity with, biomedical care. This community is also knowledgeable about other local remedies, including traditional forms of healing and faith healing due to the active presence of various religious traditions, as mentioned earlier.

After visiting the hospital, Adams's condition persisted, prompting friends and other members of the neighbourhood to encourage his family to explore alternative sources of assistance beyond the hospital. Following consultations with various healing practitioners, rumours began to circulate that Adams's former boss, with whom he had travelled to Côte d'Ivoire to engage in fishing, had attempted to utilize Adams and another individual for ritual sacrifices to bolster his fishing business. It was alleged that the ritual process backfired, resulting in the death of the other individual while Adams survived, attributed to his strong *sunsum* (spirit). Nevertheless, it was speculated that his condition might have been exacerbated by the ritual activities. Another rumour suggested that Adams had stolen something and, upon inquiry, had refused to confess. His refusal to confess reportedly led the victim to invoke a curse upon him, which was believed to have resulted in his 'madness'. As these rumours proliferated, Adams's condition worsened, leading his family to take him to a prayer camp. After several weeks at the prayer camp, he escaped and returned home. When I later inquired about him, I was informed that his situation had not improved, and the family had to relocate him.

Despite the background knowledge I had about healing camps and my familiarity with the story of Adams and prayer camps, I did not take an interest in the topic of prayer camps until the later years of my life when I started reading about the activities of prayer camps, following my engagement with online articles and blogs regarding the role and involvement of healing camps in mental healthcare in Ghana. I could connect the issues with my background experiences on the events that had somewhat shaped my perspectives on how society deals with mental illness. My motivation was further intensified upon discovering that the majority of existing scholarship on the relationship between prayer camps and mental health has emerged from disciplines such as anthropology, clinical psychology and psychology. This prompted me to pursue an interest from the perspective of religious studies, with the aim of examining the contribution of religion to the discourse on prayer camps and mental health in Ghana. The absence of a religious perspective was significant to me, as prayer camps are religious institutions whose activities and modus operandi warrant examination within a religious studies framework, in conjunction with other disciplines. This motivation culminated in my research on the topic for my doctoral dissertation at Åbo Akademi University, Turku, Finland.

The focus of my doctoral research was on the lived experiences of individuals who have received treatment at prayer camps for their mental illnesses and the importance of the healing procedures to their well-being. Beyond the religious and spiritual dimensions of the healing procedures or rituals, the work also explored the media and human rights dimensions associated with the healing of persons with mental illnesses at prayer camps. The findings of my doctoral research were published as stand-alone articles, which were subsequently compiled into an article-based dissertation. Portions of the data collected during fieldwork have been utilized in this book, and I have also employed some of the data in my analysis herein. It is important to note that this book contains work that has already been published elsewhere. A section of Chapter 7 has previously been published under the title 'Prayer Camps, Healing, and the Management of Chronic Mental Illness in Ghana: A Qualitative Phenomenological Inquiry' in Andrew R. Hatala and Kerstin Roger (eds), *Spiritual, Religious, and Faith-Based Practices in Chronicity: An Exploration of Mental Wellness in Global Context* (London: Routledge, 2022), 173–94. Additionally, part of Chapter 8 has been published as 'Healing and Mental Illness in Ghana: Why Prayer Camps in Ghana are Sometimes Alternatives to Psychiatric Hospitals', in *Temenos—Nordic Journal for the Study of Religion*, 59 (1), 101–23, https://doi.org/10.33356/temenos.109270. Other sections of the introduction, particularly on methodology, as well as portions of Chapters 1 and 2, were also included in the 'Kappa' I submitted for my article-based doctoral thesis at Åbo Akademi University. All of these works have been extensively revised for this publication.

The main argument of the book is that the understanding of mental illness in Ghana particularly among the Akan is profoundly influenced by cultural world-views. As individuals are shaped by the surrounding cultural perspectives during their socialization processes, such views often inform their interpretation of existing realities, including health and illness. Among Christians, and more specifically Pentecostals, this world-view is frequently evident during healing and deliverance practices for various illnesses, including mental illness. Consequently, the Akan interpretation of mental illness is recontextualized within the Pentecostal healing environment, such as prayer camps. For successful healing outcomes for individuals afflicted with mental illness, recognition of this world-view and the application of relevant techniques, including deliverance at healing camps, are essential to address any perceived supernatural realities associated with the illness. Additionally, while supernatural explanations predominantly shape the understanding of mental illness, there are also non-religious or spiritual factors, such as biological, environmental and social influences, that are acknowledged, thereby highlighting the dualistic nature of the Akan world-view.

The following conclusions are drawn: first, to effectively address mental health issues in a context such as Ghana, it is imperative to seriously consider the cultural and religious world-views that shape the people's approach to matters of health and healing. Second, while societies modernize and adopt new innovations in healthcare technologies, other dimensions of the framework that define people's social and cultural lives, such as indigenous knowledge systems, particularly in healthcare, must be recognized and further developed to support scientific approaches. In this context, the concept of personhood as articulated in relation to healthcare can be explored within new models. Third, there is a need for resources to be dedicated to strengthening collaborative efforts among different stakeholders, including faith-based healers and biomedical service providers, to offer complementary and holistic healthcare to individuals requiring such interventions. This approach not only meets healthcare needs but also yields effective outcomes, as the services provided address both the medical, social, religious, spiritual and emotional dimensions of ill health. Fourth, the call for the decolonization of psychiatry in contexts such as Ghana can be realized through intersectoral partnerships, enabling parties involved in collaborative efforts to learn from one another through appropriate channels that respect the perspectives, authority, power and rights of each stakeholder engaged in this work. Finally, effective education, advocacy and oversight are essential in mitigating the entrenched beliefs and abuses often associated with the activities of prayer camps.

This book makes a valuable contribution to the discourse surrounding mental health-seeking experiences, not only in Ghana but also across Africa and other regions of the Global South. It offers fresh insights into the role of religion and culture in mental healthcare and contributes to the development of theories and contextual epistemologies that explain and guide the processes of care and support for individuals living with mental illnesses across Ghana, Africa and beyond. Specifically, this material is essential for experts in global mental health who seek to understand the practices, approaches and treatments of mental health issues in Africa. It contributes to ongoing debates regarding the role of religion and culture in global mental health and deepens academic reflection on the intersection of these fields.

Essentially, a work of this nature cannot be completed without the support of others; thus, it is appropriate for me to express my gratitude to all who have contributed in various ways to this project. Indeed, in a project of this magnitude, where every single assistance and contribution is equally significant, it is challenging for me to determine whom to mention and whom to omit. I appreciate all the support I have received from anyone who has made this possible. I would like to thank all the participants who took part in this study. Their experiences and knowledge shared during fieldwork have been instrumental in bringing this project to fruition. I am grateful to my funders at Åbo Akademi University, who not only sponsored my field trips to Ghana but also covered the open access fees to ensure this book is accessible to all upon publication. I also wish to thank the Polin Institute at Åbo Akademi University, which provided funding at various stages. My special thanks go to the Overseas Ministries Study Centre, Princeton Theological Seminary, New Jersey, United States, for awarding me the Lamin Research Prize. The grant was instrumental in the final data collection stage. I extend my gratitude to Måns Broo and Aminkeng Atabong Alemanji, my supervisors during my doctoral studies at Åbo Akademi University, and I would also like to thank the Centre of African Studies and the Centre for Privacy Studies at the University of Copenhagen for granting me the time and space to complete the final phase of this project. Special thanks are due to centre leaders Karen Jenny Lauterbach and Mette Birkedal Bruun for their support whenever I needed to be away. There are many others who offered significant assistance, whom space does not allow me to mention. I hope that the publication of this book will bring satisfaction to all of you.

INTRODUCTION

Religion permeates almost all aspects of healthcare in Africa. In Ghana, in particular, the influence of religion and/or religious world-views with regard to health can be observed in every facet of healthcare delivery services. At the institutional level, several religious bodies, including churches and Islamic organizations, provide healthcare services. Indigenous healthcare providers also warrant mention. Certain religious bodies offer logistical support to facilitate the delivery of healthcare (Walker 2022). At the personal level, the role of religion becomes evident in the ways individuals' world-views and beliefs shape their understanding and approach to seeking healthcare (Olsen and Sargent 2017; Janzen 1978). Indeed, the intersection of religion and healthcare has remained a principal focus of research in several studies in Africa (Kilonzo and Chitando 2025; Fancello and Gusman 2022; Lloyd et al. 2024).

The primary motivation of this book is to demonstrate how individuals' culture, religious world-views and beliefs shape their understanding and interpretation of illness and their approach to healthcare, particularly concerning mental illness and other ailments in general. A pertinent question that arises when discussing the nexus between religion and health in Africa is how religion and spirituality is often associated with health in various African societies. The answer to this question is that, in Africa, a person is viewed as a relational being whose body, mind and spirit are conditioned by critical relationships with diverse entities within the cosmos and their environment (Grillo et al. 2019; Pobee 2001; Westerlund 2006). These entities include family members (both living and deceased), malevolent and benevolent beings such as witches, God, deities and other human agents, such as diviners, magicians and *juju* practitioners, who are believed to possess the power to affect the human body through supernatural means. To ensure good health and well-being, one must maintain a harmonious relationship with the environment and the spirit world. In other words, 'ailments and afflictions are understood to be the result of a disturbance in this web of relations' (Grillo et al., 2019: 178). From this perspective, illness is viewed as a spiritual or moral dilemma; consequently, symptoms cannot be treated as a medical matter alone (Grillo et al. 2019).

This perspective of affliction as a holistic matter requiring spiritual intervention transcends all the major religious traditions in Africa, including Christianity, Islam and traditional African religions. Mbiti (1970) has emphasized that in

African societies, disease and misfortune are religious experiences, necessitating a religious approach for their resolution. In most instances, human suffering is deemed part of the evil strategies employed by an enemy or an angry spirit; thus, suffering associated with illness is attributed to the devil or evil forces, offending parties and broken relationships. In this context, 'moving to alleviate misfortune may entail addressing questions of accountability by identifying a possible agent and adjusting relationships through words, exchange, or ritual action' (Whyte 2018: 167). The ritual action may involve invoking spirit beings to restore healing, seeking forgiveness from offended parties (both human and divine) to mend broken relationships as well as utilizing herbs and other elements deemed potent for such actions. The rituals are performed by religious functionaries who are trained specialists in various healing methods. Among the Akan, for instance, the practice of medicine, health and healing is the preserve of herbalists, midwives and traditional priests or priestesses, referred to in the local parlance as *odunsinni* (herbalist), *awogyefo* (traditional birth attendant) and *ɔkomfo* (traditional priest). These practitioners have historically been known to possess curative powers in treating illnesses (both natural and supernatural) in contemporary Ghanaian traditional societies.[1]

Alongside the role provided by traditional religious functionaries in medical care, Western medicine emerged through the work and activities of colonial administrations and Christian missionary groups tasked with spreading the gospel while simultaneously providing care for the sick. Indeed, the efforts of missionary groups in healthcare provision as part of their holistic ministry have served as the foundation for several faith-based health programmes and facilities catering to numerous remote communities in Ghana and other parts of Africa where governments have been unable to provide such services.

Historically, as faith-based healing centres, prayer camps can be considered part of the legacies of colonial missionary enterprises. Currently, there are several hundred of them dispersed across the country. In every city, town and village, one is likely to find one or two prayer camps. The popularity and appeal of prayer camps as healing centres resonate with the majority of Ghanaians because they have become an integral part of Ghana's religious culture, often replacing the traditional healing shrines that previously fulfilled similar roles (Onyinah 2012; Asamoah-Gyadu 2007).[2] Contemporary Christian prayer camps in Ghana respond to indigenous traditional spiritual quests that previously directed individuals to traditional shrines. In this sense, they resonate strongly with the country's indigenous cultures and maintain continuity with the health, healing and recovery heritage of the people.

The reinvention of prayer camps as indigenous healing cults and their implications for modern healing practices and healthcare in Ghana have rarely been examined in the growing literature on Ghanaian Pentecostal studies and, more broadly, in the intersection of religion and healthcare. To date, there has not been a single textbook that extensively addresses the issue of prayer camps and mental healthcare in Ghana; this book aims to fill this gap in the literature by closely examining the social and cultural realities that shape the understanding of mental illness and the therapeutic interventions deemed appropriate and efficacious by those affected. In doing so, the book maps healing practices for mental health patients[3] in Ghana's prayer camps within traditional Akan indigenous frameworks and illustrates how such practices reflect the surrounding local cultural understanding and common-sense interpretations of mental illness. The Mental Health Authority of Ghana (MHA 2018) has underscored how culture and religion influence the value societies place on mental health, the understanding of causative factors, the management of conditions, the extent of stigma and discrimination, access to services and pathways to care. This book significantly highlights how these factors manifest in the lived experiences of individuals with mental illness who have undergone treatment at prayer camps in Ghana. The book underscores the need for substantial attention to be devoted to religious institutions, such as prayer camps, which seek to provide health relief, community and social support for individuals in low-income countries with limited healthcare resources, particularly for those living with mental illness.

Cosmologies of Mental Health does not purport to answer every question pertaining to prayer camps and mental health in Ghana. However, it offers a comprehensive analysis and overview of the contemporary landscape regarding prayer camps and their role in providing both faith healing and spiritual and medical care to individuals who seek their services in Ghana. It explores the lived experiences of individuals who have received treatment at selected prayer camps in Ghana. The discourse emphasizes the importance of prayer camps in delivering services that have been neglected by the state while simultaneously addressing a need or void inadvertently left by state actors due to their conflicting roles with scientific and modern medical culture. Furthermore, it aims to respond to the challenges surrounding the operation of prayer camps and the competing views on them as healing centres for individuals with mental health issues.

The main question explored in the book is: What are the perceived causes of mental illness for participants at prayer camps, and what do participants consider therapeutically effective in the treatment of these perceived causes? In answering this question, *Cosmologies of Mental Health* analyses the lived experiences of individuals who have received treatment at prayer camps in Ghana. In so doing, the book examines the influence of traditional or Akan[4] cultural world-views on the conceptions and perceived causes of mental illness among supplicants at prayer camps. Furthermore, it examines the methods employed to address these perceived causes within the healing rituals for individuals seeking treatment at these camps. Thus, *Cosmologies of Mental Health* examines how surrounding cultural world-views shape or influence people's aetiological explanations, particularly for mental illnesses, and how these explanations influence help-seeking behaviours for participants who utilize prayer camps.

It is important to emphasize that whether one identifies as a Christian or not, he or she is a cultural being, having been born, raised and socialized in a society that possesses its own cultural values, ways of life and approaches to understanding and addressing issues, including health and healing. In many ways, individuals are encrusted by cultural and religious world-views that intertwine as part of the process of their socialization. Therefore, it is crucial to acknowledge that the Akan Pentecostal Christian is, first and foremost, a cultural being who has been socialized within a specific cultural framework that influences his or her way of being, thinking and acting. While I am acutely aware of and acknowledge the tension of being a Christian while simultaneously being a person of culture, these social realities will inevitably influence the ways one practices his or her Christianity and behavioural actions when illness arises.

Although religion, spirituality and faith healing are prominent in addressing issues of mental illness for many Ghanaians, the degree of awareness regarding the importance of religion, culture and spirituality in psychiatry appears to remain low, and achieving consensus among professionals remains challenging. In some instances, attention to aspects of religion and spirituality in the care of mental health patients is contingent upon the interests of individual professionals. This book aims to raise awareness among practitioners about the growing necessity to consider cultural and religious issues in mental healthcare in Ghana. While I do not claim expertise in psychiatry, the conceptual clarity provided in this book regarding the definition of mental illness from Akan traditional frameworks will be beneficial not only to clinicians and healthcare practitioners within their fields but also for the welfare of the patients they endeavour to treat. Consequently, this book advocates for an important dialogue between technocrats in the field of mental healthcare and religious practitioners.

The importance of understanding cosmology in mental healthcare

A growing body of literature on global mental health and transcultural psychiatry has underscored the significant role of culture in mental health and psychiatric practices (Moreira-Almeida et al. 2021; Kpanake 2018; Kirmayer et al. 2015). One of the primary components of cultural identity, particularly among populations in the Global South, is religion and spirituality. The importance of these elements in mental healthcare has not gone unnoticed by professionals in the field of psychiatry (Ofori-Atta et al. 2018; Kirmayer et al. 2013; Maercker et al. 2019). Consequently, several initiatives, including scholarly contributions and practical resources, are being developed to enhance practitioners' understanding of appropriate diagnoses and interventions in mental healthcare (Kirmayer et al. 2013; Verhagen 2017; Lewis-Fernandez et al. 2017).

These initiatives indicate a recognition of the diversity of cultures and worldviews, particularly in relation to the understanding of mental health. There is a pressing need to address the differences that arise from these diversities through methodologies and interventions that are culturally salient and meaningful. A critical aspect of these interventions is the necessity of understanding individuals' explanations for illnesses through their cosmological lenses. This phenomenon is universally applicable, regardless of a nation's advancement in medical technologies. For instance, Canadian psychiatrist Laurence Kirmayer has been a leading advocate for the incorporation of cultural considerations into psychiatric practice, alongside the influential work of scholars such as Arthur Kleinman and others (Kleimann 1980; Kirmayer 2025, 2007, 2004). A substantial body of scholarship has emphasized how indigenous African world-views regarding mental illness resonate with traditional cosmologies in various global contexts (Ratele 2019; Ayinde et al. 2021). This is exemplified in the Akan culture of Ghana, where understandings of mental illness and other determinants of mental health issues are deeply embedded in traditional cosmological frameworks (Ayim-Aboagye 2006).

In this context, the term *cosmology* is employed to refer to the world-views of individuals, including their thought patterns and systems (see also Adogame 2022). These world-views are not formed in isolation; rather, they develop over time through cultural practices, historical events, beliefs about nature – such as the universe and the environment – and socialization processes involving interactions with various cultures and social groups outside one's primary culture. Adogame (2022: 78) has emphasized that 'local cosmologies are themselves dynamic, complex, and variegated' in response to external cultural contacts, influences, syntheses, interethnic trade, marriage and migratory trends. Konadu (2007: 38), drawing upon the ideas of Akoto and Akoto (1999), defines cosmology as 'a system or body of thought rising out of a people's history and culture that addresses issues of reality and creation, truth and value, meaning, and process, and that people's place in creation'. Regarding the central role of creation and individuals' understanding, interaction and relationship with it, Adogame (2022: 77) argues that in most African communities, delineating the anatomy of a people's cosmology involves classifying and understanding 'the significance of mythical images and religious imaginaries concerning the cosmos, the origin and structure of the universe, how humans relate in and to the cosmos, and how and to what extent their thoughts and actions are shaped by it'.

Among the Akan and several other African communities, the structure of the religious cosmos is largely influenced by the understanding of the spirit entities that inhabit the universe and their relationships with humans, as well as by folk myths, proverbs, music and so on. Describing Akan cosmological views entails discussing how the Akan live and act within an understanding of the universe and the environment, which is believed to contain spirit beings (both malevolent and benevolent), including the Supreme Being or God (*Nyankopon*), deities, ancestors and witches, among others. The belief in the existence of these spirit beings is prominent, and they are thought to affect every facet of human life – both positively and negatively – depending on one's relationship with them. The articulation of cosmological views is often demonstrated when addressing existential issues, such as illness, and other difficulties in life, whether social or economic.

In this book, I engage in an extensive discussion of Akan views of the human person and unpack how their conceptions of the human person and its relationship with the cosmos have implications for how the Akan conceptualize health and illness. The concepts of health and illness are interconnected with other beliefs about the organization of the universe (Foster 1976). In essence, the medical ideologies of a culture are not separate from the prevailing cultural ideologies; rather, they are integral to how individuals comprehend aspects of their environment (Helman 1984). Indeed, Csordas (1997: 165) argues that 'how evil spirits are conceptualized as forces, beings, or entities offers insight not only into the structure of a cosmology, but into the structure of the behavioural environment that evil spirits share with humans'. Among the Akan, for example, the beliefs and rituals associated with spiritual forces constitute a distinctively indigenous pattern of religious thought and action regarding health and illness.

To understand how people construct and perceive social realities such as health and illness, it is essential to consider their cosmological views, which shape the construction of illness narratives and the ways they address these narratives. This process is not uniform; even when particular symptoms of illness are universally recognized, illness narratives are defined and shaped by local or indigenous epistemologies. The cognitive understanding of an illness situation influences the ritual actions and performances invoked when such knowledge is revealed through consultation with appropriate channels or individuals, such as a diviner, priest or prophet at a healing centre or prayer camp.

Among the Akan of Ghana (as well as in other parts of Africa), as demonstrated throughout the discussion in this book in the context of prayer camps, individuals often resort to divination when confronted with illness, danger or misfortune, particularly when the causes of these afflictions remain inexplicable. The objective of consulting appropriate mediums, such as the *okomfo* (traditional priest) or prophet at a prayer camp, is to find solutions to illnesses, especially when the illness defies scientific treatment, although this is not always the case. In many African communities, one of the primary functions of a priest is to provide healing, and members of religious communities expect their leaders to fulfil such roles during times of illness (Lartey 1986). In local African communities, those who assume special ritual roles or function as healers typically undergo a period of specialized medical training lasting no more than three years (Ayim-Aboagye 2006; Adogame 2022).

The recourse to various therapeutic interventions in addressing illnesses, such as mental illness, as illustrated in this book, reveals the diversity of world-views regarding the causes of mental illness. The variations in the interpretation of illness stem from differing understandings of the cosmos, human relations and what constitutes a flourishing life. The argument presented in *Cosmologies of Mental Health* posits that the understanding of the cosmos and conceptions of health and illness differ from one society or community to another, leading to distinct interpretations of illnesses. Consequently, individuals' understandings of illnesses cannot be assumed to be uniform, even when similarities in symptoms exist. In the case of mental illness in Ghana, *Cosmologies of Mental Health* maintains that the understanding and interpretation of mental illness are largely shaped by local cosmologies, which in turn influence help-seeking behaviours. The practices of healing at prayer camps, particularly in relation to mental illness, are particularly appealing to the populace because they are framed within traditional interpretations of healing, thereby enhancing their influence.

Understanding the culture and cosmology of a given people is crucial for providing holistic healthcare. Societies that neglect these significant cultural aspects in the face of modern scientific advancements risk failing to deliver appropriate medical care that is meaningful, acceptable and symbolic to the people. Indeed, Konadu (2007: 37) argues that 'if culture and cosmology determine or are closely linked to health care systems and all illness and healing are culturally interpreted, then the recent call' for an integrated approach to illness and health matters cannot overlook the challenges posed by opposing world-views or ways of making sense of the world. In other words, a proper understanding of the nature and dynamics of African medicine and healing necessitates a firm grasp of a people's cosmology (Konadu 2007). Not to get far ahead of the conclusion, I argue in the concluding chapter that culture and cosmology are significant not only for understanding illness narratives but also as integral components of the frameworks to be considered in the decolonization of psychiatry.

Material and methods

This study employed interpretative phenomenological analysis (IPA) to investigate the lived experiences of individuals concerning their perceived causes of mental illness and the role of prayer camps in aiding their recovery (Smith and Osborn 2015). IPA was utilized during interviews to elicit participants' views regarding their experiences with healing rituals at prayer camps, including their perceptions of these rituals and practices such as Bible studies, counselling, fasting and prayer, and how these contributed to or facilitated their recovery. This investigation also encompassed shared experiences within the camp as a community. This methodological approach was essential to highlight the participants' own shared experiences in contrast to an etic construction of the camps, thereby avoiding the risk of making unsubstantiated claims.

The application of IPA was significant for two primary reasons. First, the approach was instrumental in addressing prior scientific hypotheses or abstract conceptualizations regarding the camps. In other words, the methodology enabled me to relinquish some of the preconceived notions I had formed about the camps prior to the commencement of my study. The prayer camps in Ghana have been the subject of considerable criticism, and I had developed certain perceptions based on my readings of these critiques. This allowed me to set aside some of those preconceived ideas about the camps.

Second, the dynamic nature of the methodology ensured my active involvement in the process, allowing me to comprehend the participants' own experiences. For instance, while participants shared their experiences related to healing, the methodology also provided the opportunity to derive implications from these accounts, a process that Smith and Osborn (2015) describe as an 'interpretative activity and/or the hermeneutic development of phenomenology'. IPA is 'intellectually connected to hermeneutics and theories of interpretation' (Smith and Osborn 2015: 26). However, various approaches to interpretation exist, and in this study, I employed an 'empathetic hermeneutic with a questioning hermeneutic' (Smith and Osborn 2015: 26). This signifies that while there was an effort to understand participants' healing experiences through their personal narratives, there were also moments of personal reflection on the participants' experiences. My reflections were informed by their explanatory models regarding their experiences of mental illness. These reflections were conducted within the broader framework of cultural relativism and how this influenced help-seeking behaviours. This enabled me to derive meaning from some of the participants' shared experiences. In other words, IPA provided me with the opportunity to interpret and elucidate the participants' accounts of their situations and the meanings they ascribed to them.

It is crucial to acknowledge that questions may arise regarding the phenomenological approach, particularly concerning claims related to the religious experiences of phenomena such as prayer and fasting (McCutcheon 2001; Chitando 2005; Blum 2012; Wiebe 1999; Heinämaa 2022; Davis 2019). In the context of this study, for instance, the inquiry would centre on how individuals or visitors at prayer camps perceive their relationship with God, how this relationship is experienced and in what forms. In this context, the interpretation of religious consciousness and experience would involve exploring the implications of these experiences concerning rituals of prayer, fasting and other activities such as worship and the reading of the Bible. This does not imply that the investigator must necessarily endorse the claims made by the religious subjects regarding their attitudes, beliefs and practices but rather seeks to interpret, through empirical evidence, the meanings such practices hold for the religious subjects.

In some instances, readers might perceive my views on certain reported findings in the study as uncritical. This is largely because I adopt an empathetic stance that aims to understand the perspectives and logic of my participants as a useful tool for critically analysing taken-for-granted assumptions and often unforeseen implications of their experiences at prayer camps. Despite this stance, readers should remember that 'methodological empathy does not imply sympathetic feelings of agreement with the subjects under study, but rather an effort to see things from the perspective of those studied and to step outside that perspective to analyse broader causal and contextual frameworks that sometimes complement and at other times challenge the interpretations made by our subjects or participants of the study' (Brown 2011: 6). For instance, to comprehend the participants' healing practices – practices that often require considerable effort and commitment – one does not necessarily have to concur with participants regarding their views on the causes of illness (or mental illness in this case) and their explanations regarding the effectiveness of non-medical healing methods. What is crucial is that 'we do listen to them carefully, appreciating that their beliefs, practices, and experiences may operate with a different logic from that of biomedicine yet be completely reasonable' while also acknowledging that certain aspects of these practices may conflict with biomedicine and even with certain orthodox religious practices (see McGuire 2008: 137).

Data were gathered through semi-structured interviews and participant observation. The interviews were conducted across three distinct phases of fieldwork in the central and eastern regions of Ghana. The initial phase occurred from October 2019 to January 2020, while the subsequent phases extended from February 2021 to April 2021 and from April 2024 to May 2024. The interviews were audio-recorded with the consent of participants and transcribed for thematic analysis. In total, forty-five individuals were interviewed, comprising religious leaders, prophets, academics, health professionals, caregivers, patients and family members or relatives of patients seeking treatment at prayer camps.

The number of patients at each camp I visited ranged from 10 to 150. Reports from caregivers and a psychiatric nurse working at one of the camps indicated that some patients had previously sought hospital treatment and had been diagnosed with mental health conditions, including psychosis, schizophrenia, mania, bipolar disorder and depression. Others had a history of substance abuse involving substances such as cocaine and cannabis. The prayer camp, in collaboration with a nurse, took the initiative to refer patients without a proper diagnosis to the hospital for formal assessment and appropriate care, alongside the support provided at the camps.

Interview transcripts were analysed using thematic methodology. This process involved both coding and interpretation. The coding and interpretation facilitated a systematic analysis of the data, permitting the extraction of emerging patterns and ideas (Lindlof and Taylor 2017). During coding, MS Word was employed to search for keywords such as fasting, prayer, counselling, mental illness and witchcraft, which were pertinent to the discussion of the study. In this manner, each transcript was coded twice to capture every detail of the conversation. The meanings that participants attributed to their experiences were not readily apparent and were extracted through engagement with the text.

The ethical considerations surrounding engagement with prayer camps have been extensively documented in the expanding literature on prayer camps and mental health in Ghana (Taylor 2019; Coleman 2019). The focus of this study on vulnerable populations inevitably raises several ethical concerns (Hugman et al. 2011; Riandey and Quaglia 2009; Liamputtong 2007). Moreover, there are significant moral implications associated with such research, particularly

Table 1 Overview of key data on the interviewees for this study

Interviewees	No.	Place of interview	Age range
Patients	21	Prayer camp	23–60
Caregivers	8	Prayer camp	26–65
Family members or relatives	7	Prayer camp	49–71
Prophets in charge of prayer camps	5	Prayer camp	50–68
Religious leaders/academics	2	Office/home	60–65
Health professionals	2	Workplace	30–40
Total	45		

given that individuals living with mental illness are often perceived to have compromised decision-making capacity. Additionally, one must acknowledge the ethical and epistemological challenges inherent in interviewing individuals with a history of mental illness who have attained a notable level of wellness. The ethical dimensions of this study were reviewed and evaluated by the Ethics Board of Åbo Akademi University, Turku, Finland. Ethical considerations included obtaining informed consent, guaranteeing anonymity and maintaining the principles of confidentiality to uphold the ethical commitment to 'do no harm' (Buchanan and Warwick 2021) and securely managing the data.

Limitations of the study include the possibility that some accounts from participants may be biased, primarily reflecting their cultural beliefs and potentially obscuring an objective assessment of their experiences, which may be regarded as solely spiritual in nature. Additionally, the methods did not permit further probing of some claims made by patients. In other words, the assertions of participants are highly subjective, shaped by their experiences within the prayer camps. However, the subjective nature of these experiences does not negate the importance attributed to the role of religion and spirituality in aiding their recovery. Finally, it is necessary to remind readers that this study is approached from the perspective of religious studies and may not address all the questions that scholars from disciplines such as anthropology, psychiatry and psychology might have concerning some of the findings presented.

Structure of the book

The book comprises ten chapters. Chapter 1 provides the contextual background for the study by elucidating the theoretical framework of cultural relativism and linking it to Akan perspectives on personhood and well-being. This is followed by a discourse in Chapter 2 addressing the implications of the cultural concept of the person for mental healthcare within Akan perspectives. The chapter emphasizes how the understanding of Akan personhood influences treatment therapies and the care of sick relatives during periods of illness. Chapter 3 examines Akan indigenous epistemological frameworks of disease aetiologies and mental illnesses. The chapter also elucidates how the Akan indigenous epistemic framework of disease aetiologies is reinterpreted within a Pentecostal context, further demonstrating the relevance of seeking mental healthcare assistance at prayer camps for certain individuals. Chapter 4 provides a comprehensive overview of prayer camps in Ghana by contextualizing their development within the framework of Ghanaian Pentecostal historiography. In terms of historiography, the chapter underscores the cultural historicity of prayer camps in Ghana, positing that while they can be regarded as a continuation of the colonial legacies of Western missionary Christianity, they concurrently offer religious healing rituals that merge Christian and indigenous forms of spirituality. The chapter endeavours to typologize prayer camps by distinguishing between existing camps in Ghana based on their operational styles and administrative structures. These typologies are significant in elucidating the extent of control as well as the power dynamics and hierarchical structures that prevail in the operation of prayer camps in Ghana. Furthermore, the chapter articulates the religious and/or theological motivations for visitors to prayer camps, alongside the backgrounds of both the visitors and the leadership present at these camps. Chapter 5 extends the discussion from Chapter 4 by situating prayer camps within the medical pluralistic landscape of Ghana and presenting an argument on the relevance of integrating religion and/or spirituality into mental healthcare. It identifies gaps in mental health research in Ghana and argues for the importance of prayer camps as significant stakeholders in mental healthcare delivery sector. Chapter 6 offers a religious ethnography on the everyday lived experiences of individuals with mental health conditions at prayer camps, alongside their families and prayer camp staff. The chapter highlights their perceived causes of mental illness and the intervention strategies employed to remedy these conditions. Chapter 7 discusses how prayer camps operate as spaces for managing social issues such as stigma, discrimination and exclusion, which are frequently faced by individuals suffering from chronic illnesses, including mental illness. Chapter 8 focuses on various factors that influence why participants deem the therapeutic interventions at prayer camps as appropriate and adequate alternatives for addressing mental illness. Chapter 9 engages with ongoing discourses regarding the collaboration between prayer camp staff and healthcare practitioners, drawing on the experiences of patients, prayer camp staff and health professionals to underscore the importance of intersectoral partnerships between prayer camps and health professionals. A further discussion is presented regarding the necessity to decolonize mental health through local or indigenous epistemic frameworks and methodologies. Chapter 10 serves as the concluding chapter, synthesizing the various arguments articulated throughout the work and offering recommendations.

Chapter 1

CULTURAL RELATIVISM AND THE AKAN CONCEPT OF PERSONHOOD AND WELL-BEING

This study is theoretically grounded in cultural theories, specifically cultural relativism, alongside two interrelated concepts of health and healing from Ghanaian Akan perspectives. This framework provides a relevant theoretical and conceptual basis for analysing how Ghanaian Akan traditional notions of health and healing are reinterpreted within the context of Ghanaian Pentecostal interpretations of health and healing, particularly as evidenced in the healing rituals for individuals living with mental health issues at prayer camps in Ghana.

Cultural relativism has been defined as 'the differences in beliefs, feelings, behaviours, traditions, social practices, and technological arrangements that are found among diverse peoples of the world. Such differences are related because they are believed to result from differences in culture' (Fabrega 1989: 415). Within the context of psychiatry, cultural relativism encompasses 'the claim that at least some, if not all, of the parameters of psychiatric illness among a people, are variable, different, and more or less unique precisely as a function of their culture' (Fabrega 1989: 415). At the core of this theory is the imperative to recognize how individuals perceive and interpret illnesses differently based on their cultural beliefs, dispositions and social relationships, which are often intertwined with or influenced by the cosmological structures of their environments or the universe in which they reside.

The cultural relativist perspective acknowledges 'humans as holistic and symbolic creatures' who are not abstracted from their environment but are instead integrated into and symbolically connected to social institutions (Fabrega 1989: 416). This approach positions humans at the centre of psychiatric discourse and seeks to understand psychiatric illness through the lens of fundamental cultural features such as personhood, beliefs and the social institutions that form the foundations of these belief systems. The fundamental significance of this theory in discussions related to psychiatry and mental health lies in the assertion that psychiatry fundamentally concerns human beings. Consequently, any endeavour to comprehend the human experience, behaviour and the delineations of what is considered normal and 'abnormal' without a thorough understanding of their cultural contexts and the structures that inform such notions may fail to yield an objective assessment, thereby undermining the efficacy of any appropriate interventions, whether religious, spiritual, social or medical.

Another perspective that underpins the cultural relativist approach is that each individual experiences illness in a unique manner, with their responses influenced by factors such as personal physiological composition, immune system robustness, cultural background and historical context. Essentially, illness is a subjective experience, and this principle extends to the ways in which societies and diverse cultures around the world perceive, respond to and treat illnesses. Indeed, the definition of what constitutes illness may vary significantly from one society to another, and the understanding of the conditions associated with illness can differ markedly across various contexts (Hahn 1996). From a cultural relativist perspective, the symptoms of mental disorders may be specific to particular contexts. In other words, mental disorders exhibit variations across different cultures, and their manifestation and articulation are influenced by a complex cultural framework of meaning. This, in turn, shapes the affected individual's understanding of their condition and necessitates the application of treatments that possess cultural significance (Fabrega 1989; see also Patel et al. 1995).

One notable aspect of this theory is the manner in which the concept of the individual or person is invoked to assert its relevance to the field of psychiatry. Consequently, the notion of the person has stimulated the development of cultural relativistic theory and reinforced its application to the construction of illness. Scholars engaged in the study of culture and personality, who have focused on the characteristics of individuals within diverse cultural contexts, have underscored the significance and central role of understanding personhood in the domain of psychiatry. Given that psychiatry places considerable emphasis on behavioural characteristics in the diagnosis of a range of psychiatric disorders, proponents of the cultural relativist perspective contend that the criteria defining a person in one culture may not be applicable in another. This fundamental divergence in the understanding of personhood subsequently influences the comprehension and interpretation of illness across cultural boundaries (Fabrega 1989; Comaroff 1982).

This viewpoint is exemplified in Fabrega's assertion (1989: 416) that 'even if a key lesion or biological marker were found for each psychiatric illness, the social and symbolic importance of psychiatric illness would not diminish because realizations of psychiatric illness have far different meanings and consequences in modern contemporary society than, for example, realizations of diabetes or pneumonia, because *the core of the self* is affected by them' (emphasis mine). As previously mentioned, Fabrega further acknowledges that 'both psychiatric illness and culture meaningfully' involve 'humans as holistic and symbolic' beings. The complete individual cannot be replaced merely by an abstract structure or reduced to a lower-order system. Understanding the essential attributes of an individual necessitates recognizing their integrated and symbolically rooted complexity, as well as their interconnectedness with social institutions (Fabrega 1989: 416). Ultimately, 'it is these shared features of psychiatry, personhood, psychiatric illness, and culture that render the construct of cultural relativism central to psychiatry' (Fabrega 1989: 416).

In contrast to other approaches, such as the universalist and absolutist perspectives, the cultural relativist approach emphasizes the utilization of qualitative behavioural and phenomenological data to explore how psychiatric illness is constructed, particularly in terms of interpreting the self (personhood) and behaviour. Anthropologists and cultural psychiatrists employ fieldwork techniques to document how language is utilized to describe illness, the conceptualization of the body, engagement with external ontological agencies and the understanding of these concepts within the context of illness and social disequilibrium (Fabrega 1989).

The cultural relativist approach is, nonetheless, significant in various respects in relation to the central arguments posited in this book. The primary contention is that culture profoundly influences the understanding and interpretation of mental illness across different global contexts. If culture plays a crucial role in shaping how individuals comprehend and interpret mental illness, as well as illnesses in general, then cultural considerations become a vital framework for establishing the explanations and causal patterns of diseases.

Cultural explanatory models in psychiatry

Psychiatrist-anthropologist Arthur Kleinman (1978) and his colleagues have emphasized the importance of culture within medical settings for physicians. They assert that understanding the cultural perceptions surrounding sickness and healing in any given context is essential for determining appropriate treatment. Kleinman (1978) and his colleagues encapsulate their arguments within the 'clinical social science' framework of 'explanatory models', which is defined as a set of ideas regarding sickness. According to their perspective, both patients and healers possess explanatory models. While patients acquire their models in cultural contexts, healers or physicians develop additional training that intersects with their initial cultural learning through formal education, such as professional schools. The explanatory models articulated by Kleinman (1978) and his colleagues can be categorized into five components: (1) an explanation of the cause(s) of a sickness, (2) a description of precipitating circumstances and initial symptoms, (3) an explanation of the physiological aspects of the sickness, (4) an outline of the illness's progression and appropriate patient behaviour, and (5) a delineation of available treatments.

In my view, patients' explanatory models may be contextually shaped, significantly influenced by cultural conceptions of illness and cosmological world-views pertaining to theories of disease causation. The five points outlined by Kleinman (1978) and his colleagues are mutually exclusive, and the determination of each point or category can occur within a continuum of routine health-seeking practices across various healing spaces or modalities. For instance, among the Akan of Ghana, the journey to identify the cause of an illness may be affected by the application of different healing interventions, often prompted by narratives shared by the patient and others in close social proximity (Olsen 2017). Such narratives reveal core events, symbolic codes and social processes that may further communicate meanings associated with the illness (Olsen 2017). Moreover, to fully appreciate the experiences of both the sick individual and their family, clinicians must first assemble the illness narrative as it emerges from the patient's and family's complaints and explanatory models; subsequently, they must interpret it in light of the various models of illness meanings – symptom symbols, culturally salient illnesses and social contexts (Kleinman 1988). Michael Taussig (1980: 4) has emphasized that 'in any society, the relationship between doctor and patient is more than a technical one. It is very much a social interaction which can reinforce the culture's basic premises in a most powerful manner.'

Indeed, diagnostic measures and tools are predominantly influenced by surrounding cultural and religious world-views. Consequently, culture provides explanations for affliction derived from local ontologies and ethno-physiological systems (Kirmayer and Swartz 2013: 47). This understanding assists in comprehending the meanings individuals assign to their health conditions or problems. In the quest for healing and recovery, affected individuals and families will gravitate towards approaches that are culturally symbolic and therapeutically effective. I assert that the healing rituals observed in prayer camps settings are embedded within 'local meaning systems that confer upon them a degree of social value and potential efficacy' (Kirmayer and Swartz 2013: 48). Given that religion is intricately tied to culture, factors such as world-views and religious beliefs become salient within the broader cultural spectrum, particularly regarding health and healing. This perspective potentially enhances the understanding of the phenomenon under consideration within its proper context and concurrently provides an analytical framework for examining a complex and nuanced concept, such as mental illness.

In the Akan context, the causation of an illness may be attributed to a supernatural force (both malevolent and benevolent), natural or biological factors or may be associated with the patient's social or human relationships. Frequently, the identified symptoms are indicative of broader belief systems, which influence healthcare-seeking behaviours and treatment interventions (Kleinman 1980). Thus, it is not uncommon to observe that among the Akan, both biomedical and non-medical approaches are integrated into the therapy process. In this context, the 'disease symptoms determine the cause of the pathology and its treatment methodology' (Olsen 2017: 51). Complicated or prolonged illnesses, such as mental illnesses, may be subjected to various modes of interpretation, resulting in differing medical recommendations from biomedical and non-medical relatives and friends.

The implicit role of understanding the concept of 'person' from a cultural framework is acknowledged by scholars across various disciplines, including psychology, psychiatry, anthropology, mental health and healing (Ratele 2019; Kpanake 2018; Kirmayer 2007). The significance of comprehending the concept of 'person' stems from the fact that health and healing practices focus on individuals, groups or communities from diverse backgrounds, histories and cultures, each possessing unique notions and understandings of what constitutes a person, health and healing. These differences are particularly evident in the various interpretations posited by indigenous and/or traditional communities, societies or groups regarding the concept of 'person', health, well-being and, notably, mental illness and disorders (Hatala et al. 2015). One such traditional community, the Akan of Ghana, sustains multiple active medical healing systems, which include indigenous or traditional healers, faith-based healers and biomedicine, due to their understanding of the human person, health and healing.

Despite the accumulating evidence indicating that the concept of 'person' is gaining prominence in discussions surrounding mental health and healing, current studies in Ghana reveal that these concepts have generally been secondary to broader ethnographic and clinical research objectives concerning mental health (Ofori-Atta et al. 2018; Yendork et al. 2019). While individuals occupy a central and integrative role in mental healthcare, it remains unclear to what extent those who engage with or treat individuals experiencing mental illnesses truly comprehend the backgrounds of the patients they serve, including their interpretations of illness and the perceived causes of that illness. The perceived causes of illness, as elucidated in the Akan concept of health and healing, assist in appreciating the application of the theory of cultural relativism as an overarching framework for the discussion in this book. As previously mentioned, cultural relativism prioritizes the use of behavioural and phenomenological data in examining how psychiatric illness is constructed across different cultures through the lens of the concept of the person.

Akan concept of the person

In Akan philosophy, the concept of a person encompasses both physical and spiritual dimensions. These two aspects are intricately interconnected and cannot be separated from one another. The Akan people refer to the corporeal entity or physical component of a person as *nipadua*, which serves as the vessel for one's spiritual elements. In the realm of spirituality, a person is understood to possess non-material constituents, specifically the *sunsum* (spirit), the *okra* or *kra* (soul) and the *mogya* or *bogya* (blood).[1]

Kra or ɔkra (soul)

The Akan people hold the belief that the soul is a life force that animates the body and defines one's existence. The soul, referred to as the *kra*, is invisible but can be discerned through the actions of the individual (Akesson 1965). The *kra* is responsible for providing energy and vitality to the person, serving as their source of life (Akesson 1965). Meyerowitz (1951) describes the *kra* as the vital force of life, a divine spirit that influences inspirations, dreams and instincts and acts as a protector for the individual.

Moreover, the *kra* is believed to determine good and bad luck, as individual fate is often influenced by uncontrollable impulses (Meyerowitz 1951). It can be conceptualized as analogous to what Freud designates as the 'Id' or what Jung defines as the 'unconscious' psyche or the universal mind (Meyerowitz 1951).[2] The Akan world-view also recognizes the human being as a composite of physical and spiritual elements, with the soul regarded as an immortal entity that existed with God prior to its incarnation (Kudadjie and Osei 1998). Upon death, the soul returns to God. Kwame Gyekye (1995) notes that the *kra* is perceived as a divine essence, a spark of God that resides within each individual. This divine nature of the *kra* is encapsulated in the Akan *adinkra* symbol and proverb, *Nyame bewu ansa na mewu* (If God can die, then I would too) (Danquah 1968). Abamfo Atiemo (2013) elucidates that the Akan consider a person to be a child of God because it is God who bestows the soul. This belief is reflected in the proverb *nipa nyina ye nyame mma obi nye asaase ba*, meaning 'every human being is God's offspring; no one is the offspring of the earth'. Ephirim-Donkor (2015) argues that this proverb signifies that every human being possesses a divine origin and is not solely constituted of earthly matter.[3]

Within Akan culture, an individual's soul is determined by the day of the week on which they are born. For instance, there are seven distinct types of *kra*, corresponding to the seven days of the week (Ayim-Aboagye 2006; Meyerowitz 1951). Children born on the same day are regarded as having the same *kra*. The day of an individual's birth is termed *akrada*, which translates to 'soul day'. *Akrada* also assigns a *kra* din (soul name) to each person. Every Akan individual possesses a *kra din* that signifies their birth day. For example, a male born on Tuesday is named *Kwabena*, while a female is named *Abena*. In Akan culture, surnames are perceived as formal, whereas *kra din* carries a sense of affection. Each day is believed to be under the influence of a deity whose character impacts those born on that specific day (Meyerowitz 1951; Atiemo 1998). The *kra* also determines one's destiny, known as *nkrabea* (Gyekye 1984).

The link between kra, health, illness and well-being

In Akan beliefs, there exists a profound connection between the physical body and the soul. The *kra*, which is understood to possess its own emotions, can significantly impact the individual as a whole. The treatment of the *kra* influences its mood, which in turn can lead to disturbances in the person's overall well-being. Atiemo (1998) observes that neglecting the promptings of one's *kra* can offend it and substantially disrupt one's peace of mind. Akan proverbs such as *ne kra werɛ ahow* (his or her soul is sad), *ne kra atwe ne ho* (the soul has withdrawn from him or her) and *ne kra ani agye* (the soul is joyful) illustrate the varying moods that the *kra* can assume. These proverbs are frequently employed to describe individuals who have experienced unusual illnesses or misfortunes.

The Akan concept of *kra* is closely related to the notion of conscience (Ephirim-Donkor 2015). The disturbance of one's conscience or any mental distress can precipitate physical illness (Debrunner 1961). This phenomenon occurs because the *kra* responds to sins and grief. For example, when an individual's life force diminishes due to shock or grief, Akan expressions such as *me kra adwane afiri me ho* (my soul has gone away) or *me kra atu ayere* (my soul has flown away) are used (Meyerowitz 1951: 24). Meyerowitz (1951: 24) further explains that when a person's conscience troubles them to the extent of losing weight and vitality, it is said that *ne kra ayera neho* (he/she is losing his/her soul). Among the Akan, such statements are commonly used to describe someone who is seriously ill. The *okra* is regarded as the life force of an individual; without it, one is considered dead. Debrunner (1961) summarizes this concept by asserting that anger, bitterness and resentment towards others – especially when left unexpressed – are widely recognized as causes of illness. It is believed that harbouring rancorous thoughts undermines the attainment of good health. Additionally, Debrunner (1961) posits that individuals with a good *kra* may meet their demise if they bring disgrace upon it. Akesson (1965: 287) contends that the Akan's awareness of the purity of the *kra* renders them 'sensitive to wrongdoing'.

Another significant aspect of the relationship between the soul and illness is what the Akan people refer to as *kra biri* or *ɔkrabirifo*. The etymology of the word *biri* implies darkness or blackness; therefore, *biri* or *birifo* can be interpreted as a state in which the soul is darkened or blackened. Atiemo (1998) observes that the customary colour of the *kra* is white, symbolizing purity. When an individual's *kra* is white, it is believed that they will prosper and be protected. Conversely, a soul that has become darkened (*kra biri*) is thought to attract misery, troubles, tragic accidents and other negative experiences. Christaller (1933: 264, cited in Atiemo 1998: 26) concisely captures this concept by stating, *sɛ obi kra yɛ tuntum a en'de ɛyɛ mmusu, okrabiri ne no; wope sika a wunnya bi, wonam a wonnkyɛ na wunya amanne*, which translates to 'if a person's *kra* is black or dark, that person is *mmusu*; if you desire wealth, you will never obtain it, and you will frequently encounter troubles'. *Mmusu* is a grave form of evil. In the following section, I will provide an explanation of *mmusu*.

When an individual is ill, the Akan express it as *ne kra ebiri* (the soul is darkened). As previously mentioned, the soul is regarded as the centre of life and a spiritually intrinsic entity within the body. If not properly attended to, the soul can become darkened, resulting in misfortune (Bartle 1983). Bartle (1983: 98) suggests that 'just like a person whose face becomes dark (the idiomatic way of saying "angry"), the *kra* will be annoyed at being neglected'. Furthermore, misfortune may manifest as premature or undesirable death, as well as occurrences of witchcraft, illness, infertility or poverty. By honouring, respecting, appeasing, praising and offering drinks to the *kra*, one can attract good fortune (Bartle 1983). Therefore, *kra biri* is commonly employed to describe someone who is sick or unwell. For example, an Akan individual might say *me nyare, nso me nte apɔ*, which translates to 'I am not sick, but I don't feel well'. In such cases, the person typically turns to a traditional shrine to seek guidance and healing. As part of the healing process, purification rituals are performed to restore the soul's brightness, which the Akan refer to *as ɔdware ne kra* (the washing or cleansing of the soul) (Meyerowitz 1951; Adubofuor 1987). This involves providing specific food to the individual and dressing in white garments or applying white clay (*hyire*) to the body. Through these actions, the soul is revitalized and fortified against various attacks, including sicknesses perceived to be caused by witchcraft. This is because witchcraft is perceived as an evil force that can cause injury to someone's soul that might result in sickness or death (Parrinder 1951).[4]

Sunsum (spirit)

The distinction between the *kra* and the *sunsum* remains a subject of ongoing scholarly debate, with various interpretations posited by researchers (Gyekye 1995; Wiredu 1992).[5] One significant difference between the *kra*, or life-soul, and the *sunsum* lies in the belief that the *kra* originates from God (*Nyame*) and is associated with the maternal bloodline of ancestors known as the *abusua*. Conversely, the *sunsum* is perceived as existing within the physical realm and is linked to the spirit of male ancestors referred to as *ntoro*. It is only when an individual becomes a living soul that the *sunsum* becomes an active component. According to Gyekye (1995), in Akan ontology, the term *sunsum* specifically denotes the activating principles within a person.

Individuals can be categorized as possessing either a 'light' *sunsum* or a 'heavy' *sunsum* (Debrunner 1961; McCaskie 2000). When an individual has a 'heavy sunsum', they are often described as *ne sunsum ye duru* or *ne sunsum ye den*, which translates to 'my spirit is heavy' or 'my spirit is strong'. In contrast, an individual with a 'light' *sunsum* is referred to as *ne sunsum ɔhare*. These distinctions can have implications for an individual's well-being, particularly concerning health and protection, which will be elaborated upon in the subsequent section.

British anthropologist Robert Sutherland Rattray, who extensively studied and documented Ashanti culture, customs and traditions, characterizes *sunsum* as 'that spiritual element in a man or woman upon which depends not life, i.e., breath, for that is the KRA – but that force, personal magnetism, character, personality, power, soul, call it what you will, upon which depend health, wealth, worldly power, success in any venture, in fact, everything that makes life worth living' (Rattray 1923: 46).

Unlike the *kra*, the *sunsum*, which represents the personality-soul residing within the body, possesses the ability to depart from the body at will and engage in independent experiences in free space, such as in dream adventures (Parrinder 1951). The life-soul, in contrast, does not appear to exert influence over other souls in the manner that the *sunsum* does. Furthermore, the *sunsum* ceases to exist upon the death of an individual (Twumasi 2005). A near-death experience recounted by Palgrave Boakye-Danquah, executive director of the Kandifo Institute, after contracting Covid-19 in 2021, as reported by Ghanaweb, an online news portal in Ghana, provides valuable insights into this phenomenon:

> And then on the 9th January, I think I was completely dead because I had a whirlwind experience where my spirit left my body. I went to my home, my office, I went to a few other places where I worked, and then I suddenly came

back. I even remember that there were some documents that I actually read when *my spirit left my body*, and it was really quite an experience that I had. (emphasis mine)

The aforementioned experience, as recounted by Boakye-Danquah, exemplifies the notion that one's spirit can depart from the body and engage in independent experiences. In Boakye-Danquah's case, he would have been presumed dead had his spirit not returned to his body, as, according to Akan philosophical thought, an individual's spirit ceases to exist upon death. Within the Akan context, the expression *me kra adwane afiri me ho* (my soul has fled away) is analogous to the experience encountered by Boakye-Danquah. This expression is often used when an individual is unwell. Following recovery from the trauma or near-death experience, the individual may state *afei na mekra aba me ho* (it is now that my soul has returned to my body). It is important to note how the terms 'soul' and 'spirit' are used interchangeably to refer to the same concept. It is somewhat evident that in many instances, it is difficult for people to differentiate between the *kra* and *sunsum* because they are so interrelated and what affects one affects all.

The link between sunsum, health, illness and well-being

Sunsum is conceptualized as the spiritual element of an individual, which activates the body during periods of distress and illness (Olsen 2017). *Sunsum* is characterized by its volatility, as it can be influenced by external forces that exist beyond the corporeal self (Boaheng 2024). For example, the Akan community holds the belief that individuals can manipulate external malevolent forces to target a person's *sunsum* (Konadu 2007). Rattray (1923) elucidates that an individual's *sunsum* may interact with and be affected by other *sunsum*, potentially resulting in illness or even death. As previously mentioned, individuals possessing a 'light' *sunsum* are deemed more susceptible to witchcraft attacks or malevolent influences. When subjected to such attacks, an individual's *sunsum* may weaken, thereby facilitating the onset of sickness or death. Consequently, certain symptoms of illness are regarded as being associated with *sunsum* (Olsen 2017). These illnesses are sometimes commonly referred to as *sunsum yareɛ*, which translates to spiritual sickness or illness caused by spiritual factors. Although these conditions can be diagnosed, they are not amenable to treatment through Western biomedicine or pharmaceuticals.

Children are particularly vulnerable, as their *sunsum* may not possess the same strength or development as that of adults, rendering them more susceptible to harm, even from their own parents (Olsen 2017). Furthermore, an individual's *sunsum* may counteract their well-being, resulting in misfortunes and adverse luck, particularly when the individual engages in wrongful actions or harbours negative intentions towards others. As Parrinder (1951: 48) notes among the Akan, 'The spirit is troubled by evil-doing, for which it is not responsible. If a man has a good spirit and does something to disgrace it, the spirit may sicken and die.'

Certain individuals are believed to possess a 'heavy' or strong *sunsum*. For these individuals, their robust *sunsum* acts as a protective barrier against illness symptoms induced by witchcraft (Olsen 2017). Among the Akan people, it is posited that the optimal defence against witchcraft is the possession of *sunsum ɛyɛ den*, referring to a strong personality-spirit. This notion is encapsulated in the Akan saying *sɛ wo sunsum ɛyɛ den a ɔbayifoɔ ntumi wo*, meaning 'if your personality-spirit is strong, witches cannot harm or overpower you'. Debrunner (1961) observes that his interlocutors underscored this protective aspect, known as *sunsum ɛyɛ duru* or *sunsum ɛyɛ den*. As previously noted, individuals with *sunsum ɛyɛ den* are characterized as bold, forceful, fearless and strong-willed. Witches cannot assail their soul (*kra*) due to the protective nature of their strong *sunsum*. Generally, adults are considered to possess stronger *sunsum* than children, which accounts for their greater resilience to illness. The relationship between *sunsum* and illness highlights the Akan community's reliance on religious and spiritual frameworks in matters of healthcare and medicine. The association between strong *sunsum* and health, as evidenced by the healing and deliverance of mentally ill individuals in prayer camps in Ghana, is examined in Chapters 6 and 7.

Mogya or bogya (blood)

In addition to the *sunsum* and *kra*, another essential component of the Akan person is blood, known as *moyga* in Twi or *bogya* in Fante. *Mogya* is an intangible aspect of the human body, closely associated with the spirit of an individual. According to Akesson (1965), *kra* or the *ɔkra* is intricately linked to the body's organs, particularly the blood. Parrinder (1951: 19) also notes that blood is regarded as one of the most vital components of the body and is 'closely associated with the soul'. While *mogya* is non-physical, it possesses a material nature and differs somewhat from other non-physical or immaterial substances such as the *sunsum* and *kra*. Unlike the *sunsum* and *kra*, *mogya* can be observed in its raw state or when it is external to the body. Despite this characteristic, the Akan still consider *mogya* to possess spiritual elements or dimensions.

The spiritual elements of *mogya* are determined by the *sunsum* (spirit), which is believed to be conferred upon a child by the father during conception. Rattray (1923: 36) elucidates this by explaining that among the Asante, pregnancy or conception occurs through the 'mingling' of a woman's *mogya* with a man's *ntoro* (which is his *sunsum*). Each *ntoro* is believed to be connected to a specific *obosom* (deity). For instance, the Fante refer to the *ntoro* as *egya bosom* (father's deity) (see Atiemo 2013; Chukwukere 1978). The *ntoro* is thought to regulate individuals' conduct within the unit (see Atiemo 2013; Gyekye 1984).[6] Therefore, the well-being of the Akan largely depends on the harmonious relationship between the *kra*, the life-soul and the *sunsum*, the personality-soul.[7]

Consequently, kinship relationships, which are also influenced by customary beliefs and personal behaviour within the groups, are believed to be sanctioned by the supernatural. Despite the predominant matrilineal structure, the Akan inclination towards the father's role in kinship is rooted in the theory of *sunsum*, which the father transmits to all his children, thereby sanctioning behaviour within the family or unit. Within Akan culture, *mogya* holds paramount significance as the essential essence of an individual. This is because the social unit or clan (*abusua*) is formed and defined by one's blood relations, traced through the maternal lineage. As a result, Akan society operates under a matrilineal structure. Therefore, the mother-child relationship within the *abusua* carries great importance, serving as the fundamental basis for the relational personhood of matrilineages among the Akan and the primary means through which this is established and expressed. The Akan believe that blood is transmitted through the mother to the child; hence descent is traced through her, and the mother-child bond confers rights or obligations. Consequently, *mogya* determines one's lineage, kin relations as well as succession to traditional offices such as kingship or chieftaincy positions, inheritance of property, one's status as a citizen (commoner or royal) and one's connections with the spiritual world (Chukwukere 1978; see also Schneider and Gough 1961).

The link between mogya, health, illness and well-being

Among the Akan people, there exist diseases referred to as *mogya mu yareɛ* (Warren 1975). *Mogya mu yareɛ* are ailments that arise from natural or physiological factors; however, certain cases of *mogya mu yareɛ* can be categorized as *sunsum mu yareɛ*, depending on the method of transmission or the response to treatment (Konadu 2007). Further information regarding disease causation will be provided in subsequent sections. However, this particular section will focus on exploring the connection between conception and illness as well as examining the correlation between the health of kin groups during times of sickness.

The understanding of the mother-child relationship through *mogya* holds implications for matters pertaining to health and illness. Some diseases are recognized as being inherited or caused through blood relations. The anthropologist Warren (1975: 124) suggests that certain diseases are 'inherited through the matriclan', which falls under the subcategory of 'spiritually caused illnesses' known as 'sunsum mu yadeɛ'. Warren (1975: 124) employs the term 'awosanne/abusua' yadeɛ (*awosanne* meaning inherited through birth and *abusua* referring to the family or clan) to describe diseases inherited through the matriclan. While this categorization may hold some truth, it also gives rise to various disputes. For example, within the Akan community, diseases such as hypertension, diabetes and glaucoma may be considered hereditary or influenced by genetic factors rather than being solely attributed to spiritual causes. Thus, classifying diseases inherited through the matriclan as exclusively spiritually caused diseases may be an exaggeration.

Nonetheless, there are circumstances in which individuals may perceive such diseases as spiritually caused illnesses based on their own personal experiences, especially in relation to their individual narratives about the contraction of the disease and their treatment outcomes. Another way in which diseases inherited through the matriclan may be interpreted as spiritually caused is when they are viewed as a generational curse within the family. These types of diseases are referred to as *abusua yadeɛ* and are regarded as *yadeɛfo*. McCaskie (2000: 93) observes:

> These were 'diseases' with physical symptoms but social and metaphysical causes. They were said to be occasioned by conflicted or antagonistic interpersonal relations and arose most commonly (but not exclusively) within the lineage or between the sexes. They were grave complaints in that they struck at the fundamentals of kinship, marriage and procreation. If untreated, they might develop into abusua yadeɛ, transmitted by and blighting descent ('spoiling') descent.

As previously mentioned, *ntoro*, the paternal *sunsum* transmitted during conception, not only influences the behaviour, character and personality of an individual but also has significant implications for their well-being. The Asante community firmly adheres to the belief that the separation of a father's *sunsum* from their child can lead to various misfortunes, including illness (Chukwukere 1978; Rattray 1929; Busia 1954). This notion is further substantiated by Appiah-Kubi's argument (1981) that a child's illness can be attributed to the anger of their father, and severe offences towards the father may even result in the child's death. The Asante people expect individuals to show utmost respect, particularly towards fathers and paternal kin groups, as it is believed to be essential for maintaining one's health, peace and tranquillity (Appiah-Kubi 1981). Similarly, Janzen (1978) has examined how, in Zaire, Congo, a child's sickness was perceived to be caused by a rancorous relationship or strife within a family, resulting in the mother's recourse to traditional and faith healing instead of conventional medicine.

It is noteworthy that each *ntoro* group has unique dietary restrictions or food taboos; however, a detailed examination of these restrictions is beyond the scope of this discussion. Nevertheless, it is crucial to emphasize the correlation between *ntoro* taboos (*akyiwade*) and illnesses, an aspect that has often been overlooked in existing literature. Among the Akan, an important aspect of the *ntoro* taboos is the food taboos. This belief is considered significant because it is connected to the spirit of the individual. Parrinder (1951: 48) succinctly captures this notion:

> Food is thought to please the spirit, being spiritually and not merely physically satisfying. A hungry man gets faint and tired because his spirit is starving or neglected. Food enlivens his spirit, and so cheers the whole man. If a man is ailing and spiritless, it is because his spirit is sulking. A doctor is called in and prescribes some food that the spirit will like, or forbids another dish on the ground that the spirit does not want it. A medium may be called in for more difficult cases and, on going into a trance, she is asked to find out what the spirit needs.

Parrinder's (1951) observation encapsulates profound social realities among the Akan concerning the role of food in sickness, healing and well-being. What renders Parrinder's (1951) observation significant in light of this discussion is that his statement unravels both the scientific and traditional perspectives on the importance of food in relation to the Akan's comprehension of the nexus between food and well-being and how that is connected to the spirit of an individual. An individual may forbid a particular dish because it is against their *ntoro* group, and failure to adhere to such rules is believed to aggravate one's state of well-being.

For instance, members of the *Bosomburu ntoro* group are prohibited from consuming certain foods and animals, including bull, dog, mouse, *kwakuo* (a species of monkey) and maize, on Tuesdays, which are considered sacred days for spirit observance associated with the *ntoro* (Meyerowitz, 1951). Similarly, the *Bosompra* group forbids the consumption of specific foods or animals, such as *adowa* (a species of antelope), white fowl, *afaseɛ* (water yam), *tamiriwa* (large edible snail) and palm wine on Wednesdays (Meyerowitz 1951). Among the Akan people, a proverbial saying aptly encapsulates the essence of these dietary restrictions: *sɛ yɛre pae afaseɛ a, na Pra ada*[8], meaning 'if someone is announcing the sale of water yam, *Pra* just goes to sleep'. This proverb signifies that *Pra*, an *ntoro*, holds no interest in the sale of water yam due to its taboo nature (Meyerowitz 1951).

Atiemo (1998) has identified *akyiwade*, such as dietary taboos, as an example of *mmusu* due to its association with the sacred. *Mmusu*, an Akan term that denotes an evil of significant consequence, possesses the capacity to undermine the spiritual foundations of an individual or community and disrupt peace and harmony. It can only be resolved through the performance of prescribed rituals by religious functionaries, such as traditional priests (Atiemo 1998).[9] *Mmusu* is invariably linked with a sense of mystery or the supernatural, and its impact extends beyond individuals to encompass entire families, clans or even states. Disregarding prohibitions such as dietary taboos, as Atiemo (1998) warns, can have tragic consequences, effectively inviting evil in the form of *mmusu bɔ*. The ritual process of warding off *mmusu* is known as *mmusuyi*. In Pentecostal context, particularly in relation to prayer camps, this could be similar to aspects of healing rituals meant to expel demonic powers or neutralize evil spirits through deliverance rituals. A similar term used by the Ewe of Ghana is *busu* and the process for removing it referred to as *busuyiyi* or *nuvɔ̃ɖeɖe* where the afflicted person goes through a 'symbolic procedure (often including taking a herbal bath) which restored his or her spiritual and physical integrity so that life could continue' (Meyer 1999: 88).

If individuals violate their *akyiwade*, it has deleterious effects on both their physical and spiritual well-being. The transgression of these cultural norms undermines the protective power that safeguarding one's personhood provides, leaving individuals vulnerable to the influence of malevolent spirits. This is exemplified by instances in which individuals experience inexplicable ailments and seek medical attention, only to be informed that there is no discernible pathology. Nonetheless, a persistent feeling of malaise lingers, indicating that something is amiss. Such occurrences represent a manifestation of *kra biri*, wherein the soul is being mistreated. Adubofuor (1987) offers a salient illustration of the repercussions of *akyiwade* within Ashanti households. He elucidates that Ashanti tradition dictates that married women must be cognizant of and adhere to their husbands' food taboos. Failing to observe these prohibitions adversely affects the husband, who is considered the head of the household. For instance, if the husband's *akyiwade* pertains to water yam and the wife, either unaware or knowingly, continues to serve him dishes containing water yam, it is believed that the husband becomes contaminated, rendering him feeble and powerless. This, in turn, precipitates a cascade of consequences, as the impaired husband is impeded in fulfilling his responsibilities as a man, particularly the critical task of procreation. Moreover, economic instability befalls him. It is important to note that while these dietary restrictions or food taboos may have diminished in prevalence in modern Akan communities due to the influence of Christianity and the societal changes accompanying modernization, they still retain significance in Akan traditional societies.

Unbeknownst to many Akan community members, these dietary prohibitions can be conceptualized as food allergies or food taboos within the realm of Akan anthropology, contingent on one's *ntoro* group. For instance, a colleague shared with me the advice her mother gave her to abstain from consuming pork due to its taboo status in their family. However, she disregarded this counsel and consumed pork during her time in senior high school. Consequently, she developed peculiar skin rashes. Although the rashes eventually subsided, their reoccurrence upon reingestion of pork prompted her to seek alternative treatment after conventional medical interventions proved futile. Herbal remedies appeared to ameliorate her condition. Subsequently, she abstained from consuming pork and has since remained free of skin rashes. Although this account may be considered anecdotal, it serves as an empirical exemplification of the impact of food taboos within Akan society. Further investigation into these facets of Akan belief systems, health and well-being within contemporary Akan communities would be a valuable endeavour.

Kra, sunsum, mogya and its ontological links with the spirit world and well-being

From the discussion thus far, it can be inferred that the Akan people of Ghana, similar to many other traditions and cultures, regard the individual as interconnected with the cosmic and social order. Atiemo (1998) highlights an aspect of the Akan understanding of the human person that is often overlooked by scholars in their examination of its constituent elements. This oversight lies in the failure to recognize the divine origin of *sunsum* and *mogya* alongside *kra*. While *kra* is acknowledged as being directly bestowed by God and, therefore, possessing a divine origin, *sunsum* and *mogya* are attributed to the mother and father, respectively. However, it is important to note that *sunsum* and *mogya* are not entirely devoid of spiritual associations. Atiemo (1998) argues that akin to *kra*, which originates directly from God and links the human being to the divine, *mogya*, transmitted through the mother, connects the individual to their ancestors (*abusua*). Conversely, *sunsum*, transmitted through the father, links the individual to the gods. Thus, it can be concluded that all three components of the human person are intricately tied to the spiritual realm.

Consequently, the human being is essentially regarded as a child of the spiritual world. Within the framework of this world-view, the Akan comprehend the human person and navigate life. Every entity possesses a spiritual essence, and 'changes occur as the result of the action of spirit upon spirit' (Atiemo 1998: 17). The physical realm is not entirely distinct from the spiritual realm, and occurrences in the spiritual realm have tangible implications for the lives of the Akan, whether positive or negative. Therefore, it is imperative to uphold a harmonious relationship between the physical realm and the spiritual world in order to attain and enjoy good health, peace and tranquillity.

In this vein, to ensure well-being, individuals are expected to maintain harmony between themselves and their environment, as well as the cosmos, which are animated by various spiritual beings, including deities and ancestors. A person's health is contingent upon their interactions and relationships within this ontological realm (Larbi 2015; Obeng 2004). The components of the human person (*kra*, *sunsum* and *mogya*) and their relationship with the cosmic world must be maintained in harmony to avoid disruption. Thus, among the Akan, an individual is considered healthy only when none of these elements are disturbed or impaired. Disease, and consequently death, arises when one, two or all of these components are not in an appropriate condition (Sarpong 2019). To elaborate further, true health is attained when these elements exist in perfect harmony, with each component intact. It is only then that one can speak of an individual's well-being. Any disruption or maladjustment of these elements results in a state of ill health, necessitating healing depending on the affected element and the resultant disease and malaise (Sarpong 2019).

Thus, the *kra*, *sunsum* and *mogya*, as described, are elements that contribute to the holistic nature of the Akan individual. Disharmony among these dimensions of the human person leads to a state of incapacity, social disconnection and spiritual misfortune. This threefold composition establishes ontological connections not only with various metaphysical entities but also with social units. As Atiemo (2013: 130) succinctly states:

> Each person is thought to have been created by God with an independent soul that is said to carry something of God's essence. Each soul is viewed as unique in relation to other human beings and creatures and their unique destinies. But people are born into the world of humans, which is deemed to interact unceasingly with the world of the deities and the ancestors.

Kwasi Konadu (2007), an expert in African histories, cultures, medicine and healing, posits that among the Akan, the human being is characterized as 'spirit-encapsulated' rather than 'matter animated', indicating the metaphysical nature of the individual. It is widely acknowledged that the concept of the person and its ontological connections within the Akan community in Ghana have significant implications for health, healing and overall well-being. Therefore, it is the responsibility of each individual to ensure their welfare and that of the entire community by living in harmony with others and maintaining a proper relationship with the cosmic order.

From the Akan perspective, health is recognized as a holistic and interconnected phenomenon. This understanding of health is shared by both educated and non-educated members of Akan society. The Akan conceive of health not solely as the absence of biological pathogens or the proper functioning of bodily organs but rather as the mental, physical, spiritual and emotional well-being of oneself, family members and the community as a whole. This viewpoint is rooted in the belief that the body serves as a vessel for the *kra* and *sunsum*. Consequently, any detrimental impact on the body has repercussions for the *kra*. As Akesson (1965: 287) suggests: 'If there is a conflict between the two (kra and sunsum), in other words, if the equilibrium is disturbed as a result of a sinful act or wrongdoing, the life-soul may decide to evacuate its casket' – which is the body (Akesson 1965: 287).[10] For instance, an individual experiencing emotional distress or mental disturbance may become ill.

This conception of health is further elaborated in the argument presented by Kenyan theologian Philomena Njeri Mwaura (2014: 326) that within the African context, when an individual falls ill, it is believed that the ontological balance between the human world and the spiritual world has been disrupted. This is due to the notion that one's health is contingent upon being in harmony with, or being an integral part of, the 'life force'. Illness, conversely, is regarded as a misfortune and an indication of falling out of this delicate equilibrium. Moreover, illness is perceived as a social sanction, with the adherence to societal norms and the maintenance of harmonious relations with neighbours, the environment, God, spirits and ancestors deemed essential for safeguarding oneself and one's family against disease.

The ancestors are integral to the societal fabric and play a critical role in shaping morality, ethics and collective solidarity (Adjei 2019; Gyekye 1995; 1984). Kwesi Dickson (1984: 70), a Ghanaian theologian, has noted that the African sense of community necessitates the recognition of the presence of the ancestors as the focal point for group solidarity. As custodians of law and morality, they possess the authority to reward or punish in order to maintain equilibrium within the group. The prioritization of communal support and togetherness over individualism is evident in African societies. Dickson's observation aligns closely with Fisher's (1998) assertion that elaborate and sophisticated traditional African medical and mental health systems have long existed. These systems aim to promote the well-being of both the community and lineage, considering the welfare of the community and lineage as the foundation of social and political life. Moral obligations are inherent in social life, and an individual's worth is determined by their personal and social relationships, which guarantee success in life, good health and fertility. In this context, wealth and health primarily refer to overall well-being encompassing the mind, body and spirit.

Consequently, the concept of health and wellness is understood as a state of cosmic equilibrium in an individual's physical, mental/emotional and social domains (Onyinah 2002; Asamoah-Gyadu 2013). Health is perceived as complete well-being and encompasses all aspects of life that are considered valuable, including mental, physical, social, spiritual and cosmic harmony. It signifies a harmonious relationship between individuals and their environment, as well as with one another and with God (*Nyame*), ancestors and deities (Mwaura 2014). This elucidates why traditional medicine in Akan society addresses both the spiritual and physical aspects of human well-being. Ancestors also hold significant importance in the Akan perception of good health, as a proper connection with the ancestors is believed to greatly influence one's health. Maintaining a healthy relationship with the deceased is crucial, with the expectation that the living exhibit virtuous behaviour to receive protection and blessings from the ancestors. Conversely, engaging in unethical conduct, such as neglecting family property or disregarding sanctioned ethical behaviour, can result in punishment, sometimes manifested in illness.

Given that good health and well-being depend on maintaining a balance between the visible and invisible worlds, it is widely acknowledged that there are various explanations for the causes of diseases or afflictions. The invisible world is perceived to be inhabited by a range of spirits whose actions affect the living, including deities, ancestors, witches and individuals believed to possess supernatural abilities to inflict illness or harm upon chosen targets. Consequently, it is not unusual for individuals to interpret their illness as a form of divine retribution for wrongdoing or as an affliction caused by malevolent spirits or demons. This understanding informs the diagnosis of illnesses and shapes the selection of treatment options aimed at restoring one's health.

Importance of the cultural understanding of the person in psychiatry

In any clinical setting, a physician's comprehension of a patient's condition plays a critical role in delivering an accurate diagnosis and implementing appropriate interventions to facilitate the healing or resolution of the patient's illness. In the domains of psychiatry and psychotherapy, a comprehensive assessment of the patient's circumstances by a psychotherapist or psychiatrist serves as a foundational basis for establishing an objective and meaningful interpretation of the patient's mental disorder. Furthermore, this assessment aids in identifying suitable interventions for remedial purposes (Janus 2019). An integral aspect of this process involves understanding the patient's social background, which encompasses their beliefs, religious affiliation, spiritual history, culture, identity, family and other external relationships (Kao and Peteet 2021).[11]

This approach enables clinicians to not only focus on the symptoms but also consider what is significant to the patient. For instance, Kao and Peteet (2021: 325–6) suggest that inquiring about spirituality can be a valuable method for clinicians to discern the patient's concerns while also acquiring pertinent mental health information. The importance of foregrounding a patient's medical and social history to inform clinical judgements has been extensively addressed in psychiatry from a cultural perspective (Bila and Carbonatto 2022; Kirmayer 2012; Kleinman and Good 1986). Within the fields of psychiatry and psychotherapy, a cultural understanding of individuals has now been recognized as a crucial factor in clinical judgement (Kpanake 2018; Osafo 2012; Kirmayer 2007). Indeed, it has been posited that cultural conceptions exert systematic influences on clinical judgements within psychiatry (White and Marsella 1982). Kirmayer (2007: 251) has also highlighted the significance of 'recognizing the diversity of cultural concepts of the person', asserting that this 'presents the clinician with certain imperatives'.

Conflicts, tensions and disruptions may often arise between clients and clinicians when there is a misunderstanding of an individual's cultural background or a failure to acknowledge and consider their cultural perspectives or knowledge of an illness (Taylor 2003). Kirmayer (2007) underscores the importance of this polarity by asserting that effective psychotherapy should integrate values that are comprehensible within the individual's cultural context while also addressing the tensions between traditional beliefs and the new choices or opportunities engendered by social change or migration. This is due to the fact that each cultural community embodies a unique concept of the individual and a specific vision of a fulfilling life. Significantly, it is essential to examine how the cultural understanding of a person is implicitly present in therapeutic discourse and practice to evaluate its compatibility or conflict 'with the concepts, values, and way of life of the patient' (Kirmayer 2007: 232).

My observations in Ghana regarding treatment of mental illnesses indicate a failure, whether conscious or unconscious, on the part of some healthcare professionals to effectively address the implicit cultural dimensions of mental illness that are often expressed or invoked by patients seeking assistance at hospitals or clinics (see Draicchio 2020; Goldstone 2017). The issue becomes even more concerning when considering human rights observers and NGOs that, to some extent, neglect these important attributes or values in their mental health advocacy efforts in Ghana.[12]

Fundamentally, human beings are inherently cultural entities, and their development into functioning adults is influenced by cultural processes (Sarpong 2020; Gyekye 1998). Therefore, in order to make effective clinical judgements, it is crucial to possess an understanding of the individual, including their personality traits. This necessity arises from the fact that the concept of a person varies across cultures, with the boundaries of personhood differing within each culture. Kirmayer (2007) emphasizes the importance of considering the internalized concept of the person in psychotherapy, as neglecting this concept can leave patients without a coherent understanding of themselves or the means for meaningful social interaction. A comparative cross-cultural perspective allows for a critical examination of how our psychotherapeutic practices depend on specific cultural concepts and values (Kirmayer 2007). For instance, the notion of the individual and individualism in Euro-American contexts differs significantly from that in many other cultures, necessitating variations in therapeutic goals and methods of change (Kirmayer 2007).

However, the concept of the person is complex and poses challenges for explanation within comparative research (White and Marsella 1982). Even within the African context, the concept of the person cannot be assumed to be universal across all cultures, owing to factors such as cultural variations, cultural dynamism, ethnic diversity, normative values, systems of thought and the ever-evolving nature of culture influenced by external or global forces (Kpanake 2018; Mbembé and Rendall 2002). Nonetheless, there exist similarities in belief systems and patterns of thought across different cultures in Africa. It is important to note that this analysis does not seek to represent African peoples as a homogeneous entity but rather offers a practical framework that reflects communal values, practices and indigenous and/or traditional systems of thought endorsed by African cultures, particularly the Akan of Ghana.

Summary

In this chapter, the concept of the person among the Akan and its relationship to health and well-being has been examined. The focus has been on understanding the definition of the human person and how it influences approaches to health, healing and well-being within Akan society and how this reinforces the views of cultural relativist framework in the understanding of illness and well-being. The objective was to emphasize the significance of this cultural framework in comprehending how mental health and healthcare are addressed, particularly within the Akan community. The discussion also aimed to highlight the importance of appreciating diverse ways of life without undermining the value of other contexts. In Ghana, the exploration of various healing practices pursued by individuals and their families not only demonstrates their agency in addressing illness but also underscores the deep-seated and enduring cultural meanings associated with illness. It is essential to recognize that diverse understandings of health and healing across the globe result in the development of unique medical taxonomies that may not be universally applicable.

However, the potential of any medical or healing system, whether scientific or unscientific, cannot be overlooked. This potential largely depends on how individuals benefiting from these systems perceive and value them. In other words, what may be considered positive in terms of medical care is contingent upon the outcomes experienced by patients who utilize these services. Despite advancements in medical science and healthcare treatments, there remain individuals who rely on traditional, religious, spiritual and alternative forms of medicine for their healthcare needs. Even in developed countries with sophisticated medical systems, people continue to seek alternative medicines, including religious healing (Brown 2013; McGuire 2008).

The aim is to establish a practical framework that can inform the practices of healers (both traditional and faith-based), psychologists, psychiatrists, psychotherapists and other therapists working with Akan or African clients who subscribe to this concept of 'person'. It is anticipated that this framework will facilitate a deeper understanding of the interpretation of mental illness within a specific cultural context. With respect to prayer camps, therapists will gain insights into the meanings attributed to mental illness and the ritual interventions that occur within these camps. This understanding will aid in elucidating many of the challenges associated with mental illness, particularly in reconciling illness explanations and interventions based on incompatible ontologies. This explanation is important because previous authors addressing mental health in Ghana seldom discuss or possess extensive knowledge of how healing is practised and how culture influences medical and healing practices.

The next chapter continues the discussion by teasing out the implications of the cultural concept of the person for mental healthcare.

Chapter 2

CULTURAL CONCEPT OF THE PERSON AND MENTAL HEALTHCARE: AN AKAN PERSPECTIVE

The notion of culture in mental healthcare has been a subject of scholarly debate in medical anthropology, transcultural psychiatry and psychology (Antić 2021; Patel et al., 2000; Kleinman 1980). The cultural conception of mental health has been defined as the 'common sense knowledge which is used to interpret social and medical experience, and which plays an important role in shaping both professional and everyday views of mental disorder' (White and Marsella 1982: 3). Numerous works published in the past four decades have sought to establish culture as a significant factor in understanding mental health and its treatment (Moreira-Almeida et al. 2021; Patel and Martin 2010; Andary et al. 2003). The central premise of these studies is that 'illness experience is an interpretive enterprise which is constructed in social situations according to the premises of cultural theories about illness and social behaviour generally' (White and Marsella 1982: 3). In other words, culture shapes the understanding and meaning attributed to a particular illness within a specific cultural context. Consequently, the interpretation assigned to a specific form of illness will not necessarily be the same in another culture or social space. Therefore, the articulation of illness experience in cultural settings and belief systems cannot be disregarded if holistic or comprehensive healthcare is to be achieved. In mental healthcare, for instance, such articulations of beliefs about disorders are crucial in addressing questions concerning the universality and specificity of aspects of mental disorders.

However, studies that have provided accounts of cultural beliefs about mental illness in Ghana have given scant attention to the concept of the person and its interrelatedness to illness. This oversight is not surprising, as research conducted thus far in Ghana on mental health has primarily emerged from disciplines such as psychology, clinical psychology and anthropology, albeit still in its developmental stages. Furthermore, a considerable portion of these studies has been undertaken by researchers from Western countries. Consequently, there is limited knowledge regarding the concept of the person and its connection to aspects of mental disorders, which imbue illness experience with cultural meaning and social significance (see Kpanake 2018; White and Marsella 1982). The primary objective of this chapter is to examine the conceptions of mental health as culturally ordered systems from the perspective of the concept of the person presented in Chapter 1. The aim is to underscore the significance of understanding and treating mental disorders in different cultural settings where such views are deemed important.

Akan concept of personhood and its implication for mental health

What are the implications of the concept of the person discussed in Chapter 1 for mental health? It can be argued that if mental illnesses or disorders are interpreted as behavioural disturbances and dysfunctions of human cognitive abilities, or as disruptive and abnormal behaviours, then comprehending the concept of the person is crucial in establishing a dissociative disorder and discerning what constitutes normality versus abnormality. In an article published in the journal *Theory and Psychology*, Stephen B. Adjei (2019), a Ghanaian cultural and development psychologist, elucidates the implications of the African concept of personhood for psychological science and practice. He notes that in Africa, for example, 'psychological phenomena such as mental health, interpersonal aggression, enemyship, friendship, and suicidal ideations have been empirically studied and associated with communal self-perceptions and embedded social referencing in Africa' (Adjei 2019: 492; see also Osafo 2012). The concept of the person as a relational being, along with its association with the cosmic order as perceived in the African world-view, influences well-being and mental health (Adjei 2019). Adjei (2019: 492) articulately describes the broader implications of the concept of personhood for mental health as follows:

> The relational sense of personhood in Africa goes beyond structural and subjective dimensions to capture the spiritual dimensions as well. That is, people do not live interdependently and derive belonging, warmth, respect, value, meaning, and purpose, but they also desire to experience a sense of transcendence by maintaining harmony and unity with an ultimate being. Thus, connectedness serves as the glue that holds the self, others, nature, and God in cosmological balance. As long as this balance is maintained, in the worldview of the African, there is wellness and mental health.

In Chapter 1, I highlighted the folk orientation of the Akan concept of the person and its connection to the cosmic order. I noted that a void among the components that constitute the human person results in the destabilization of identities and relationships, thereby creating social disequilibrium. In many African societies, mental illness and emotional disturbances are predominantly associated with social, economic and spiritual factors that impact an individual's life (Kpobi and Swartz 2019; Kyei et al. 2014). Such occurrences typically disrupt the individual's somatic and psychological equilibrium as well as the smooth functioning of the self, family or society. For any clinician, psychotherapist or therapist operating within this context, understanding the concept of the person is crucial for clinical diagnosis and psychological assessment. In the context of illness events or episodes of disturbance, the underlying assumptions regarding the nature of the person and ordinary social experiences can serve as a pivotal entry point into the local constructions of the self or the knowledge systems aimed at explaining, diagnosing and treating the disorder (Gallagher 2023; Hammack 2008). This understanding is essential as the notion of the person encompasses a cultural inventory of the psychosocial universe, alongside the forms of reasoning employed in interpreting events within that universe (Kpanake 2018; White and Marella 1982).

Scholars in transcultural psychiatry argue that any attempt to comprehend an individual's behaviour without an understanding of the cultural, linguistic and philosophical models employed within the respective society is fundamentally flawed (Cox 2018; Kirmayer 2007; Kleinman and Good 1986). Indeed, 'both clinical ethics and effectiveness demand careful attention to potential discrepancies between the concept of the person inherent in any given therapeutic practice and the cultural models that underwrite patients' self-construal' (Kirmayer 2007: 251). Furthermore, across the globe, mental health issues, which encompass conditions such as depression, anxiety and somatic and dissociative symptoms, have been elucidated through a diverse range of cultural lenses. Some of these perspectives may refract these issues not as health problems in themselves but rather as personal challenges, moral dilemmas or manifestations of dissonance or disharmony within familial or communal contexts (Kirmayer and Swartz 2013). Consequently, 'expressions of psychiatric illness in thought and behaviour are of necessity mediated by the symbolic forms of language and culture' (White and Marsella 1982: 3). In other terms, 'cultural theories of mental disorder lie at the intersection of conceptions of personhood and conceptions of illness, both of which are probably universal aspects of cultural knowledge' (White and Marsella 1982: 14). It is crucial to acknowledge that the relationality or interconnectedness of personhood is reflected in the understandings of health and illness within the Akan concept, as well as in many African communities.

In the article 'Cultural concepts of the person and mental health in Africa', Lonzozou Kpanake (2018: 198), a psychologist based in Africa and Canada, reinforces the notion that:

> many African cultures promote a relational-oriented personhood, in which an individual manifests his or her personhood through connections to three distinct forms of agency: a) spiritual agency including God, ancestors, and spirits that influence the person; b) social agency, including the family, the clan, and the community, with extension to humanity; and c) self-agency, which is responsible for the person's inner experience.

These forms of agency, as elucidated by Kpanake (2018), impact the understanding of the concept of the person and have significant implications for the mental well-being of individuals.

Social agency and its implications on mental health

Within the context of the Akan cultural framework, social agency can be conceptualized as the agency that arises from the effects of unified relationships and interdependence among individuals within a society. In regard to social agency, a person cannot be regarded as a discrete entity to be understood and addressed individually but must always be perceived as embedded within a social context or social relation (Gyekye 1987; Kpanake 2018). This concept differs somewhat from the Euro-American notion of the individual, which places significant emphasis on individualism and personal autonomy as distinctive characteristics in the pursuit of life goals (Kirmayer 2007). John S. Pobee, a Ghanaian theologian, has argued that 'if Descartes' *cogito ergo sum* represents the Western person's understanding of reality, i.e., individualism,[1] *homo Africanus* would rather say "*cognatus sum, ergo sum*", i.e., "I am because I am related to others by blood"' (Pobee 2001: 59–60). This perspective is reflected in the widely cited statement of Kenyan philosopher John Mbiti, who articulated that 'I am, because we are, and since we are, therefore I am' (Mbiti 1970: 141), emphasizing an understanding or assessment of the status of the individual within African culture. Mbiti (1970: 102) further affirmed that the African is a being that 'can be only understood as a being characterised by interrelationships'.

In examining the relationship between community epistemology and ontology concerning health among the Akan, Fisher argues from the Akan perspective that 'physical or mental illness is not merely biological but is more appropriately psychosocial in both etiology and diagnosis. Misunderstanding of this viewpoint by colonial governments and Christian missionaries has resulted in ineffective denouncements of sorcery and traditional medicine as pagan and unscientific' (Fisher 1998: 113; see also Mohr 2013). Within Akan thought, 'the human person in community is where the cosmos lies. Akan and most African cosmologies are therefore anthropocentric, human-centred' (Fisher 1998: 65). Each individual is expected to uphold harmonious social relations with others in society, including the environment, to ensure societal equilibrium. The maintenance of social equilibrium encompasses not only peaceful coexistence with neighbours but also with ancestors, deities and other spiritual beings. For instance, individuals are expected to adhere to certain taboos and observe specific rites to facilitate harmonious interactions between the living and the non-living. Failure to maintain this balance may lead to repercussions not only for the individual but also for their family and the broader community. Manifestations of such consequences may include the onset of mental disorders as a form of punishment. In the context of Africa, Kpanake (2018) has contended that individuals experiencing mental illness 'typically dwell in a threatening world in which they feel in disharmony with entities belonging to one of the ontological realms or levels of personal agency'. It has been suggested among the Akan that a 'lack of balance and harmony between the human, the physical and the spiritual has in its trail all forms of psychological and social strains that may eventually result in psychological and mental disorder of individuals' (Amoah 2014: 210).

Another social implication of the Akan concept of the person in relation to mental illness is articulated through the Akan maxim *ne safoa ayera*, which translates to 'has lost a key' or 'his or her key is missing'. This reference to the key is believed to signify the key to life, encompassing all necessary tools required for achieving one's aspirations and overall well-being. The key may also represent an individual's mind, which is essential for the proper functioning of human behaviour (Amfo et al. 2018; Amoah 2014). When a person's 'key is missing', this leads to the malfunctioning of the brain, hindering the formation of meaningful social relationships and disrupting the sense of harmony that is crucial for ensuring one's well-being within society. This includes the inability to coexist harmoniously with oneself and with individual members of the community, being attuned to the spirits, fulfilling social, moral and spiritual obligations and achieving a sense of accomplishment. Such a disjunction can result in confusion, disorientation, ill health and a diminished will to live (Amoah 2014).

Understanding mental illness through the lens of social agency and disharmony highlights the reconciliatory dimensions of healing rituals at healing centres, which are designed to address fractured relationships and restore harmony. It is often believed that an individual's state of mental well-being can be influenced by broken relationships, which may include those between a child and their parents, couples or connections with lost loved ones, among others. Agyekum (2020) elucidates that the death of an individual's mother can provoke distressful and sorrowful moments, typically expressed by the Akan in the saying '*Me Maame wuo no a-ma me werɛ a-ho*', which translates to 'my mother's death has made me sad'. Agyekum (2020) further explains that the expression of *awerɛhoɔ* (sorrow) or sadness is derived from the Akan word *werɛ*, which is connected to the body part soul or heart, and refers to a situation in which the soul or heart becomes excessively light due to physical, mental, psychological or social pressures. In other words, the person is semantically distressed due to the loss of a loved one and 'that situation can lead to "depression" ' (Agyekum 2020: 9).

At both prayer camps and traditional healing centres, individuals suffering from mental illness engage in healing rituals that encompass confession and reconciliatory processes, including sacrifices to the spirits within traditional healing contexts. If it is determined that the individual has committed a sin or wrongdoing, or if the illness is attributed to a broken relationship resulting in feelings of guilt, the person is encouraged to make an open confession. Following the confession, suitable reconciliatory rituals are performed, including prayers for forgiveness, aimed at restoring broken relationships and alleviating guilt from one's life. The reconciliation of broken relationships and the feeling of being forgiven after confession liberate the individual from any guilty conscience and mental distress that may contribute to their becoming mentally traumatized.

Additionally, within the Akan context, elders in the family, particularly elder siblings, are expected to care for their younger relatives. Moreover, individuals who have attained wealth and are in a stable financial and economic position are often expected by their extended family members to provide assistance in times of need. The moral obligation to cater for the needs of members within a close-knit family (*abusua*), especially those related by blood, can exert pressure and distress that may potentially affect an individual's mental well-being. Among the Akan, for example, uncles within the matriclan are typically expected to support their nephews and nieces. Parents are also expected to take care of members of their nuclear family. However, individuals burdened with such responsibilities may become psychologically distressed when they encounter difficulties in their own lives such as job losses, unemployment and collapsed businesses that impede their ability to fulfil these obligations. Unemployment, lost productivity and the desire of the employed (both part time and full time) to seek better job opportunities have been found to be part of the reasons accounting for psychological distress among Ghanaians (Sulemana and Anarfo 2021; Canavan et al. 2013). Agyekum (2020: 8) posits that the Akan use the term 'distress' to refer to a state in which one becomes psychologically disturbed when circumstances are not favourable. In such instances, the individual may experience stress and depression due to the numerous and overwhelming demands from extended family that exceed their capabilities and resources.

Consequently, the person who is depressed due to these pressures may become emotionally numb, mentally and physically disturbed, inactive and hopeless, believing that the situation will be permanent (Agyekum 2020: 8). According to Agyekum (2020), in such scenarios, the Akan express *adwendwene* (stress) in terms of unbearable demands as *menhunu me ho ano* (lit. 'I cannot see the end of myself') and *menhunu deɛ menyɛ* ('I am clueless'). In the Akan language, the closest term to the concept of depression is *adwendwenentrasoɔ*. As elucidated by Agyekum (2020), the nominal *adwendwene* is a combination of *adwene* ('brain') and the verb *dwene* ('think'). *Tra* means 'beyond', and the adjective *ntraso* implies 'excess or extreme'. Therefore, *adwendwenentrasoɔ* signifies excessive thinking (Agyekum 2020: 13). He argues that *adwendwene* ('stress') and *adwendwenentrasoɔ* ('depression') are metonyms that indicate emotional states affecting the entire personality of an individual. 'In Akan culture and traditions, "stress", "distress", "sorrow", and "depression" are closely related, since they all create problems for the mental and emotional abilities of the SELF' (Agyekum 2020: 7), particularly in challenging situations.

Individuals who are in a state of despair and depression due to their inability to fulfil their social responsibilities may become mentally traumatized. *Adwendwenentrasoɔ* is articulated in expressions such as *agye me nsam* ('it has stripped out of my hand'), *megye me ho baabiara a ɛnnye* ('there is no way I can release myself') and *meto m'ani a ɛnsia* ('when I cast my eyes around, they do not fall on anybody') (Agyekum 2020). Indeed, such outward bodily expressions of self-experiences during challenging moments have been shown to be predominant in first-person accounts of individuals who exhibit signs of schizophrenia. Gallagher (2023) has emphasized how psychiatric disorders are self-disorders. These self-descriptions include 'aberrant self-experiences such as the loss of a coherent sense of the self, blurring between the self and other, loss of body ownership and agency' (Lee et al. 2021: 263). According to Lee et al. (2021: 263), 'the phenomenology of losing one's own self-boundary' is succinctly captured by Elyn Saks in her memoir,

The Center Cannot Hold, in statements such as 'I am dissolving ... like a sandcastle with all the sand sliding away'. They argue that these kinds of self-experiences are always present long before the first episodes of schizophrenia, which may, in turn, lead to social impairments and social disconnection due to disruptions of agency, body ownership and other boundaries which are related to personhood.

While some of these issues may be attributed to malevolent forces, they also underscore how social problems, particularly expected roles within the family that are reinforced by strong social ties stemming from maternal blood relations, can adversely affect the mental well-being of certain individuals. In this context, the problem impacting the individual's mental health may be physical, although spiritual dimensions are occasionally not entirely disregarded. In Ghana, when individuals face such hardships in life, they sometimes turn to prayer camps to seek divine intervention in hopes of transforming their circumstances. The interventionist prayers conducted at these camps help to soothe confused and traumatized minds, instilling hope that improvements will occur despite challenging and trying circumstances.

Spiritual agency and its implications on mental health

With the concept of spiritual agency, the integration of supernatural or invisible entities into the daily lives of individuals must be acknowledged. Kpanake (2018: 202) posits that 'cosmology in many African cultures represents life as such a tragedy that the self alone, as a vulnerable and mortal entity, could never achieve its aspirations'. Consequently, personhood necessitates the intervention of other spiritual entities that can provide a form of protection and security against malevolent spiritual forces, whose actions can be either detrimental or beneficial to human life (Kpanake 2018). As previously indicated, human beings are believed to possess a spiritual component, and their interactions with other spirits within the cosmos can result in harm. Indeed, among the Akan, it is perceived that when an individual's spirit (*sunsum*) is assailed by an external evil force, such individuals may exhibit signs of distress that can adversely impact their mental well-being.

In Akan religion and culture, as previously argued, there exists a robust belief in impersonal forces that inhabit the cosmos. Given that human beings are integral to the cosmos, human activities are thought to have repercussions on both spiritual and physical occurrences. The powers within the cosmos can be harnessed by individuals for either benevolent or malevolent purposes. Among the Akan, there is a prevailing belief that an individual, driven by jealousy, may consult spirit mediums to inflict illnesses upon their target. These ailments can include mental illness (Benyah 2024; Opare-Henaku 2013). Jealousy may arise from envious sentiments towards another person's successes in various aspects such as education, business or marriage. These perceptions are widely articulated by participants in literature concerning the perceived causes of mental illness in Ghana (Kpobi and Swartz 2018). Furthermore, jealousy can also stem from witchcraft activities. Additionally, individuals may face repercussions in the form of mental illness for failing to heed an invitation from a deity to serve as its priest or priestess or for neglecting to perform specific rites or rituals that are expected of them (Amoah 2014).

Previous studies have indicated that the belief in spiritual agency as responsible agents for mental illness is prevalent among individuals within Akan indigenous religions and Pentecostal traditions (Yendork et al., 2019; Kpobi and Swartz 2018). Consequently, both Pentecostal and indigenous healers engage in the practice of casting out evil spirits perceived to influence those with mental illness (Benyah 2024). Furthermore, individuals unable to overcome certain addictive behaviours, such as the consumption of alcohol and substance abuse, are often believed to be under the influence of spirit agents. These perceived spirit agents, typically malevolent in nature, compel individuals to engage in such practices until their lives become severely affected, potentially leading to the manifestation of mental illness. In prayer camps, such individuals undergo counselling and prayer interventions aimed at helping them break free from their addictive behaviours.

The widespread belief in the power of supernatural forces to induce illness – whether as a result of punishment for wrongdoing (intentional or otherwise) or through the malicious actions of living human agents – often compels individuals to seek supernatural means of protection against malevolent influences. This practice of seeking additional security against evil forces is described by Pobee (2001) as 'double insurance', where some Africans concurrently consult medical practitioners or seek assistance from biomedicine while also turning to traditional shrines, prophets or healers. The utilization of diverse healing modalities in pursuit of assistance raises various paradoxes regarding patterns of causality that must be addressed to attain a comprehensive understanding and provide balanced solutions to individual challenges.

Thus, an appreciation of the African medical landscape should be favoured over outright rejection or dismissal, considering the persuasive nature and behaviour of those seeking assistance, who often invoke different patterns of causality depending on the context of the healing environment. Bernhard Udelhoven (2015), writing on pastoral care for the afflicted in Zambia, has argued that spirits are typically experienced in disruptive, negative and afflicting ways; however, metaphysical conceptions of their nature can easily shift within healing contexts. A single individual may label their afflictions as 'demonic' when seeking help from a Christian pastor, 'witchcraft' when consulting a traditional healer analysing family constellations and 'virus' when receiving treatment in a modern hospital. A nuanced understanding of such world-views and patterns of interpreting causality is essential to provide culturally resonant responses to afflicted individuals.

Agency of the self and its implications on mental health

Aside from the social and spiritual dimensions, another significant aspect of personhood in African cultures is the concept of the self, which distinguishes an individual from others and is typically articulated through deictic terms such as 'I' or 'me' (Kpanake 2018). Kpanake asserts that 'this self is a locus of agency that is responsible for introspection, feeling, and questioning, and an entity that one is proud of and seeks to improve'. He further posits that 'the self is responsible for the individual's social presence and accommodates the life essence'.[2] However, the self is also perceived as an extension of oneself, transcending 'its bodily, anatomical, and physiological substrate' (Kpanake 2018: 205). Consequently, in certain African cultures, the self may manifest as an invisible self or an environmental self. This phenomenon elucidates why an item used by an individual could be employed by another to perpetrate an evil act against that individual. This concept aligns with James Frazer's classification in his seminal work, *The Golden Bough*, where he described the 'law of similarity' and the 'law of contact or contagion'. The law of contagion operates on the principle of contiguity, whereby items previously associated with a person can be manipulated to inflict harm until the contact is severed. Examples of such items include hair, towels, shoes, jewellery and footprints, among others.

Parrinder (1951: 19) articulates similar concepts when he contends that, among West Africans, including the Akan of Ghana, an individual's body is not considered a mere empty vessel but rather as an entity 'filled with energy which may be hurt or helped by other forces'. Furthermore, he observes that the belief in the dynamistic powers of the body is evident in the significance attached to bodily appurtenances such as hair, nails, spittle, washing water, sleeping mats and any objects that have been in intimate contact with the body. Such items are disposed of, based on the belief that improper disposal can enable practitioners of black magic to cause harm or inflict pain, including illness, upon their targets (Parrinder 1951). The notion of utilizing items that have been in contact with individuals is prominent in the practices of magic and sorcery, where individuals often attempt, through deliberate actions, to employ magical powers to harm others due to feelings of jealousy, envy or perceived wrongdoing on the part of their targets. This concept is grounded in the theoretical framework of magical practices and rituals within traditional cultures, as articulated by Frazer and also by Marcel Mauss (1972). The law of contagion, as mentioned, suggests that items or entities that have been in contact with one another may influence each other through the transfer of certain properties via an 'essence'. This influence is believed to persist even after physical contact has ceased, potentially becoming permanent, functioning on the premise that 'once in contact, always in contact' (Rozin et al. 1986). In magical practices, contact is frequently embodied as a personal residue, such as fingernails. These residues are thought to retain essential properties of their original owner or source, with the 'essence' remaining in these residues in a form of non-physical connection with its origin. This provides the potential for actions taken against the essence present in a residue to impact the original source (Rozin et al. 1986). Here, the 'essence' is sometimes regarded as the person's soul or spirit; that is, an individual's soul or spirit is perceived as being connected to the item by virtue of prior association or contact. In this sense, the item becomes an extension of the individual's body or an extension of oneself as articulated by Kpanake (2018). The extension may include the invisible self. The invisible self refers to the unseen aspects of human existence or the components of the human being that are not visible to the eye. This may include the *kra* (soul) or the *sunsum* (spirit).

In Akan cultures, the concept of contagion may be observed in the practice of *aduto* by medicine men or *juju* men. In the Akan indigenous medical systems, medicine is not always beneficial; there exist both detrimental and beneficial medicinal practices (Konadu 2007; Mohr 2009). *Aduto* conveys a notion of negative medicine, which is often employed by individuals to inflict pain, suffering or even pronounce death upon their targets or those perceived as offenders. In this context, the illnesses contracted are invariably harmful (Konadu 2007). Common knowledge among the Akan indicates that, in the practice of *aduto*, practitioners may utilize items such as clothing, towels, slippers or any objects that have been used by their target as mediums to enact harm. The afflictions imposed upon these offenders may sometimes encompass mental illness. Thus, *aduto* serves as one avenue through which sickness, including mental illness, is explained within Akan cultures.

Kpanake (2018: 206) observes that 'each of these agencies is associated with particular ways of self-understanding and self-representation that are invoked in causal explanations and interventions of actions and events'. Illness or any misfortune that befalls individuals is often interpreted as the consequence of malevolent spirits' activities, such as witchcraft or sorcery, or as a result of committing an offence through immoral acts or neglecting to observe certain ritual practices. Consequently,

> personal misfortune, including illness, may be attributed to the actions of spirits or malign magic. These explanations are caught up in local notions of proper social and moral behavior: observing the moral code, performing the required rites, and maintaining good relations with others, including ancestors. These systems provide explanations for what otherwise might seem inexplicable and satisfy the need to maintain a coherent worldview. They may influence help-seeking and the acceptability of treatment. (Kirmayer and Swartz 2013: 47)

This cultural understanding of personhood and illness is emphasized by Jean Comaroff, an anthropologist and scholar of African studies, who contends that healing across diverse cultures relates to 'human intervention in disorder' and is exemplified in the efforts of a community 'to mend the physical, conceptual and social breaches entailed in illness' (Comaroff 1981: 368). Comaroff (1981: 368) perceives illness as 'a particular expression of a universal feature of human experience, that of threat to the normal state of being, or to survival'. In this regard, illness engages with universal paradoxes of human existence and their symbolic representation within specific cultural frameworks. Comaroff (1981) posits that human selfhood manifests through the physical body, which serves as the symbolic framework in which the paradoxes of human existence are most vividly articulated. This assertion is based on the premise that

> the perception of the body is culturally ordered, and everyday social action serves to reinforce or transform the mutual interdependence of physical and social being. But the body … is not merely a convenient source of symbols

> which provides a functional image of social form. It is a scheme through which universal contradictions are shaped by historically specific values, but it also permits such values to be 'naturalised' – i.e. to achieve the status of transcendent truths, or realities which are above temporal interests. (Comaroff 1981: 368)

Comaroff also underscores illness or bodily dysfunction as both a result of and an indication of the disruption of harmony among the physical, social and moral dimensions of existence, thus 'setting in motion the search for reconstitution'. Given that part of the human being or an individual is viewed in spiritual terms, the pursuit of reconstitution may, at times, incorporate elements of divination. She thus asserts:

> In the face of the doubt and anxiety which often accompanies illness, healing processes powerfully reinforce the validity of meanings drawn from the dominant forms of knowledge in the wider culture. Healing affirms the hegemony of established images of self and context. It touches upon deep-seated paradoxes of the human condition, addressing them through definition of reality which imply specific interests. Explicit medical knowledge provides the rationale for the process, presenting as 'natural' what is actually a culturally constituted and socially motivated image of man. (Comaroff 1981: 369)

Occasionally, individuals may experience a lack of inner peace due to perceived transgressions against others. Additionally, the sorrow that envelops a person engaging in self-guilt practices is thought to affect the individual's soul, thereby impacting overall well-being and self-perception. This discontent may have repercussions on the individual's mental state. As previously noted, a fractured relationship can also lead to mental instability. Forster (1962), who authored an extensive and informative treatise on mental health practices and values in Ghana, identified the disintegration of social units as a principal factor influencing complex psychiatric profiles among the populace. Beyond social disintegration, a disconnect between an individual and their higher power can engender anxieties and disrupt inner peace. These issues can lead to emotional trauma and mental health problems that may necessitate either the restoration of strained relationships within the social framework or the performance of certain rituals to facilitate feelings of forgiveness or purification, particularly when the individual perceives that the source of their illness or malaise has spiritual implications.

Understanding of the concept of the person and treatment therapies

In the preceding discussion, I have highlighted the implications of the Akan cultural concept of the person on mental health and well-being. The discourse endeavoured to demonstrate how an understanding of this concept aids in elucidating certain induced mental health issues. As previously articulated, it is maintained within Akan society that spiritual forces possess the capacity to induce various afflictions, including illnesses. To comprehend how these forces exert their influence over human beings, it is essential to grasp the local doctrine concerning human personality.

The Akan conception of the human being as comprising the body (containing the *mogya*), *sunsum* and *kra* serves to elucidate the aetiologies of illness. As noted previously, *sunsum* is perceived as volatile and susceptible to harm from malevolent forces when subjected to spiritual attack. Furthermore, the *kra* may be affronted through an individual's misdemeanours. The quality of an individual's social position, in terms of their relationships with neighbours and the environment, is believed to have profound implications for their overall well-being, as health is understood to be communal (Sarpong 2019).

This understanding of the human person and its relationship with the environment must be contextualized to comprehend certain aspects of the Akan explanatory models of psychiatric disorders and the selection of therapeutic interventions for such conditions. Grasping this perspective on the Akan explanatory models is a crucial element in assessing the role of culture in psychiatric disorders. This is significant because the explanatory model is grounded in the notion that reality is socially constructed (Kleinman 1980). These models are associated with specific categories of illness that reveal labels and cultural idioms for articulating the experience of illness (Kleinman 1988). For many Akan individuals, the perception that malevolent supernatural agents may assault one's spirit and cause illness, that an individual with ill intent can manipulate the spiritual realm to inflict harm on their targets and that one's transgressions could be penalized by ancestors, deities and other entities are lived and existential experiences encountered routinely.

Given the understanding of the human person's bodily structure and the belief that malevolent beings can attack it, individuals who fall ill seek therapeutic options that link their bodily symptoms to models of cultural explanation and local therapeutic systems. In other words, while the Akan acknowledge that certain illnesses may stem from natural factors and thus require hospital care or biomedical treatment, their understanding of the human person – including its other bodily constituents and associated agencies, as described earlier – suggests that they are vulnerable to diseases in ways that may not be adequately explained or treated by biomedicine. Similar to other African communities, the Akan perceive that 'natural realities are also social facts, and the biology of the body … maintains a vibrant cultural dynamic'. This dynamic becomes particularly pronounced during periods of change, stress, transition and decay (Olsen 2017: 59).

Understanding the cultural dynamics of the Akan conception of the human person, along with its bodily constituents and agencies, helps illuminate the conditions of medical pluralism during periods of illness. In Pentecostal prayer camps, individuals seek solutions to the perceived malign forces behind their ailments. Furthermore, they often attend these camps to pray for forgiveness for sins and to seek liberation from behaviours that induce guilt and adversely affect their well-being, including mental health. Individuals also visit these spaces to garner support in reconciling fractured relationships with relatives or families. Additionally, some individuals seek divine intervention for their distressing social and economic circumstances, which may lead to depression. This engagement occurs within the context of spiritual warfare, addressing perceived supernatural and demonic influences on health conditions (including mental illnesses), familial relationships, business dealings and employment matters, among others. While hospital environments are generally deemed effective for many medical issues, they are frequently viewed as inadequate for addressing these specific challenges, as caregivers and professionals in such settings are not trained to comprehend the multifaceted aspects of the human person and its bodily constituents, nor the ways in which they respond to various stimuli as understood in traditional cultural contexts. Chapters 6 and 7 present numerous ways individuals and their families pursue therapeutic interventions based on these cultural notions of personhood, cosmological understandings and the perceived origins of mental illnesses.

The kin group or family (abusua) as therapy management group

As elucidated in the previous discussion regarding the concept of personhood among the Akan, an individual is categorized as a member of the *abusua* through maternal blood ties. Membership in the *abusua* designates an individual as part of the family's collective identity, obliging the family to provide care for its members during periods of illness. Crentsil (2007) posits that the act of caregiving highlights the vital role played by the Akan matrilineage. According to Akan culture, every individual is regarded as belonging to the family or *abusua*.

Consequently, when misfortunes such as illness occur, the responsibility of caring for the sick primarily falls upon family members, particularly uncles, aunts and relatives from the maternal side. Caregiving typically takes the form of contributions from family members in terms of personal resources, including financial support and time dedicated to caring for the sick individual. The objective is to restore the sick person to a 'normal' state of life while also conveying the Akan's general understanding of illnesses (Crentsil 2007). In subsequent chapters, I will further explore how this commitment to care is manifested in the social support provided by family members as they assist their kin seeking treatment at prayer camps in Ghana.

In the quest for the afflicted individual's recovery, all available healing modalities – encompassing both biomedicine and divinatory consultations – are pursued with the intent of restoring the individual to a state of normalcy. Robert B. Fisher, a Euro-American Roman Catholic theologian and liturgist, who spent nearly thirteen years as a Divine Word Missionary teaching and serving within Akan communities in Ghana, astutely observed that when illness strikes within these communities, the suffering extends beyond the individual to encompass the entire family unit. He noted:

> While the family and community are central to this equilibrium of wealth and health, individual achievement is the mark of life well lived. For that reason, when illness does strike, the individual suffers, but normally not alone ... Elders

> are summoned who first observe if the sickness can be cured with herbs. With the white man's medicine, this first stage is called the social palaver ... The kin group shares the expenses of the treatment ... The kin group is like an 'extended patient'. (Fisher 1998: 133)

Within the Akan context, kin members, particularly those from the matriclan, frequently perceive the illness of a relative as a familial or private matter (Crentsil 2007). Indeed, in numerous African societies, an individual's illness is regarded as a dysfunction affecting the entire family or clan (Janzen 1978). Janzen (1978: 4) asserts that in Central Africa, for instance, the management of illness and therapy by close relatives constitutes a central aspect of medical practice, forming what is referred to as a 'therapy management group'. He contends that 'a therapy management group comes into being whenever an individual or a set of individuals becomes ill or is confronted with overwhelming problems' (Janzen 1978: 4). In his research, Chavunduka (1978: 45) discovered among the Shona people that 'when a person is ill, he does not often act on his own. His kinsmen both educated and uneducated jointly take the decisions throughout the illness and are responsible for paying the medical fees.' In Ghana, the care and support provided by family members for individuals seeking treatment at prayer camp facilities exemplify social concern and family solidarity during episodes of illness.

This provision of care for individuals experiencing mental health issues has been observable throughout both the colonial and post-colonial eras. Despite the use of mechanical restraints (Figure 1), colonial observers did not overlook the ways in which families accommodated and supported the mentally ill within their communities. Geoffrey Tooth, a British medical doctor commissioned by the colonial government in the Gold Coast (now Ghana) to conduct what is now recognized as the first comprehensive report on mental illness in Ghana, reported: 'There appears to be little social stigma attached to madness, lunatics are well treated in their homes and even when shackled to a log in the traditional manner, the madman is seldom alone for long, is well fed and enjoys the company of his children and friends' (Tooth 1950: 30).[3]

Tooth's observation resonates with a Ghanaian Akan maxim which states that *obodamfoɔ biara wo wura*, which translates as 'every mad person or lunatic has a relative' or, alternatively, 'every lunatic has someone who takes care of him or her'. This maxim illustrates how families of individuals affected by mental illness continue to value, initiate and invoke processes aimed at restoring the individual to his or her 'normal life'. Tooth's insights were not unique. Robert Cunyngham-Brown, a British psychologist and medical administrator, was commissioned in 1936 by the British government to inspect 'the care and treatment of lunatics' within their West African colonies, commencing his work in the Gold Coast. Contrary to his expectation that the majority of mentally ill individuals would be confined to asylums, he discovered, to his astonishment, that more mentally ill persons were cared for by their extended families or by 'native doctors'. After evaluating fifty 'wandering lunatics', Cunyngham-Brown (1937: 24) extolled the merits of 'family care of the insane' as 'a natural growth of age-long custom'

Figure 1 Native method of restraining the insane with the use of logs as mentioned by Tooth. This practice is similar to the modern-day use of chains or shackles at prayer camps or at indigenous healing centres. *Courtesy*: Picture taken by the author at the Bodleian Library Special Collection from the archival records of Leonard Goodman, a British surgeon who worked in the Gold Coast (now Ghana) from 1939 to 1952, MSS.Afr.s.709, University of Oxford on 17 May 2022.

and 'in entire harmony with the officially encouraged strengthening of native administrators'. His conclusion is particularly revealing:

> The general attitude of the native peoples … to the vagrant lunatics … is one of kindly commiseration, tolerating much and giving alms as a matter of course … Elsewhere when visiting patients in their own homes, I found the same kindly bearing to the insane, and though many were chained or put in stocks, to my thinking often needlessly, it was evident that they were seldom neglected but instead were in receipt of kindly and assiduous though often ill-directed attention. (Cunyngham-Brown 1937: 13)

The aforementioned quotation draws attention to the role of the family as a primary unit in providing care for individuals with mental illness. Margaret Field, a British anthropologist and psychiatrist, conducted an extensive study of mentally ill individuals in rural Ghana at traditional healing shrines in Ashanti. She reported, 'The majority of chronic schizophrenics in rural districts are treated with … patient and sustained kindness by their relatives and tolerance by their neighbours' (Field 1960: 453). Such forms of tolerance and care were considered influential in the recovery process. Meyer Fortes, an anthropologist, and his wife, Doris Mayer, a psychiatrist, also conducted research on psychosis in Northern Ghana during the 1960s. They noted, 'Schizophrenia, at least when treated in the family setting and with the very real support of the whole family, seems to be a more reversible process than it is in more complex societies' (1966: 40). The emphasis here is on the family as a social unit within the Akan cultural context, highlighting the significance it assigns to individuals not as isolated entities but as beings embedded in social relationships. This perspective contributes to a broader understanding of health, healing and well-being within society. Subsequent studies conducted by the World Health Organization on schizophrenia appear to affirm the views expressed by Fortes and Mayer.[4]

During my visits to prayer camps, I observed that no patient had arrived at the camp voluntarily. Most, if not all, were referred to the prayer camps by parents, relatives or family members (and even in some cases by medical professionals) in search of remedies for their illnesses. Indeed, camp leaders informed me that they were unable to accept any individual without prior approval from a family member or parent. They emphasized that they did not actively seek out mentally ill individuals to bring them to the camp for treatment. Furthermore, some family members stayed at the camps to assist in caring for their relatives during treatment and even engaged in fasting on behalf of their ill relatives. A challenge highlighted by certain camp leaders was that some family members would leave their relatives at the camp and fail to return to check on their well-being, even after recovery.

Despite this challenge, what is of concern in the context of this discussion is the initiative taken by the family to seek a solution to a health problem of a relative. It reflects how the family, as a social unit in Akan society, takes a keen interest in the well-being of its members and the processes that are initiated to seek redress when an illness strikes. Indeed, the prayer camp environment, despite its infrastructural challenges, is organized around a similar motive of providing care and hospitality to people afflicted with mental illness. Patients who visit the camps are predominantly sent there by their family members, and some of them stay with their relatives until they recover and are charged by the camp (Read and Nyame 2019; Goldstone 2017).

The 'dark side' of kinship on health and well-being

In the preceding discussion, I referenced several spiritual agents that can be considered responsible for illnesses. These include witches, ancestors, magicians, *juju* men, sorcerers and demons. For the purposes of the discourse in this chapter, particularly concerning the significance of matrilineal kin in the care of person living with a mental health issue, I shall elucidate the concept of witchcraft among the Akan. My focus will primarily be on the negative dimensions of witchcraft within the context of relational personhood among the Akan.

While the Akan hold the belief that witchcraft can be employed positively by those who possess it to attain personal gains in various aspects of life, such as education and business ventures (Appiah-Kubi 1981), witchcraft practices are predominantly perceived in negative terms. Some even contend that there can never be a form of 'good' witchcraft as 'witches are wicked people and it is their wicked feelings – their hatred or envy – that cause harm' (Appiah-Kubi 1981: 13). Witches are believed to engage in 'mystical cannibalism' by spiritually consuming 'the blood of victims, which results in the onset of diseases' (Asamoah-Gyadu 2015a: 23). However, these cannibalistic tendencies are believed to be enacted only upon individuals with whom the witch shares blood ties. Thus, witches 'destroy these ties by feeding on relatives' blood and flesh' (Meyer 1999: 192). It is posited that 'a witch may invite other witches to participate in the cannibalistic meal' and that in order to gain access to a person, a witch must utilize familial connections (Meyer 1999: 192). Meyer (1999) recounts instances where individuals perceive family members as the source of their misfortunes in business and health issues attributed to witchcraft practices stemming from envy. The ramifications of such accusations among family members are severe, leading some to refrain from discussing the matter openly for fear of provoking familial conflicts (Meyer 1999). Onyinah (2012) presents cases in which accusations of witchcraft have resulted in significant disputes among family members. Asamoah-Gyadu (2005: 79) also recounts an incident involving a Ghanaian man who lured his mother into a secluded area and murdered her with a machete after having been informed through a 'prophetic revelation' that his chronic stomach pain was caused by his mother's witchcraft.

The notion of witchcraft as an evil supernatural force responsible for the causation of illnesses 'thus make[s] the cosmology of the Akan "human-centred"' (Crentsil 2007: 129). Witchcraft spirits are believed to be possessed by individual human beings who manipulate these powers to inflict harm upon those in close proximity to them. A popular Akan proverb, *aboa bi beka wo a na ofiri wo ntoma mu* (literally translated as an insect will bite you only from within your cloth; or your closest acquaintance is your worst enemy or adversary), exemplifies this concept. The proverb conveys the idea that one's destroyer is situated nearby, possessing greater knowledge of one's vulnerabilities than any other individual. Consequently, in Ghana, when calamity or misfortune befalls an individual, it is common for them to assert *wei diɛr efie foɔ nim ho bi* or *efie foɔ ka ho*, which literally means, as for this problem, my household or family has masterminded it, or my household or family is behind the cause of the problem. This suggests that a witch within one's family unit is responsible for the misfortune. Indeed, 'witchcraft is a crude way of expressing tensions within the kin group' (Pobee 2001: 60). In other words, 'sickness and troubles are attributed to envy on the part of relatives and their spiritually powerful allies' (Asamoah-Gyadu 2015a: 23), with such beliefs often emanating from the matrilineal group, closely bound by blood relations.

Within the Akan context, when an individual who is unwell (or a member of their group) perceives that their illness has stemmed from witchcraft, suspicions and accusations frequently arise within the clan (*abusua*) or kin group (Rattray 1927). Indeed, the discourse surrounding witchcraft as aetiological to illness has been well documented among the Akan. Field's (1960) work, *Search for Security*, recounts how individuals who visited shrines while ill or confronted with life's challenges during the 1940s attributed their predicaments, as well as their feelings of insecurity, to the fear of envious machinations perpetrated against them from within their kin group.

Certain parts of the lyrics from a popular Ghanaian highlife song titled *Fie nipa sei woa a* by J. A. Adofo capture this sentiment succinctly:

Fie nipa sei woa a saa
Fie nipa sei woa saa oh
Wo di wo yadeɛ bɛ Kyini amanso, amanso!
Nanso wonya ano aduro ara da ah ooh
Ɛba no saa wo brɛ oooh

Translated as:

If someone from your household destroys you
If someone from your household destroys you
You will go to places with your sickness
But you will never find a solution or cure for it
When that happens, you suffer a lot

The song effectively conveys the notion and affirms the prevalent belief that it is solely a witch within one's own household or from within one's own family who can bring about their destruction. According to the song, when an individual suffers from illness due to a family member's actions, efforts to identify a remedy for the affliction are often rendered futile. Consequently, 'witchcraft and destruction in circumstances such as illnesses' are commonly perceived to emanate 'from the matrilineal group' (Crentsil 2007: 131). This perspective among the Akan – that a witch has the capacity to harm or destroy exclusively within their kin group – resonates with anthropologist Peter Geschiere's (1997, 2003) well-known characterization of witchcraft as 'the dark side of kinship'. Within Akan culture, a witch is believed to act within the matrilineage (*abusua*) and to consume the blood (*mogya*) that constitutes it, thereby epitomizing antisociality.

Moreover, Crentsil (2007: 132) explains that the Akan theory of witchcraft within a kin group resembles the relationship between an owner and an owned object. This analogy reflects the Akan understanding of jural rights over the individual. Consequently, 'by virtue of blood (and the womb), a person belongs to the matrilineage; lineage concepts determine the individual's position within the group – as the "bona fide property" of the matrikin'. This also grants the witch (or witches) within the kin group dominion over the individual, permitting them to 'kill him or her at will' (Crentsil 2007: 132). Thus, an illness episode attributed to witchcraft is not seen as external but rather as immediate to the kin group and/or close relations. While the importance of the family (*abusua*) in the care of the sick is paramount, there also exists an additional dimension of kin relations that is perceived as detrimental to the survival and well-being of members within the kin group.

Summary

This chapter has examined the implications of the concept of the person as understood in the Akan context for illness and mental illnesses in particular in Ghana. The discussion focused on three aspects of agency that are derived from the concept of the person and how these aspects affect issues related to the mental health and well-being of individuals within Akan communities. It emphasizes that the overall understanding of how the Akan conceive the concept of the person and its ontological relationship with the cosmos has significant implications for mental health. While good health is contingent upon the harmony of the mind, body and soul within an individual, it is also necessary for one to maintain a relationship with society in order to be regarded as healthy. Moreover, the general understanding of, and belief in, the existence of supernatural beings in the cosmos renders human beings particularly susceptible to their environment. On one hand, individuals may experience fear regarding the afflictions that could befall them if they contravene society's sanctioned moral codes or established norms. On the other hand, there exists a strong belief in the manipulation of cosmic powers by certain individuals for malevolent purposes, resulting in the affliction of various illnesses, including mental disorders.

These factors collectively influence the ways in which individuals relate to their environment, interact with one another within society and construct the concept of illness, particularly mental illness. The Akan construction of mental illnesses must be understood within this contextual framework. In seeking solutions to the issue of mental illnesses, the Akan do not exclusively rely on biomedical treatment but also pursue alternative healing interventions, such as religious healing, which are congruent with their cultural beliefs and practices.

In contemporary Ghana, such belief systems and understandings continue to shape individuals' attitudes and approaches to the treatment of mental illnesses and other health conditions in general. Post-colonial writers who have addressed African psychiatry have aimed to decolonize the discourses surrounding mental health in Africa and facilitate the integration of perspectives that resonate with psychiatric practice in post-colonial societies. The prayer camps in Ghana represent one such institution where the integration of belief systems in the care of the mentally ill can be observed.

The next chapter complicates the discussion by unpacking the notion of mental illness as *sunsum yareɛ* (spiritual illness). The objective is to provide a critical review of the aetiologies of mental illness in Ghana and help-seeking preferences.

Chapter 3

UNPACKING AKAN DISEASE AETIOLOGIES AND THE CONCEPT OF MENTAL ILLNESS AS *SUNSUM MU YAREƐ* (SPIRITUAL ILLNESS)

While the Akan perspective on disease aetiologies is often characterized as predominantly supernatural, it is undeniable that the Akan do not invariably rely on metaphysical explanations for the causes of diseases. Indeed, it has been posited that the Akan resort to supernatural explanations and remedies primarily when attempts to address a disease condition through biomedicine have failed (Onyinah 2012). This paradoxical approach to illness among the Akan becomes comprehensible when viewed within the continuum of Akan disease interpretation. The classification and categorization of disease, whether perceived as physically or spiritually caused, do not occur in isolation. Such interpretations are frequently informed by the outcomes of specific causal relationships, which are subject to various layers or mediums of testing and experimentation. This chapter provides insights into this array of disease taxonomies by explaining how factors responsible for a disease or illness, whether categorized as spiritual or physical, are determined, and the pathways that are employed in seeking solutions.

Among the Akan, an illness, depending on the predetermining factors before its onset, medium of contagion and response to treatment, often influences its interpretation as either physical or supernatural; mental illnesses are perceived to almost always fall into the latter category. In such instances, evil forces, particularly witchcraft or the use of *juju*, are often invoked as the causal factors. In this case, the illness assumes the interpretation of what is referred to as *sunsum yareɛ* (literally translated as spiritual illness). However, the question arises: Is the category of *sunsum yareɛ* always determined by evil spiritual forces such as witchcraft? What specifically do the Akan mean when they refer to an illness (in this case, mental illness) as *sunsum yareɛ*? The chapter further complicates the discussion by nuancing the discourse on mental illness as *sunsum yareɛ*. It argues that culturally, *sunsum yareɛ* is not always perceived to be influenced by witchcraft, as it is sometimes portrayed. There are other factors that might influence illnesses, such as mental illness, to be perceived as *sunsum yareɛ*, and this understanding can only be obtained when an individual has a broader and more comprehensive understanding of the Akan religious environment as well as the concept of the person and well-being.

Furthermore, the chapter explains how the Akan understanding of the causes of illness is reframed within a Pentecostal interpretation of illness. In so doing, the chapter foregrounds the ways in which aspects of Akan cultural understanding of illness are sustained, relived and addressed in Pentecostal settings, such as prayer camps. In other words, prayer camps appeal significantly to the Ghanaian populace because their belief systems and understanding and practices of healing align closely with Akan indigenous healing therapies. These understandings influence health-seeking pathways and determine what kinds of agency are employed in addressing an illness situation. Particularly for mental illnesses, the causes and effects determine who is consulted for remediation.

Akan concept of disease causation

The preceding discussion regarding the Akan concept of the person has established a foundation for comprehending the Akan perspective on illness. Gyekye (1995) posits that the Akan doctrine of being offers a suitable metaphysical framework for understanding and interpreting causality.

The Akan people of Ghana, prior to the introduction of Western medicine, possessed extensive knowledge of diverse categorizations of causality through observation, testing and experimentation (Gyekye 2013). In fact, numerous empirical studies have demonstrated how the Akan classified and treated diseases using observation and testing methods (Warren 1975, Warren et al. 1982; Wyllie 1983). These studies reveal that the classification process was based on the expertise of traditional priests, spiritual or prophetic healing church practitioners and herbalists within Akan society. These experienced healers were adept at identifying the nature of specific health conditions (Konadu 2019; Wyllie 1983). Although their approach primarily relied on traditional healing methods, their extensive experience in determining, categorizing and treating various diseases brought them recognition not only among society members but also from medical experts and researchers in the field of medical anthropology. In his work *Our Own Way in This Part of the World*, Kwasi Konadu (2019) highlights how the disease classification of renowned traditional healer Kofi Donkor, hailing from the Techiman-Bono area of Ghana, became the cornerstone for disease classification among medical experts and anthropologists, such as Stanford-trained biologist Dennis Warren.

What is evident in nearly all studies on the Akan concept of disease causation is the classification of two taxonomies: (1) natural or physical and (2) supernatural or spiritual. Obeng (2004) characterizes these two models of disease classification as the 'bipartite' concept of diseases among the Akan.[1] The Akan understanding of disease causation is not significantly different from disease categorization in other traditional African societies or non-Western contexts (Olsen and Sargent 2017; Brown 2013). Of particular importance is Foster's (1976) frequently cited categorizations of 'personalistic' and 'naturalistic' explanations for non-Western disease aetiologies. Personalistic causation occurs when an illness is believed to be caused by deliberate, purposeful intervention of human agents through malevolent practices, such as witchcraft, sorcery or juju, or by non-human agents such as ancestors, malevolent spirits, ghosts and supernatural entities as retribution for wrongdoing. Naturalistic causation refers to diseases caused by natural factors, including biological causes or pathogenic agents such as bacteria or viruses.

David Westerlund (2006), a historian of religion who writes on African indigenous religions and disease aetiologies, has expanded Foster's personalistic category into three subdivisions to facilitate comprehension and to encapsulate the essence of the framework for his study on *African Indigenous Religions and Disease Causation*. However, there appears to be no compelling rationale for Westerlund's compartmentalization, as it does not fundamentally alter the agent-oriented nature of Foster's categories. While articulating the claim of personalistic aetiologies poses certain challenges, the scientific basis for such explanations remains unrefuted. In fact, the personalistic principle has also been recognized in 'scientific' medicine (Munson 1981). Similarly, Allan Young's (1976) classification of medical systems as 'internalizing' or 'externalizing' within an Ethiopian context exhibits similarities to Foster's categorizations. According to Young (1976), internalizing medical systems attribute the causes, mechanisms and solutions for afflictions to factors within the individual, such as toxins, germs, evil spirits or trauma, which may be addressed to alleviate the individual's suffering. This process can be physical, psychological or metaphysical, aimed at removing any undesirable elements or malevolent entities from the individual's body. It may also involve the replenishment of nutrients that have been depleted, such as vitamins and other bodily nutrients. In contrast, externalizing medical systems attribute the causes of illness or affliction, along with their remedies, to factors outside the individual, primarily interpersonal, social or spiritual elements (Young 1976).

Akan view on supernatural/'personalistic' causes

One noteworthy aspect of the Akan's explanation of illness is their conception of the person. As previously discussed, the Akan believe that an individual consists of a spiritual component that continuously interacts with the cosmos or surrounding environment, which is teeming with spirits. Individuals possess the ability to engage with the realm of the spirit for both benevolent and malevolent purposes. Furthermore, since humans are partially composed of spirit, they may experience affliction when another spirit 'knocks them out'. Consequently, the interplay between spirits can result in tumultuous outcomes, underscoring the necessity for balance within the cosmos. Thus, health and wellness are interpreted as a state of cosmological balance in an individual's physical, mental/emotional and social life (Onyinah 2002).

Within the realm of spirits, there exist both human and non-human entities. Kwasi Sarpong, a Ghanaian anthropologist, elucidates that among the Akan, 'human spirits are believed to be spirits of people, animals, or trees, rivers etc. that have appeared in the visible form before, but are no longer perceptible' (Sarpong 2019: 248). Conversely, non-human spirits do not possess visible or tangible manifestations and encompass both benevolent and malevolent categories. The non-human agents comprise the Supreme Being (referred to as God, *Onyame* or *Onyankopon*), deities, ancestors and malevolent forces such as witchcraft. Sarpong further asserts that the Supreme Being, *Onyankopon*, represents the pinnacle of spirits, being the creator of all beings, including humanity, other spirits, the world and the universe, along with their contents and implications (Sarpong 2019).

In contrast to the Supreme Being, deities and ancestors derive pleasure from inflicting pain, misery and disaster. Other entities capable of causing pain and distress include the devil, witches, sorcerers and monsters residing in the sea or forest, among others. The Akan people of Ghana attribute the origin of disease to these spirits for several reasons (Sarpong 2019). For instance, as the orchestrator of life and death, the Supreme Being (God) is believed to punish wicked individuals or those who engage in malevolent practices by afflicting them with illness. Furthermore, it is posited that ancestors cause disease and death when the living transgress specific moral codes or violate established laws and customs. However, the punishments enacted by ancestors are confined to the members of their respective clans or families. For example, Pobee (2001: 58) notes that disease such as stroke is often believed to come about as a result of 'the wrath of the ancestors on a member of the clan who has cheated his brother's wife and children of their due in a deceased brother's estate'. According to Pobee (2001) the Akan call such illness *saman yarba* meaning an illness afflicted by the ancestors. Thus, 'ill health and good health are the doing of the ancestors and the nature of the case has to do with right relationships and justice in the kin group' (Pobee 2001: 58).

The tutelary spirits, known as *abosom*, also dispense unpleasant retributions to their adherents or to the adversaries of their adherents when offences are committed that are considered abhorrent (Sarpong 2019). It is also widely believed that both witches and magicians possess the ability to inflict sickness or disease upon their targets. However, a clear distinction exists between witches and magicians, or juju men, as there can never be a good witch, as previously argued; the archetype of a witch is inherently selfish. Conversely, there are instances of benevolent magicians (Sarpong 2019; Obeng 2004). Another factor contributing to the occurrence of disease is one's destiny. According to the Akan belief system, individuals declare to God their intentions prior to entering the world. This declaration is referred to as *hyebre*. In turn, God reveals to each individual what their responsibilities are, known as *nkrabea* in Akan culture. *Nkrabea* is considered inevitable, as encapsulated in the proverb, *Onyame nkrabea nni kwatibea*. It is important to note that one's *hyebre*, such as a negative habit or lifestyle, can lead to illness or poor health (Sarpong 2019).

When an individual falls ill and their condition cannot be remedied using scientific or Western medical methods, it is often posited that the illness has a spiritual origin. This belief is not isolated; rather, it is part of a spectrum of therapeutic interventions that may encompass biomedical treatments (Olsen 2017). The determination of whether a disease has a spiritual origin is typically conducted by a diviner, shrine priest or prophet-healer. Once it is confirmed that the illness is indeed spiritually induced, it is referred to as *sunsum yareɛ*.

As previously mentioned, *sunsum yareɛ* can be precipitated by the utilization of witchcraft motivated by jealousy. Such witchcraft attacks may readily afflict individuals whose *sunsum* is inherently vulnerable or 'light'. The term *sunsum* is invoked to indicate that the person has been afflicted by a disease through spiritual manipulation by a malevolent individual, either through witchcraft or by employing a *juju* man to induce the illness. Or that the illness might be influenced by a spiritual medium that is not necessarily a witchcraft.

Additionally, *sunsum yareɛ* may also arise from familial conflicts or as a form of ancestral punishment. In both instances, it is the diviner's responsibility to identify the root cause of the malaise and provide appropriate remedies. In cases of witchcraft-induced ailments, the malevolent spirit is expelled from the individual's body to restore health. Conversely, when the affliction is attributed to ancestral or family discord, sacrifices may be administered to appease the offending spirits, or the individual must confess, seek forgiveness and reconcile with those aggrieved before healing can be accomplished. The process of seeking forgiveness and reconciliation is known as *nteteho* among the Akan (Ayim-Aboagye 2006). It is imperative to note that not all diseases are ascribed to witchcraft, as some scholars argue. John Janzen has emphasized that, while researchers may be inclined to attribute illness in Africa to 'human relations and human society', it is misleading to assume or assert that witchcraft underpins or influences every aspect of health and illness (Janzen 1992: 196).

Akan view on natural/biological causes

Apart from the belief in supernatural causes of disease, Akan society also acknowledges that illness can arise from external factors such as bacteria or viruses. For instance, the Akan understand that consuming food with unclean hands can lead to a bacterial infection and subsequent illness. Similarly, exposure to mosquito bites can result in malaria. However, what is particularly noteworthy about the Akan's interpretation of natural events is the emphasis on the underlying causes behind them.

While the Akan recognize that consuming food with unclean hands can lead to illness, they are more concerned with determining who or what may have influenced the individual to eat with contaminated hands. In other words, the focus is not solely on the unclean hands as the direct cause of the disease but rather on identifying the spiritual entity or force that influenced the individual's behaviour (Asante 2017). Consequently, although the Akan may possess an awareness of scientific or empirical explanations for causality, they do not regard these explanations as sufficiently comprehensive or satisfactory (Asante 2017).

To illustrate this perspective, consider the following scenario presented by Sarpong (2019): If a child is involved in a fatal car accident, the parents may attribute it to witchcraft. When one explains that the accident was actually caused by a mechanical failure, such as a burst tyre, an ordinary Akan individual might respond with a series of 'why' questions. They would seek to understand not only how the accident occurred but also why it happened, why that particular tyre burst, why previous instances of tyre bursts did not result in accidents and why not all the passengers died. This emphasis on the 'why' highlights the Akan's desire for thorough explanations (Sarpong 2019).

Akan disease classification: Some divergences

Let me clarify that the purpose of this book is not to present an Akan disease classification, as this task falls within the domain of medical anthropologists. However, it is essential to provide fundamental background information regarding Akan disease classification to enable readers to comprehend the context of the ensuing discussion and analysis within the book.

In the preceding section, I indicated that the Akan employ two primary forms of disease categorization: natural and supernatural. I also furnished examples of various potential causes of illnesses. While this categorization does not purport to offer a specific disease classification, it provides a general outlook on how the Akan perceive illnesses, irrespective of whether they are spiritual or physical, biological or natural, and irrespective of whether they result from external or internal factors within or beyond the individual. As previously mentioned, Warren (1975) endeavoured to create an all-encompassing categorization of Akan disease classification or a lexical inventory of diverse Akan diseases. Yet, his work has encountered substantial criticism for its lack of representativeness, as it is based on an abstract and generalized model of Akan medical knowledge, confined to one specific Akan locality in Bono-Techiman, Ghana (see Konadu 2008). Examples of disease categorization offered by Warren include 'mogya mu yadeɛ' (diseases with a natural causation), 'sunsum mu yadeɛ' (diseases with a spiritual causation), 'nsane yadeɛ' (contagious diseases) and 'bayifoɔ yadeɛ' (diseases caused by witchcraft power used for malevolent purposes), among others. Konadu (2007) has also offered similar categorizations.

It is crucial to emphasize that, among the Akan, an illness is attributed to either spiritual or physical causes. Thus, irrespective of the classification proposed by Warren (1975) and Konadu (2007), the Akan only acknowledge or recognize two potential causes of diseases. This is typically classified as *sunsum mu yareɛ* (spiritually caused disease) or *honam mu yareɛ* (physical or natural illness). Scholars such as Fosu (1981) and Obeng (2004), both Ghanaians, have upheld the binary distinction between physical and spiritual as the basis for Akan disease classification.

Another noteworthy aspect is that the binary distinction between natural and supernatural disease causation among the Akan is not rigid but rather fluid. A particular type of disease can be classified as both natural and supernatural, contingent upon the medium through which the disease was contracted. In other words, the binary distinction can be context-specific and does not invariably lend itself to straightforward identification or classification. Allow me to employ Warren's own example, which he asserts was provided by one of his priest-healer informants, to elucidate my argument further:

> If a man slept with a married woman and later learned that the husband had visited a local medicine man, followed by the man contracting gonorrhoea (babaso), the babaso would be classified as a spiritually caused disease. The person would not have known that the married woman had contracted gonorrhoea, but would have realized that a cultural norm had been broken and that the spouse had visited a healer, probably to obtain means to punish the social deviance. The babaso would be considered to be that punishment. If the victim had, on the other hand, visited a prostitute, from whom it is common knowledge that babaso can be contracted, the disease would be classified as a naturally-caused disease. (Warren 1975: 119)

From Warren's illustration, one can argue that the differentiation between diseases as either natural or supernatural primarily hinges on the mode of transmission or the method by which the disease was acquired. Indeed, Warren (1975) acknowledges that a particular disease can belong to both the natural and supernatural categories. In certain circumstances, the outcome of the treatment determines or influences the interpretation one assigns to their ailment, whether it is perceived as being of a spiritual or natural nature. For example, experiencing occasional headaches is a commonplace occurrence. Typically, headaches can be addressed with an over-the-counter pain reliever obtained from a pharmacy. However, if the headache persists after several days or months of treatment, the question of why the affliction continues becomes significant. In such instances, a variety of interpretations are considered, including potential spiritual influences as causes. This is why chronic illnesses are often presumed to possess a spiritual dimension or influence.

Furthermore, a thorough inquiry may be conducted into whether the traditional Akan ideology encompassed a belief in the dualism of disease causation, whether it was natural or supernatural, prior to the arrival of Western influences. Additionally, it is feasible to explore whether the classification of diseases into dichotomies represents a recent development influenced by Western discourses. However, it must be acknowledged that addressing this question presents considerable challenges, primarily due to the scarcity of documented discourse on these matters during the pre-Western encounter era. Nevertheless, it has been substantiated that the Akan possessed knowledge of employing herbs for the treatment of various ailments through experimentation and testing, even prior to their engagement with Westerners or Europeans. Therefore, it is evident that the Akan's pre-encounter way of life demonstrates their awareness of diverse diseases and their corresponding treatments.

Consequently, it can be asserted that the Akan comprehended that specific diseases could be remedied solely through the use of herbs, without necessitating any spiritual interventions. However, even in the utilization of herbs, certain spiritual rituals were involved in the preparation of particular plants, such as the act of pouring libations prior to plucking leaves or bark used for treating specific ailments. Some leaves are even collected specifically at night. As the documentation of these practices emerged only during the post-Western encounter phase, reliance on Western sources may be necessary to ascertain how the Akan classified diseases. As a result, making a definitive claim on this matter becomes particularly challenging.

Mental illness as spiritual sickness (sunsum mu yareɛ)

It is important to note that there is no universally accepted definition of mental illness. Rather, mental illness encompasses a variety of different disorders (Thornton 2022; McNally 2011; Patel et al. 1995). Furthermore, the meaning of mental illness varies across different societies. There are numerous factors that contribute to the understanding of mental illness, including causation, symptoms, treatments and outcomes. Research conducted in Ghana has revealed a lack of consensus regarding the concept of mental illness (Yendork et al. 2017; 2019; Kpobi and Swartz 2018). The MHA (2018) states that existing studies on mental health in Ghana cannot be generalized due to their lack of epidemiological robustness.

In Ghana, the most commonly associated disorders with mental illness are psychotic and affective disorders, such as mania, bipolar disorder and schizophrenia. These disorders are often labelled as *abodam*, which translates to 'madness', and are frequently observed among individuals seeking treatment at psychiatric clinics (Yendork et al. 2019; Arias et al. 2016). Additionally, there are cases of mental disorders resulting from substance abuse and alcoholism, as well as anxiety disorders and depression (Aning 2019). When referring to mental illness in this book, the focus is primarily on psychotic and affective disorders, including mania, schizophrenia, bipolar disorder and other forms of mental disorders induced by substance abuse, such as narcotic drugs, marijuana and alcoholism. It is important to note here that these categorizations of mental illness as found in the prayer camps are not based on clinical judgement as that is not the focus of this book. My reference to the above-mentioned mental disorders at prayer camps in Ghana is based on conversations with health professionals assisting the care and support of individuals with mental illnesses at prayer camps in Ghana as well as literature categorizing the various kinds of mental illnesses send to prayer camps or Pentecostal healing centres for healing (Kpobi and Swartz 2018; Ofori-Atta et al. 2018).

Despite the various biological, physiological, social and environmental factors that may contribute to the development of the aforementioned mental illnesses, there is a prevalent belief among the Akan that some of these illnesses may be caused or influenced by personal or impersonal evil forces, such as witchcraft and *juju*. However, in order to elucidate the complexities of mental illness within its contextual framework, I aim to clarify the terminology that has caused confusion in the existing literature.

Previous studies investigating traditional healing and faith-based approaches to mental illness in Ghana have consistently classified mental illness as *sunsum yareɛ*, attributed to *bayie* (witchcraft), curses, offending individuals and ancestral spirits (Yendork et al. 2019; Read, 2017; Opare-Henaku and Utsey 2017; Arias et al. 2016;

Ayim-Aboagye 2006; Field 1960). While these studies have relied on the accounts of their participants and should not be criticized for any inaccuracies, and possibly for not critically examining the broader significance of *sunsum* within Akan illness narratives due to it not being part of their main objectives, I would argue that the neglect, whether conscious or unconscious, has had implications on how the term is used in broader analyses of mental illness among the Akan. Among the Akan population, the concept of *sunsum*, which refers to the spirit, is multifaceted and requires conceptual clarity when applied to diseases or illnesses such as mental illness.

Prominent scholars such as Rattray (1927), Danquah (1968), Gyekye (1987) and Konadu (2007) have provided definitions of the Akan term *sunsum*, which is commonly translated as spirit. However, *sunsum* also encompasses the concept of 'anything intangible or unseen' (Ephirim-Donkor 2015: 40). The Akan people believe that spirits exist in some form and have independent existence. Therefore, the fact that something is not visible does not negate its existence. It is also believed that spirits have an influence on human activity and nature (Ephirim-Donkor 2015). It is important to note that the term *sunsum* does not inherently imply malevolence. Consequently, interpreting mental illness as *sunsum yareɛ*, primarily caused by evil forces such as witchcraft or *juju*, is somewhat misleading and fails to capture the true contextual essence of the term. The *Advanced Akan Dictionary* translates the word 'spiritual' as *honhom mu nneɛma* (Anane 2018), which means 'things that concern the spirit' and does not directly translate as 'spirit'. This implies that it refers to how things are mediated through spirit mediums or, in other words, things that pertain to the spirit. This has implications for how spiritual illness (*sunsum yareɛ*) is conceptualized or interpreted.

Contrary to popular belief, the Akan do not conceptualize mental illness as a spiritual affliction. Rather, they perceive it as a physical ailment that may be influenced by spiritual forces or causative spiritual means. For instance, Field (1961: 102) notes that among the Ga people in Ghana, 'madness is regarded as a disease and is treated as other diseases'. This indicates that mental illness is not invariably associated with supernatural elements or regarded as a spiritual condition. Strictly speaking, distinctions exist between spiritual illness and illness caused by spiritual factors; the two are not synonymous from the Akan perspective. This understanding arises from the belief that the spirit itself cannot become ill. In essence, it is not the spirit that suffers but the individual. Consequently, it is the attribution or interpretation assigned to the cause of the illness that renders it *sunsum mu yareɛ*. However, the illness itself is not intrinsically spiritual. The emphasis lies on the causal agent rather than the disease itself. It is this causal agent, perceived as spiritual, that is believed to have the capacity to assail the soul or spirit of the affected individual, thereby causing sickness. This perspective informs the Akan ritual process known as *kra dwaree*, which refers to the washing of the soul, particularly for individuals who are ill and receiving treatment at traditional healing shrines. *Kra dwaree* can only occur once the illness has manifested. This elucidates the strong interrelationship between the spiritual and material realms within the Akan world-view.

To illustrate this point, consider the case of an individual involved in a motor vehicle accident resulting in a severe injury that necessitates the amputation of a leg. The amputation is perceived as a physical consequence of the accident; however, the cause of the accident may be attributed to supernatural forces. Nonetheless, this does not categorize the amputation as a spiritual event or illness. This example demonstrates the dualistic nature of the Akan world-view regarding the causation of disease. Understanding these conceptual distinctions is vital for comprehending the therapeutic approaches employed by the Akan when seeking assistance for mental health conditions or general health issues.

In the field of Akan anthropology, the concept of *sunsum* serves to provide protection for an individual (Rattray 1927), particularly when understood as one of the constituent elements of human beings. However, when used in a more general sense, the term can carry multiple meanings depending on the context and the verb used in conjunction with it. For instance, when referring to mental illness, *sunsum yareɛ* can encompass various interpretations, including the widely held belief that such afflictions are caused by malevolent spirits like witches. Nevertheless, it should be noted that mental illness, as *sunsum yareɛ*, can also be understood in ways that do not necessarily imply evil or malevolence from the perspectives of Akan traditional or indigenous knowledge systems. In such cases, the use of the term *yareɛ* itself may not be appropriate for describing the individual's circumstances. The following points aim to further clarify these arguments.

First, one specific category of mental illness, commonly referred to as *sunsum yareɛ* in academic literature, is frequently discussed as being caused by witchcraft. As already mentioned, this type of illness is typically attributed to feelings of envy or jealousy, with individuals seeking the assistance of medicine men (*juju*) to afflict their enemies with a disease (Kpobi and Swartz 2018; Mullings 1984). It can also arise as a result of curses brought about by one's own actions or offenses against others, as well as punishments from deities or ancestral spirits for violating moral codes (Opare-Henaku 2013). Mental illnesses believed to be caused by any of these aforementioned means are classified as *sunsum yareɛ*, as they are believed to have been inflicted through a spirit medium. However, in traditional Akan societies, a punishment from a deity or ancestral spirit may not necessarily be viewed as evil but rather as a means of upholding moral order and decorum within the community.

In the context of Pentecostal healing settings, such as the prayer camps, the activities of ancestral spirits are interpreted as part of a legion of evil spirits that must be exorcised or dealt with in order to free oneself from any form of bondage (Meyer 1999). This is because among Pentecostals, anything that has to do with ancestral spirits or deities is perceived as demonic and must be expelled to free oneself from any forms of bondage. Another example of *sunsum yareɛ* in Akan belief is the interpretation of psychotic symptoms induced by the consumption of substances such as cocaine and marijuana. In this case, if the individual or their family members perceive that the drug use was influenced by an external force, it may be attributed to the manipulation of evil forces, such as witchcraft driven by jealousy or envy. The intent behind this attribution is that the individual who perpetuated such act against the fellow wants to hinder the individual from achieving his or her life goals. Both traditional Akan beliefs and Akan Pentecostal Christianity share similar views regarding the potential causes of mental illness in this particular case (Kpobi and Swartz 2018).

Second, another category of mental illness as *sunsum yareɛ* can also be referred to as *ebusua yareɛ*, commonly known as *yadeafo*. These illnesses exhibit physical symptoms but are believed to have social and metaphysical causes. According to McCaskie (2000), they are considered diseases that are passed down through generations within kinship relationships. Warren (1975) uses the term *awosanne/abusua yareɛ* to refer to the same type of disease. In the literature on mental illness in Ghana, this type of mental illness is often attributed to generational curse by participants (Yendork et al. 2019; Arias et al. 2016). However, in the traditional Akan context, these illnesses are not typically attributed to witchcraft or evil spirits. Instead, they are seen as a consequence of angry spirits seeking to cause suffering and pain due to the failure to fulfil a promise in covenant relationship with a spiritual entity by an individual or their ancestors. In such cases, appropriate sacrifices or rituals must be performed to appease the spirits and restore health. On the other hand, Akan Pentecostals typically interpret these illnesses as a result of demonic influence and seek deliverance through a prophet at a Pentecostal/Charismatic church or a prayer camp. This is because, in Pentecostal/Charismatic 'healing and deliverance' diagnosis, when difficulties in life follow a specific pattern, it is often believed to indicate the influence of evil forces at work (Asamoah-Gyadu 2005b). For instance, individuals visiting prayer camps in Ghana are often required to complete a 'healing and deliverance questionnaire' or be interviewed by prayer camp staff to identify recurring patterns of failure in their lives. Persistent death occurrences within a particular family, the presence of inherited disabilities and diseases and families with a history of mental issues and alcoholism, among other factors, may all be interpreted as signs of demonic powers at work (Asamoah-Gyadu 2005b). Asamoah-Gyadu (2005b: 102) argues that although some of these problems or illnesses may have natural causes, it is believed that malevolent spirits, including ancestral ones, 'may hijack the situation and worsen the plight of victims, sometimes even carrying it along the family line'. Therefore, 'Pentecostal/Charismatic ministry of "healing and deliverance" provides a Christian ritual context in which the enslaving effects of generational curses resulting from the sins of one's ancestry may be broken' (Asamoah-Gyadu 2004: 334).

Third, as already mentioned, in Akan philosophical thought, an imbalance or disharmony among the constituent elements (soul, spirit and mind) of the human person may lead to a state of ill health. The soul is closely associated with the notion of conscience (Ephirim-Donkor 2015), and any disturbance in one's conscience can give rise to psychosocial distress, ultimately resulting in mental illness. This distress can be interpreted as *sunsum yareɛ* because it is the soul, an intangible part of the human person, that is affected resulting in physical illness in the form of anxiety or depression. In certain cases, the fragmentation between body, mind and soul resulting from wrongdoing can manifest as schizophrenia, characterized by a split or divided mind, or as multiple personality disorder, also known as dissociative identity disorder (Ayim-Aboagye 2006; Scrutton 2021). When these symptoms occur, sacrifices or appropriate rituals are performed to restore harmony within the individual. However, it is important to note that this form of *sunsum yareɛ* does not necessarily imply the influence of malevolent spirits; rather, it is the imbalance of elements within the human person that brings about distress. Such imbalance can stem from broken relationships with parents, a marriage partner, friends, loved ones or even spirit entities. In such situations, reconciliation or forgiveness serves as the appropriate means of remediation, and certain ritual practices can provide relief to the individual's soul and spirit.

Fourth, in certain instances, the manifestation of spirit possession within an individual's body has been regarded as a manifestation of mental illness, thereby being perceived as *sunsum yareɛ*. This understanding emerges when the possessed individual displays disruptive behaviour, detaches themselves from social interactions and communicates in incomprehensible language or utterances. Although these symptoms may resemble hallucinations, it is imperative to acknowledge the existence of genuine religious encounters in which a person, regardless of religious affiliation, may become possessed by a spirit to convey significant messages to a religious community or to foretell or explicate the cause of an event (Schmidt 2017; Schmidt and Huskinson 2010; Schreurs 2002). Examples of such encounters encompass the perception of the presence of the Holy Spirit or the sensing of ancestral spirits striving to communicate. These sensations of possession are widespread in traditional Akan societies and are also greatly esteemed personal encounters within Christian contexts. Among the Ga, as previously mentioned, Field (1961) observes that if an individual is chosen by a deity to serve as its mouthpiece and subsequently refuses to comply with the call to act as a medium, that individual frequently experiences what is termed 'madness'. However, Field contends that this particular manifestation of madness is conceptually distinct, according to the beliefs of the Ga, from 'plain undirected madness' or actual madness (Field 1961: 102). Thus, the Ga differentiate between madness as a disease and spirit possession, which is frequently associated with the same phenomenon. If a mental health practitioner lacks awareness of the cultural milieu surrounding these encounters, they may mistakenly interpret them as symptoms of mental illness (see Patel et al. 1995). Consequently, when the underlying cause of these symptoms remains undisclosed by a diviner, such as a shrine priest or a prophet at a prayer camp, family members of the afflicted individual may also categorize these encounters as *sunsum yareɛ*.

Importantly, it should be emphasized that the above-mentioned experiences of mental illness can all be influenced by some form of spiritual element. Thus, *sunsum yareɛ* is multiplex in Akan thought and, therefore, mental illness can be *sunsum yareɛ* perceived to be caused by some spirit mediums. Nevertheless, it is vital to recognize that not all of these experiences are connected to witchcraft or malevolent forces, as some might assume when discussing the comprehension, interpretation or significance attributed to mental illness as *sunsum yareɛ*.

How Akan disease aetiologies are recast in Pentecostal interpretation

Among Ghanaian Akan Pentecostal Christians, there exists a prevalent belief in the connection between sin, the activities of demons and illness (Asamoah-Gyadu 2005). To support this perspective, sermons often reference biblical passages such as Mk 5.1-20, Mt. 17.14-21, Lk. 13.10-17 and Jas. 5.14-16. Read (2017: 168) notes that 'the pervasive influence of Pentecostal Christianity has revivified the attribution of illness and misfortune to malign spiritual forces, framed within the Biblical cosmology of the demonic'. Even prior to their adoption of Christianity, the Akan acknowledged sin and spirits as possible causes of illness. They recognized the presence of supernatural forces, including *Nyankopon* (the Supreme Being), deities and ancestors, who could inflict punishment on individuals for wrongdoing in the form of sickness. Furthermore, they were cognizant of the existence of spiritual entities that individuals could employ to inflict pain and sickness on others. With these pre-existing convictions, Akan Christians found it easy to assimilate the teachings of the Bible, as their traditional world-view corresponded with that of the biblical world, thereby reinforcing their belief in spirits and sin as potential contributors to illness.

Indeed, the understanding of illness plays a vital role in shaping the Pentecostal interpretation of health and well-being. The flexibility of the Pentecostal movement in adapting to local cultures, particularly in explaining the origins of phenomena such as illness and healing, has contributed significantly to its expansion throughout Africa and other regions. Kalu (2002) asserts that the substantial contribution of Pentecostal movements in Africa lies in their capacity to perceive a connection between African cultural forms and a biblical dichotomy between a godly covenant and the hindrances posed by other perceived evil covenants that inhibit progress. In this world-view, both Pentecostals and the Akan community affirm the notion that the visible world is composed of elements that are not visible (Heb. 11.3b), and conflicts occurring in the physical realm are initially resolved in the spiritual realm. Consequently, it is believed that 'the weapons of our warfare are not carnal'. Both Pentecostal and Akan world-views acknowledge the influence of spiritual forces on human beings.

Research conducted on Pentecostal prayer camps and traditional healing shrines in Ghana reveals that these entities share analogous perspectives regarding the perceived causes of illness. Both healing environments contend that witchcraft, sin, hostile forces and various other factors may be responsible for ailments (Benyah 2024). Omenyo (2014) posits that within the Ghanaian context, Pentecostals provide Christian interpretations of indigenous explanations for illness, which they believe can be surmounted through their practice of divine healing. Consequently, Pentecostals reinforce the causal patterns prevalent in primal world-views before offering a solution that transcends the limits of indigenous cosmology (Kalu 2008). In other words, Pentecostals have cultivated 'a culture of continuity' by drawing from primal world-views, thereby 'reproducing an identifiable character' and reclaiming a religious devotion characterized by spiritual and charismatic fervour that was evident in traditional society (Kalu 2008: 186). Prophets within prayer camps utilize divinatory and revelatory practices to elucidate the causes of illnesses, thereby linking the experience of illness to a symbolic space constructed by cosmological beliefs regarding health and healing, which holds significance for both patients and healers.

In the preceding discussion, the question concerning the origin of the dualistic perception of the causes of illness and its association with Western discourses was raised. While a definitive answer could not be provided, it is crucial to elucidate the relationship between the terms 'demonic' or 'evil forces' and the causation of disease. It was mentioned that both Pentecostalism and Akan world-views interpret healing as liberation from attacks and oppression by demonic and evil forces. This perspective reflects the broader academic debate surrounding the connection between Pentecostalism and African Indigenous or Traditional Religions, frequently examined in terms of continuity and discontinuity (Anderson 2018). Nevertheless, it is imperative to acknowledge relevant discontinuities by highlighting certain meanings and distinctions. For instance, the concept of 'demonic forces' associated with the Christian conception of the devil did not exist within Akan Traditional Religions. Although the Akan may have held beliefs in evil spirits, these entities were not typically construed as inherently evil and demonic until missionary Christianity associated them with the Christian idea of the devil. This crucial argument is presented in Meyer's (1999) book, *Translating the Devil*. Therefore, while Pentecostalism exhibits continuity with traditional world-views, it simultaneously undergoes transformation through a globalized and modern Christian discourse. Indeed, Robbins (2003) underscores the significance of recognizing the discontinuities exemplified by Pentecostals. He argues that despite apparent attempts to indigenize or localize their faith within host communities, Pentecostals ultimately introduce significant changes that engender real discontinuities in people's lives (Robbins 2003). Similar arguments have been articulated in other scholarly works (Benyah 2024).

How Akan establish a pattern of causality and method of healing

The Akan people and Akan Pentecostal Christians exhibit a specific understanding of illness and its perceived causes, which significantly influences their selection of therapeutic interventions when faced with health issues. The 'explanatory model' associated with their illness plays a pivotal role in shaping these choices. These illness narratives provide a framework for comprehending the 'experience of illness' and the meanings attributed to disease symptoms, while also guiding the pursuit of healing through particular types of therapy (Kleinman 1988: 49). Olsen (2017) underscores that illness narratives represent shared stories between the patient and their close associates, highlighting key events, symbolic codes and social processes that facilitate the conveyance of the significance of the illness. Such narratives frequently establish connections between bodily symptoms and the patient's environment. Moreover, Olsen (2017) argues that patients often contextualize their narratives within the framework of personal history, social and natural surroundings as well as mystical aspects and realms encompassing human experience, physicality and the supernatural.

Irrespective of the narratives articulated for any specific illness, treatment decisions are primarily dictated by the disease symptoms. In either circumstance, the condition may improve should the body respond favourably to treatment, or it may deteriorate in the event of treatment failure (Olsen 2017). What becomes evident when treatment proves ineffective is the emergence of cultural processes employed to elucidate the reasons behind the lack of response to treatment, particularly regarding biomedical interventions. It is essential to recognize that, in most instances, individuals of Akan descent seek medical assistance from a hospital as their initial recourse upon falling ill. Nonetheless, when treatment is found to be ineffective, alternative therapeutic methods are activated to investigate the underlying causes of the prolonged illness. The decision to explore alternative explanations for the sickness is typically made by the therapy management group of the patient, encompassing family members, friends and occasionally medical professionals. As already mentioned, an individual is regarded as the property of the clan (*abusua*), which is expected to care for its members. If an unexpected misfortune occurs, such as illness, the saying *abusua na woko abisa* encapsulates the obligation of the family to take responsibility for consultation (*abisa*) to ascertain the causes, with the goal of restoring the *odehye* (prince/princess) to the family (Onyinah 2012).

The process may involve seeking assistance from a traditional priest or diviner, a prophet-healer in Pentecostal healing camps or prayer centres and sometimes even consulting mallams. This approach does not imply a lack of faith in the efficacy of biomedicine on the part of the patient and their family; rather, it signifies that the illness transcends the scope of resolution through biomedical treatment, extending beyond the parameters of scientific intervention. Consequently, 'the body becomes subject to other illness-defining criteria that make sense within the social and cultural world of the sick person' but 'are not recognized as legitimate within orthodox medicine. Local modes of healing address these differences and complexities through medical and religious practices' (Olsen 2017: 52).

At the traditional shrine or prayer camp, the shrine priest, or prophet-healer, who also serves as a diviner, consults the divine to ascertain the cause of prolonged illness. This process is known as *abisa*. An *abisa* is defined as a 'divinatory consultation or the desire to discern the supernatural causations of events' (Onyinah 2012: 85). According to Onyinah (2012), an *abisa* represents a focal point of religious activities among the Akan and is prominent in the work of the *akomfo*, who are the principal figures in *abosomsom* (the worship of the gods). An *abisa* also constitutes a form of indigenous or traditional *akom* (possession) therapy employed to extract information from a patient.

During the practice of *abisa*, the oracle or deity being consulted communicates through the shrine priest, imparting information to the sick individual and their family members regarding the causes and persistence of the illness. If it is determined that the illness has a supernatural origin, appropriate rituals and sacrifices are conducted to facilitate the person's recovery. The role of the *Okomfo*, serving as the shrine priest, is to implement the healing process. Ephirim-Donkor (2008) has observed that the *Okomfo* possess knowledge concerning the treatment of various ailments, and prior to employing their medicinal expertise, they engage in divination to ascertain the diagnosis, thereby ensuring that the healing addresses both the physical and psychological dimensions. Ephirim-Donkor (2008) argues that this practice is crucial for addressing the spiritual diagnosis of what may otherwise be perceived as a physical affliction. The ritual process may involve banishing the malevolent spirit responsible for the illness, administering herbal baths and seeking forgiveness and reconciliation from offended deities, individuals or family members. In her work *In Search for Security*, Margaret Field (1960) documents numerous instances of individuals from rural Ghana seeking healing shrines for an *abisa* to identify the root causes of various mental disorders. She provides several examples of complaints and requests made during a routine *abisa*, which include unspecified sickness, drunkards seeking rescue, depression, mental illness stemming from physical ailments, involutional psychoses, schizophrenia and more.

Abisa, while a widely practised custom within Akan Traditional Religion, has gained prominence in healing practices at prayer camps in Ghana and within neo-prophetic churches (Quayesi-Amakye 2013; Onyinah 2012). At prayer camps, family members send their sick loved ones to consult with a prophet, who is believed to possess the ability, conferred by the Holy Spirit, to probe beyond the physical realm, similar to the shrine priest. The prophet is capable of discerning the cause of the illness and recommending the necessary remedy.

Depending on the outcome of the *abisa*, appropriate recommendations or directions (*akwankyere*) are made for rituals to restore the individual's health. These recommendations may include periods of fasting and prayer, deliverance processes to expel perceived supernatural forces believed to be responsible for the illness, seeking forgiveness for sins and reconciling broken relationships. Thus, 'during healing rituals, issues may be raised that are relevant to others who attend the ritual, and some of the effects of the intervention may be through its ability to change the afflicted person's relationship with family and community' (Kirmayer and Swartz 2013: 48). Kirmayer and Swartz (2013) further argue that 'healing then works not only to relieve symptoms and resolve illness but also to restore proper relations with ancestors and within the community'. Consequently, healing is not solely directed towards expelling perceived demonic or spiritual forces but also aims to rectify disturbances within social structures. This aspect of the healing process contributes to improving the individual's physical and emotional well-being, ensuring the proper functioning of the self. Among the Akan of Ghana, this framework of interpretation serves as a lens through which the causes of mental illness are understood. The set of ideas regarding sickness often derives its meaning from this body of cultural knowledge about health and healing. The patient's condition is frequently interpreted within this knowledge framework to name the condition and determine a course of therapy.

It is not always the case that a shrine or a prayer camp can provide a remedy for an illness that persists even after treatment at a hospital or clinic. In such instances, patients and their families may seek the guidance of alternative practitioners, such as Mallams, or they may adopt a combination of diverse healing therapies, including biomedicine and faith healing, or even attempt all available therapies in an effort to restore health. It is not uncommon to encounter individuals at a prayer camp who simultaneously utilize prescribed medications while engaging in fasting and prayer. This approach reflects an acknowledgement of the dynamic nature of medical pluralism in Ghana, where the treatment of illness involves a process of trial and error, as described by Feierman (2000). This process not only underscores how family members and their suffering relatives cope with illness but also illustrates how illness narratives incorporate various medical technologies, hospital diagnoses, global pharmaceuticals and local culture.

Summary

The categorization of mental illness as *sunsum mu yareɛ* encompasses a comprehensive notion of the concept of the person and the cosmos, as well as the spirit beings believed to inhabit this cosmos. Unpacking the meaning of mental illness as expressed in the concept of *sunsum yareɛ* offers insights into the reasons individuals experiencing mental illnesses may sometimes prefer to seek spiritual support from a prophet at a prayer camp rather than accessing a hospital or medical facility. Within the Ghanaian context, the conceptualization of mental illness as *sunsum yareɛ* provides a framework for understanding the utility value of religion as a significant resource in the care of individuals requiring mental health support, as well as the role of pastor-prophets at prayer camps in delivering such care. While some individuals contend that religion does not offer substantial resources in the care of those with mental illness, the concept of mental illness as *sunsum mu yareɛ* reveals considerable pathways for recognizing religious resources as essential tools for supporting individuals afflicted with mental illness in contexts such as Ghana and elsewhere in Africa.

As illustrated in this chapter, the understanding of illness and associated healing practices are rooted in Akan traditional beliefs and concepts of health and healing. While there exist scientific methods for treating illnesses, traditional and religious approaches to healing encompass divinatory and ritual practices that hold emotional and transformative significance for participants. Although it may be challenging to measure or quantify the outcomes of healing obtained through prayer or religious rituals, it is feasible to assess the therapeutic value derived from such practices. The primary issue lies in the apparent conflict between biomedicine and traditional and/or religious healing. However, there is no inherent irrationality in integrating diagnostic processes that combine scientific and religious healing if such integration leads to desired outcomes. After all, individuals in Ghana and elsewhere in Africa navigate between different healing spaces in their search for cures for their illnesses (Gammelin 2018). This illustrates how individuals can simultaneously appreciate various medical systems while remaining open to both practices. While scientific advancements in medicine have yielded significant results, there are still regions of the world that have not yet accessed or encountered sophisticated medical technologies. In low-resource countries, for instance, there are ongoing opportunities to enhance the delivery of medical care and practice. In such contexts, it is not practical to completely dismiss practices that have historically provided effective solutions for medical conditions. Disregarding religious and traditional cultural practices as backward, primitive or outdated in light of modern technological and scientific developments can potentially undermine healthcare. Recognizing this, the World Health Organization has acknowledged the importance of integrating cultural knowledge and experiences in the treatment of diseases, including mental illness (WHO 2002).

The contextual explanation of mental illness as *sunsum yareɛ* provides valuable insights into how the Akan people comprehend and seek support for mental health issues. In Ghana, not everyone who seeks help from a pastor or prophet at a prayer camp does so because they believe their problem is caused by witchcraft. However, in some cases, the decision to seek support from a religious authority like a prophet is motivated by the desire to mend broken relationships and conflicts within the individual's mind, soul and spirit, often resulting from strained interactions with close relatives or family members, such as parents, siblings, spouse and so on. Consequently, the issue at hand may not necessarily be a medical condition but rather the quest to find a trustworthy religious figure who can provide the necessary assistance. Hence, while some individuals approach prayer camps in the hope that the perceived demons associated with their afflictions will be expelled, others go seeking emotional and communal support that may not be readily available in hospitals or clinics. In other words, the holistic approach to healing at prayer camps, which addresses not only the physical symptoms of an individual but also their spiritual and emotional well-being, is highly appealing. To put it simply, doctors treat the body, whereas pastors and prophets focus on healing relationships (Ahyi 1997).

The next chapter focuses on elucidating the historical context of prayer camps within the framework of Ghanaian Pentecostal historiography. This discourse aims to provide a comprehensive overview of prayer camps and their activities in Ghana, while also situating them within the broader context of faith-based healing practices in the country.

Chapter 4

THE EVOLUTION OF PRAYER CAMPS IN GHANAIAN PENTECOSTALISM

Prayer camps, also referred to as prayer centres,[1] are religious establishments in Ghana where individuals seek spiritual or supernatural remedies for various problems, including economic, social, political and marital issues (Omenyo 2002; Onyinah 2012; Larbi 2015). According to Emmanuel Kingsley Larbi, a Ghanaian Pentecostal theologian, people visit these prayer camps for a multitude of reasons, such as healing from illness, financial struggles, legal troubles, addiction, educational challenges, housing concerns, witchcraft accusations, demonic attacks and more (Larbi 2015). Some individuals also go to these camps to seek God's guidance and receive a special anointing for a divine calling, such as entering ministry (Asamoah-Gyadu 2007). Others visit prayer camps to seek breakthroughs in life, whether it involves starting a business or pursuing a career. Additionally, individuals who aspire to travel to countries like America or European countries for academic or economic opportunities, which may not be readily available in Ghana, visit prayer camps to pray and seek God's favour or blessings before embarking on such journeys, particularly when invited for visa appointments at embassies of their desired destination countries (Van Dijk 1997).

Visitors to prayer camps may stay for extended periods, ranging from days to months or even years, waiting upon God to heal their sickness or provide answers to their prayers and solutions to their problems. A lengthier stay at a camp can be attributed to the severity of one's illness or problem or at the instruction of a camp leader (Larbi 2015).[2] Those who seek solutions to their problems or illnesses at these camps often engage in fasting and prayer. Due to the role of prayer camps in assisting individuals with their health, economic and social challenges in an environment with limited healthcare infrastructure and social welfare systems, these camps have emerged as significant religious institutions in the public, private and religious life of many Ghanaians today.

Prayer camps have been a long-standing feature of Ghana's Christian religious landscape. Asamoah-Gyadu (2007: 75) observes that prayer camps 'have traditionally been part of indigenous independent Christianity in Africa'. In Ghana, the activities of prayer camps were popularized by Gilbert Ablorh Lawson's group, the *Divine Healer's Temple*, established in 1954 (Larbi 2015). However, the first instances of prayer camps can be traced back to Deaconess Sophia Dede

Mawulede popularly known as Mame Dede. Mame Dede's prayer group started at Kade in 1947, and she is on record to have prayed and healed many including bringing to life a woman who had died for five days (Asem 2005). A mention can also be made of the Okanta Prayer Camp, founded by Prophet Kojo Mintah in Suhum, in the Eastern Region of Ghana (Larbi 2015; Onyinah 2012).[3] These groups reportedly emerged between the years 1939 and 1953.

Despite these earlier accounts of the establishment of prayer camps in Ghana, Christian Baëta (1962) provides a narrative in his influential book *Prophetism in Ghana* that suggests the existence of a prayer camp in Ghana prior to the one initiated by Mame Dede and Prophet Mintah.[4] According to Baëta (1962), the term 'camp' was used to refer to a place where Job Cartey, described by Baëta as a 'spiritual man', pupil teacher and co-worker of Samuel Nyankson[5], directed Prophet Egyanka Appiah and his followers to prepare as a 'special place in the open for prayer' (Baëta 1962: 31).[6] This designated place was called a 'prayer camp' and served as a meeting place for Appiah and his followers. It was at this camp that they later received the Holy Spirit and performed various miracles, including instances of healing the sick. One remarkable event recounted by Baëta involves Appiah using his walking stick to kill a venomous snake while returning from the prayer camp. Baëta describes the event as follows:

> Most of Prophet Appiah's miracles were those of healing, and they were accomplished by fervent prayer; but on one occasion, when returning from the *prayer camp* with his followers, his attention was called to a poisonous snake creeping near where they were. Appiah quickly pointed at the serpent with his walking-stick, whereupon it stood still. When, after a while, the men ventured to approach the creature with sticks, intending to kill it, they found to their utter amazement that it was already dead. (Baëta 1962: 31, emphasis mine)

Although this may not mark the first instance of such a group or designated prayer place in the history of Christianity in Ghana, it is likely the first time such an event was documented in scholarly literature, using the term 'prayer camp' and contributing to subsequent academic discussions on the activities of prayer groups in Ghana.

Since the 1940s, prayer camps have proliferated and become a widespread phenomenon in Ghana, particularly with the growth and expansion of Pentecostal/ Charismatic renewal groups during the 1970s and 1980s (Onyinah 2012; Quayesi-Amakye 2011). According to Larbi (2015: 383), the charismatic revival in Ghana during the 1970s and 1980s not only gave rise to Pentecostal-type churches but also witnessed the proliferation of several prayer camps as well as the revitalization of existing ones (Larbi 2015). As of 2020, it is estimated that there are 1,016 prayer camps in Ghana.[7]

Prayer camps can be found in rural, peri-urban and urban areas. The popularity of prayer camps extends beyond Ghana to other African countries (Ukah 2016). Various factors have been identified as potential contributors to the growth and expansion of prayer camps in Ghana, including social, health, economic and spiritual issues (Larbi 2015; De Witte 2018; Van Dijk 1997). In terms of health, social and economic factors, the proliferation of prayer camps in Ghana has been linked to the economic challenges that plagued the country's economy from the 1960s to the early 2000s, resulting in severe financial hardships for its citizens. This economic crisis significantly impacted the social lives of Ghanaians, as many struggled to afford basic necessities such as food, utilities and medical expenses.

During this period, the Ghanaian government, as part of its Structural Adjustment Program with the International Monetary Fund (IMF), introduced the 'cash-and-carry' system in 1992.[8] This system, influenced by neo-capitalist ideologies prevalent in the World Bank's healthcare privatization agenda since 1987 (Yates 2009; Akin et al. 1987), involved charging patients user fees for healthcare services. The Bamako Initiative, established in 1987, saw various African health ministers embrace this initiative, resulting in the implementation of user fees in healthcare clinics across more than half of African countries by the 1990s, albeit with inherent challenges (McPake et al. 1993)

In Ghana, prior to the introduction of the 'cash-and-carry system', the government implemented cost measures in 1983 as part of its economic reforms. Under the cost recovery legislation for the health sector, healthcare fees were shared between the health seeker and the government, with variations based on factors such as the type or level of facility, treatment location, age, nationality and type of service provided (Asenso-Okyere 1995). However, a chronic shortage of, and the irrational use of, drugs precipitated the government's decision to implement the cash-and-carry system. This initiative aimed to fund the provision of drugs and enhance the efficiency of pharmaceutical services at its facilities (Asenso-Okyere et al., 1999).

Under the 'cash-and-carry' system, patients were denied medical attention, even in emergency situations, until they paid the required fees (Biritwum 1994; Asenso-Okyere et al. 1999). Numerous reports documented cases of families losing loved ones due to the inability to afford medical expenses (Biritwum 1994).[9] Additionally, qualified medical professionals began leaving the country to seek better job opportunities and remuneration abroad, further exacerbating the inadequate healthcare services provided by government hospitals (Larbi 2015). Moreover, the emergence of the private health sector capitalized on the healthcare system, making it even more difficult for individuals with limited financial means to access necessary medical services. The economic hardships compelled numerous individuals to turn to religious institutions in search of spiritual assistance, including matters concerning health (Mohr 2013).

During this time, religious institutions preached messages of hope and encouraged citizens to place their trust in God for economic recovery and spiritual deliverance from all afflictions. Frustrated individuals who were unable to afford the cost of medical treatment resorted to seeking solutions at prayer camps or healing centres which were mushrooming at the time. These healing centres held an allure due to their provision of services free of charge. Reports circulated of individuals who had sought help at these healing centres experiencing tangible testimonies of miraculous experiences, which in turn motivated others to seek similar solutions. The popularity of prayer camps grew to the extent that they became renowned as 'major healing centres' after established hospitals (Larbi 2015: 86).

While socio-economic factors contributed to the growth and prominence of prayer camps, it is crucial to acknowledge the significance of religious, spiritual and cultural factors in shaping their activities in Ghana. More details on these factors will be explored in subsequent sections.

Background of visitors/clients at prayer camps in Ghana

Previous studies and personal field surveys suggest that some individuals travel on their own to seek supernatural assistance at prayer camps, while others are brought there by their relatives (Gyimah et al 2023; Onyinah 2012). Visitors at the selected prayer camps in Ghana came from diverse ethnic groups within the country, as well as from neighbouring West African countries and beyond. Some individuals even travel from the diaspora to seek health solutions. It was found that at certain camps, individuals have travelled from places like London for treatment.[10]

Indeed, Asamoah-Gyadu (2015) has observed that prayer camps attract visitors from various denominations and foreign countries. According to Onyinah (2012), prayer camps cater to a wide range of clients, including political figures, Christians, non-Christians such as Muslims and practitioners of traditional religions. Onyinah's observation aligns with Larbi's (2015) previous findings, which indicate that people from different walks of life, regardless of their socio-economic status, age or background, visit these camps. Therefore, at prayer camps, the socio-economic divide breaks down (Larbi 2015). Although the number of visitors from different religious traditions who visit prayer camps may be small, these visits also demonstrate the broader influence of prayer camps in providing spiritual assistance to individuals in need, regardless of their religious affiliations.

The records found at prayer camps show that politicians, including Members of Parliament (MPs) and former and current presidents, have visited these camps. The famous statement by a former head of state of Ghana Evans John Atta Mills that he 'wished Ghana were a prayer camp' attested to his connection and affirmation of the role of such institutions in his personal life and administration as head of state. In a response to criticisms for making such statement, the former president mentioned that he had 'no apologies and regrets to offer' and that the men of God in charge of prayer camps 'are allies who can support the success of my [his] administration and the progress of the nation through their intercession'.[11] Mills's statement aligns closely with the perspective articulated by a former Ghanaian MP during a parliamentary debate in the early 1960s regarding the rise of indigenous healing religious movements in Ghana. While many MPs expressed support for the role of these healing institutions, demonstrating their personal connection or sympathy towards them, Mr Krobo Edusei reportedly voiced his endorsement of the healing churches or camps during this period during the debate on the floor of parliament:

> When you attend some of these [established] churches, Sir, you will find that the true spirit of worship is absent, and that is why we indigenous people of Ghana who know that freedom of worship is enshrined in our constitution go to these [newer and smaller] churches and organisations because we have surrendered ourselves to God in order that we can speak to Him and ask Him to deliver us from our sins. How many of the churches in Ghana and outside of Ghana have been able to pray for the sick to recover? But if you go to some of these churches and organisations, Sir, you will realise that they can pray and ask God to heal a sick person. (Assimeng 1995: 20)

The above quotation indicates how religious organizations particularly prayer camps whose focus are on healing and supporting people with prayers to deal with existential issues in their lives continue to attract people with diverse economic and social backgrounds.

The influence of prayer camps as religious institutions in Ghana can be seen through the range of visitors they attract. Furthermore, visits to prayer camps by individuals in high political positions, such as the president and MPs, demonstrate the extent of influence certain prayer camp leaders have in the political and public sphere in Ghana. In fact, the influence of prayer camps on Pentecostal political theology and spiritual warfare has been examined (Heuser 2015). The fact that people from economically and technologically advanced countries would turn to prayer camps for spiritual help or supernatural solutions to their problems, whether health related or economic, highlights the strong belief individuals have in the power of religion to address their needs. This indicates that prayer camps serve not only those seeking help for various illnesses or diseases but also individuals with social needs and aspirations.[12] Therefore, prayer camps in Ghana have become significant religious institutions, attracting people from diverse social, economic and religious backgrounds within Ghana and beyond.

While this study focuses on the Akan context, the diverse ethnic backgrounds of visitors at the camps also indicate an important aspect of this study in terms of the world-views of those who visit prayer camps. Regardless of whether an individual is Akan, Ewe, Ga, Fanti or from another group, the pervasive belief in and influence of supernatural evil agents in human affairs is prevalent (Atiemo 2013; Meyer 1999). The belief or perception that supernatural evil agents can cause unwanted afflictions in people's lives is not limited to Pentecostal Akan Christians or individuals but is also present among other ethnic groups in Ghana. This makes the framework of this study highly applicable and generalizable to other Ghanaian contexts.

Locating prayer camps in Ghanaian Pentecostal historiography

The use of the term 'Pentecostal' in relation to the prayer camps, as indicated in the book's subtitle, may provoke various inquiries among readers regarding the specific category or strand of Ghanaian Pentecostalism to which the prayer camps belong. This also raises the question of the prayer camps' position within the historical narrative of Ghanaian Pentecostalism. It is important to note that the prayer camps do not align with any particular typology of Pentecostalism but rather emerged historically through the activities of revival groups within various Pentecostal denominations and movements in Ghana, as well as in the established mission churches. Larbi (2015: 55) argues that the existence of 'prophet/healer centred Pentecostalist prayer camps' is a result of the evangelistic efforts of evangelical Pentecostal movements in Ghana. In doing so, Larbi seems to classify the prayer camps alongside Pentecostal renewal movements such as neo-Pentecostal churches, charismatic movements within historic mission churches and the para-church movement. However, considering their historical roots and pervasive influence within current Ghanaian Christianity, it would be important for scholars to develop a typology of the prayer camps, as they represent a complex hybrid of Pentecostal movements in Ghana.

Originating from a distinct Pentecostal ethos, the prayer camps emphasize, express and exhibit Pentecostal phenomena such as prayer, speaking in tongues, visions, healing and prophecy in their style of worship. These characteristics have led some scholars to describe the prayer camps as being 'Pentecostalist' in nature (Larbi 2015: 371). The use of the term 'Pentecostalist' encompasses the prayer camps within the broader framework or group of Pentecostal movements in Ghana and beyond. In this regard, Allan Anderson's (2010: 15) concept of 'family resemblance' is applicable. Anderson (2010) employs the 'family resemblance' approach to convey the universality and adaptability that underlie all Pentecostal movements globally, with a focus on the workings of the Holy Spirit. The 'family resemblance' approach is in line with Birgit Meyer's (1998: 321) argument that Pentecostalism can be perceived as a 'cultural complex' due to the shared religious ideas and practices present in Pentecostal churches, such as baptism in the Holy Spirit, speaking in tongues (*glossolalia*), divine healing and a strong emphasis on personal prayer. Similarly, Asamoah-Gyadu (2005) has defined Pentecostalism as Christian groups that emphasize the workings of the Holy Spirit, incorporating pneumatic elements like prophecies, speaking in tongues, visions, healing and miracles into their worship practices.

Conceptually, the term Pentecostalism or Pentecostal is used operationally and functionally to refer to the Pentecostal elements present in the activities, practices and worship style of prayer camps in Ghana. These elements include an emphasis on deliverance, healing, miracles and prophecy, as well as the operation of other spiritual phenomena like speaking in tongues, dreams and visions, which are central to the activities of prayer camps and define their Pentecostal nature and orientation.

In addition to these characteristics, it is important to situate prayer camps in their proper historical contexts. Prayer camps in Ghana emerged as a result of the Pentecostal revival and renewal movements in the country. As previously mentioned, prayer camps are firmly rooted within the broader context of the charismatic renewal in Ghana. However, it has been argued that prayer camps share similarities, at least in terms of nature and operational style, with the earlier 'gardens' operated by the Twelve Apostles Church in Ghana (Onyinah 2012). The Twelve Apostles Church traces its origins to the work and ministry of the Liberian Grebo Prophet, William Wade Warris, in Ghana in the early twentieth century.[13] The Twelve Apostles Church and other similar groups, such as the Musama Disco Christo Church (MDCC), fall under the umbrella term of African Independent Churches (AICs) (Asamoah-Gyadu 2005). In the Twelve Apostles Church, the gardens were sacred spaces that served as healing camps where prophets or prophetesses, after diagnosing the cause of afflictions, performed rituals involving exorcism to drive out any demons or supernatural forces believed to be causing the sickness (Baëta 1962: 19–21). This process could span several days, months or even years.

Therefore, it can be argued that prayer camps bear similarities to the gardens operated by spiritual churches. The issue of these similarities will be further explored in subsequent sections (see also Benyah 2024). Although spiritual churches are currently in decline,[14] I posit that the emergence of prayer camps facilitated a transition from spiritual churches and redefined their practices within the framework of a pronounced Pentecostal/charismatic culture. This demonstrates an example of how Pentecostal movements appropriate and adapt to their cultural surroundings, refining local cultures and religious identities in a manner that resonates with their constituents.

Typologies of prayer camps in Ghana

Existing literature has classified prayer camps in Ghana into two main types: residential and non-residential (Omenyo 2002; Onyinah 2012; Larbi 2015). However, I propose the inclusion of two additional categories: private/independent prayer camps and non-private/non-independent prayer camps. The addition of these categories is necessary to differentiate between the ownership and administration of prayer camps in Ghana, which previous studies have not adequately addressed. This differentiation is crucial in highlighting the level of control and supervision involved in the day-to-day operations of prayer camps in Ghana. Moreover, the distinction between independent and non-independent prayer camps has significant implications for the extent of questionable practices at these camps. These differences are often overlooked by external observers of prayer camps in Ghana and contribute to a misguided understanding of their operations, as well as the criticisms directed towards them especially by human rights activists.[15]

It is worth noting that the terms 'prayer camp' or 'prayer centre' do not imply the residential or non-residential nature of a camp, as suggested by Girish Daswani (2015) in his work *Looking Back, Moving Forward*. Daswani (2015) asserts that a prayer camp is residential, while a prayer centre is non-residential. However, in Ghana, these terms are not used to designate such distinctions. For instance, there are several residential camps in Ghana that use the term 'prayer centre', such as the Goka Prayer Centre and Mount Horeb Prayer Centre, among many others. In Ghana, these terms are used interchangeably to refer to the same entities.[16]

I would like to emphasize that although some prayer camps have transitioned into independent ministries after severing ties with their affiliated churches, prayer camps are not churches, and they do not perceive themselves as such. However, a new trend seems to be emerging, wherein some prayer camp leaders are establishing branches of their camps as churches in different cities in Ghana. One example is the Mount Horeb Victorious Church International in Teshie, Accra, established by the leader of the Mount Horeb Prayer Centre. They also have a branch of the church in London.

From a sociological standpoint, prayer camps can be likened to the prophet-healing groups described by Turner (1967: 32) as 'clientèle' in form. The prophet-healing groups functioned as healing centres where sick individuals sought treatment from practitioners renowned for their healing abilities. The process involved the sick individuals participating in religious exercises and teachings that formed part of the treatment (Turner 1967).

Furthermore, while most prayer camps in Ghana are led by individuals who identify themselves as prophets and share similarities with what has been described as neo-Prophetic churches (Omenyo and Atiemo 2006), prayer camps should not be conflated with these churches in terms of structure, leadership, organization and administration. Neo-Prophetic churches are newer forms and expressions of Pentecostal/charismatic churches in Ghana, led by individuals who identify themselves or are commonly referred to as prophets (Omenyo and Atiemo 2006).[17] Although some prayer camps are affiliated with denominations or churches, I argue that prayer camps should be regarded as separate entities, not bound to churches, as the majority of them function as private or independent religious organizations. Even in cases where they are affiliated with churches, their operational independence from the church is quite evident.

Residential camps

Residential prayer camps provide accommodation for individuals seeking longer-term stays at the camp. The decision to spend multiple days at a prayer camp is influenced by several factors, such as the severity of one's illness or problem, as well as guidance from the camp leader or religious figure. As van Dijk (1997) emphasizes, residential camps are established by prayer leaders to offer individuals the opportunity to stay for extended periods in close proximity to the healing powers associated with the presence of the prayer leader. Some of these prayer camps boast well-structured buildings and housing facilities, including guesthouses with executive suites to cater to high-profile individuals such as politicians and businesspersons. The building facilities I have seen at some include three-storey buildings and nicely designed chalet houses. Notably, the infrastructure available at residential camps in Ghana varies, with limited financial resources hindering the establishment of modern facilities. This situation particularly impacts the living conditions and welfare of individuals visiting the camp, with mentally ill individuals being most adversely affected (Arias et al. 2016).[18]

Residential camps typically charge visitors a service fee for utilizing these facilities, which may include the provision of mattresses for those unable to afford a guesthouse stay. Visitors who rent mattresses often sleep in shared rooms or tents designated for camp attendees. Additionally, some visitors sleep on their own mattresses within auditoriums utilized for worship services. User fees contribute to the maintenance and acquisition of additional facilities aimed at improving and enhancing visitors' conditions at the camp.[19]

Some residential camps have constructed dedicated sanatoriums (or houses) to provide care for persons with mental illness seeking treatment or support. It is worth noting that some of the houses within these camps are poorly constructed and exhibit numerous defects. Additionally, certain structures resemble tents, which expose the occupants, particularly those who are unwell, to unfavourable weather conditions. During one visit to a prayer camp in Ghana, camp leaders highlighted the efforts of the Mental Health Authority of Ghana (MHA) to secure external funding for the completion of a ten-bedroom apartment dedicated to improving the healthcare and welfare of persons with mental illness at the camp. While some rooms were partially completed, others were still at the foundation stage.[20] I will delve further into the treatment of persons with mental illness at residential camps in Ghana in Chapters 6 and 7.

Apart from providing hostel facilities, residential camps have also constructed large auditoriums capable of accommodating anywhere from 500 to 5,000 individuals for prayer meetings and worship services. Religious activities occur throughout the week at these camps. The location where some of these residential camps are sited has expanded to resemble vast communities in Ghana. Prominent examples include the Edumfa Prayer and Revival Centre, now known as Edumfa Heavenly Ministry, located in the Central Region of Ghana; the Bethel Prayer Camp and Goka Prayer Centre in the Bono Region; and the Okanta Prayer Camp in the Eastern Region.

In addition to their physical amenities, most residential camps possess well-established administrative systems responsible for overseeing daily operations. In some of the camps I have visited, the administrative head is referred to as the General Secretary. Notably, some of these General Secretaries, both past and present, are highly educated professionals with expertise in fields such as law and education. Conversely, certain residential camps lack structured administrative systems and rely on the leader's direction with the assistance of appointed aides. Both the camp leader and their assistants reside within the camp.

Non-residential camps

The non-residential camps function as gathering places where individuals convene for prayer on specific days of the week (Onyinah 2012). These camps do not offer lodging or accommodations for visitors. The meeting area is typically comprised of metal or wooden tents, often with aluminium or bamboo roofing, to provide shelter during prayer sessions. Due to their structure and operation, there is no established administrative system to oversee the functioning of the camp. The activities are predominantly guided by the prayer leader or the prophet in charge. Non-residential camps do not provide lodging facilities for individuals who are ill, including those with mental health conditions, who come to seek prayers.

Private/independent camps

Private or independent camps refer to camps that are owned and operated by individuals without any affiliation to a church or denomination. In essence, private camps are self-governing institutions, and their leaders are not answerable to any denomination or higher religious authority. As previously mentioned, both private and non-private camps display a significant degree of autonomy. In Ghana, several camps can be classified as private camps, as they are independent and run by their founders or leaders. It is worth noting that some well-known private camps in Ghana initially started as non-private camps until their leaders severed their ties with their affiliated churches. These separations often arose due to doctrinal or financial disagreements.[21] After breaking away, some of these camps transformed into independent ministries and churches. Examples of private camps that were formerly affiliated with churches include the Mount Horeb Prayer Centre and the Edumfa Revival and Prayer Centre, both of which were previously affiliated with the Church of Pentecost (CoP).

Non-private/non-independent camps

The non-private prayer camps in Ghana are affiliated with churches or denominations. CoP, the largest Pentecostal denomination in Ghana, had the highest number of prayer camps operating in the country. In the early 2000s, the CoP had over fifty-six prayer camps functioning under the church. However, by 2018, the number had decreased to forty-two due to some camps severing their ties with the church for various reasons.[22] Apart from the CoP, other historic mission churches such as the Methodist Church Ghana and Presbyterian Church of Ghana also have prayer camps operating under their umbrella. Currently, the Presbyterian Church of Ghana has forty-two prayer and retreat centres affiliated with the church.[23] This indicates that the phenomenon of prayer camps is widespread in Ghana, not only among Pentecostal forms of churches but also within historic mission churches. The non-private prayer camps in Ghana enjoy popularity partly due to their association with recognized denominations. As a result, they possess a high degree of credibility, which may be lacking in privately operated prayer camps that have no external control or supervision (Asamoah-Gyadu 2015).[24]

In historic mission churches, the establishment of prayer camps is often undertaken by individuals within the church who believe they are gifted with divine healing power and supernatural grace to pray for solutions to people's problems and heal their illnesses. These camps are established by these individuals with the aim of fostering the prayer needs of the church. Over time, despite occasional conflict within the church hierarchy, these groups receive recognition and support from local, diocesan and national bodies. The leaders of the prayer camps are frequently invited by their churches to lead healing and deliverance sessions during conventions and camp meetings as a form of acknowledgement for their services (Omenyo 2002). Within historic mission churches, the emergence of charismatic renewal groups such as prayer camps was a response to counter the attrition of their members to Pentecostal healing camps or churches (Omenyo 2002).

While it is not widely known that neo-Pentecostal or charismatic churches in Ghana are supportive of the establishment of prayer camps (Onyinah 2012)[25], there appears to be a new trend emerging among them. For instance, the International Central Gospel Church (ICGC), one of Ghana's prominent charismatic churches, now houses a 'Solution Centre' within one of its branches. The Solution Centre, led by Prophet Annor, operates as a non-residential prayer centre at the Holy Ghost Temple in Adenta, a suburb of Accra, Ghana (Larbi 2015). Another example is the Potters City, also known as the World Prayer Centre, which is operated by Prophet Nanasei Opoku Sarkodie in Miotso-Prampram, Ghana. The World Prayer Centre serves as a residential camp with the objective of championing economic revival across Africa and spreading the message of hope through the Gospel.[26] Similarly, Apostle Cosby Agyei of the Family House Chapel operates a similar camp in Aburi, Ghana. These new developments indicate the growing significance of prayer camps within charismatic churches in Ghana.

Although non-private prayer camps are affiliated with churches and have some level of supervision, many of them operate as independent entities within their respective churches. In terms of their management, non-private prayer camps enjoy significant autonomy in areas such as finances and construction of housing facilities. Furthermore, their activities and programme of events are distinct from those of their affiliate churches. It is important to note that the churches to which these camps are affiliated may or may not provide support for their operations (Larbi 2015). Additionally, some non-private prayer camps do not admit sick individuals, particularly those suffering from mental illness, for various reasons. These reasons may include a lack of resources to accommodate such individuals, directives from their affiliate churches to refrain from admitting such individuals or the fact that many of these camps operate as non-residential camps.

Since prayer camps in Ghana are not subject to any legal regulations, the level of control over their activities is determined by ownership and leadership. In simpler terms, non-private camps may face sanctions or restrictions from their affiliated churches if they engage in certain practices, such as using religious prophylactics for healing or teaching doctrines that contradict the church's beliefs. As a result, some churches have terminated their relationships with certain prayer camps in Ghana. Prayer camps led by private individuals do not have these controls, and the leader has the authority to sanction activities within the camp. These practices have attracted attention from health professionals and human rights observers, who question the effectiveness and ethical implications of these camps in supporting the healing of persons with mental illness, for example.

Leadership and operation at prayer camps

The activities of private and non-private prayer camps revolve around the personality of their leaders or founders. In Ghana, the leaders of prayer camps are typically not changed or replaced until they pass away or experience poor health. In some cases, the death of the leader can lead to the decline, diminished patronage or even the disappearance of the camp. In the case of non-private prayer camps, a disagreement between the leader and the church leadership can result in the removal of their position. An illustrative example is the Goka Prayer Centre in the Bono Region of Ghana. After the founder's death, a new leader was appointed by the CoP to take over the camp. However, this new leader had a disagreement with the church leadership, prompting them to report the issue to the Area Head. Consequently, the church appointed new leadership, which was sworn into office on 4 November 2022 by the CoP's Area Head, Apostle Samuel Berko.[27]

The leaders of prayer camps are commonly referred to as prophets, prophetesses or evangelists. However, the CoP discourages the use of titles like prophet or prophetess. Instead, leaders at camps are instructed to use approved titles such as elder, deacon or deaconess. This guideline from CoP stems from the fact that the appointment of a prophet or prophetess is the prerogative of the church's Executive Council and General Council.[28] Additionally, the restricted use of such titles is due to past misuse, particularly instances where individuals with these titles wielded excessive power within the church (Onyinah 2012).

Leaders in Ghana's prayer camps are seen as persons with a special God-given gift to see beyond the physical world, diagnose problems and pray for solutions with the help of the Holy Spirit (Larbi 2015; Onyinah 2012). Onyinah (2012: 188) describes prayer camp leaders as having spiritual gifts to 'reveal hidden things, predict the future, heal the sick, exorcise witches, break ancestral curses, and offer *abisa* (consultations)'. These leaders promote belief in miracles, angelic consultation and spiritual healing. As a result, they are highly respected and revered by pastors, staff members and supplicants (Daswani 2015). The day-to-day operations of the camps revolve around the leaders, who are supported by pastors and staff members. The supportive staff assist in praying for the sick, conveying visions and dreams and offering advice to supplicants (Larbi 2015). Some staff members also handle the camp's administration.

Onyinah (2012) identifies four main reasons or factors that led most leaders to establish prayer camps in Ghana. The first reason is the transformation of small prayer groups into larger camps. The second and third reasons involve individuals who, after being seriously ill and healed, felt called by God to start a camp. The fourth category consists of individuals who, after losing their jobs in unusual circumstances, claimed to have received a divine message instructing them to start a camp. It is noteworthy that these founders often describe intense religious experiences in the form of visions, dreams, voices believed to be from God, prophecies or a combination of these, which prompted them to establish prayer camps. According to Larbi (2015: 383), these founders believe that these experiences have given them a 'mission to bring healing and deliverance to the oppressed'.

Activities/practices at prayer camps in Ghana

The main activities at a prayer camp include prayer, fasting, healing, prophecy, counselling and Bible studies. Some camps also provide opportunities for socialization. The leader of a prayer camp engages visitors in lengthy prayer sessions, interspersed with healing, deliverance and prophecies. Indeed, healing and deliverance constitute the central focus of prayer camps in Ghana, which accounts for the widespread popularity of these institutions within the country. Asamoah-Gyadu (2015: 134) has emphasized that the popularity of the prayer camps can be attributed to 'their proven effectiveness as instruments of divine healing'. Healing does not only concern the healing of sicknesses but also healing from all troubles sent to the camps by supplicants for a solution (Meyer 1999).

Healing and deliverance at prayer camps are conducted by leaders, prophets or prophetesses, with assistance from their aides. This practice is integral to the Pentecostal spiritual warfare activities aimed at expelling, neutralizing or destroying any forces that impede individuals from experiencing the life intended for them by God (Onyinah 2020). Healing and deliverance in the context of spiritual warfare is one area where prayer camps and more broadly Pentecostals share similarities and continuities with African primal cosmology. Omenyo (2014: 147) has argued that 'African Pentecostals continue to embrace African primal cosmology involving spirit beings that is thought to be similar to that portrayed in the Bible. They contend that Jesus is believed in the same. Hence, there is a high degree of unanimity in their emphasis on spiritual warfare, deliverance ministry, and the miraculous healing power of Christ.'

During the process of healing and deliverance, malevolent spirits responsible for an individual's afflictions are identified and expelled from their bodies or circumstances, through the blood of Jesus Christ and the intervention of the Holy Spirit. Particularly for those seeking solutions to mental health issues at prayer camps, healing and deliverance focus on identifying and expelling evil spirits that have taken possession or control of the individual. Consequently, this possession alters their states of consciousness and produces suffering and 'unnatural behaviour', which are deemed to result from the invasion of the body by an alien or demonic spirit or even as a result of a manipulation of external evil forces. In other words, the individual's 'executive faculties' are believed to be under the influence or control of the invading spirit or demon (Asamoah-Gyadu 2005: 167). The practice of healing and deliverance is not only a component of Pentecostal spiritual warfare activities but is also employed as a form of pastoral care, as it aims to restore disturbed individuals to proper functioning and facilitate the transformation of their bodies, enabling them to achieve health and wholeness, free from any demonic spirit or bondage (Asamoah-Gyadu 2005). The discussion in Chapter 6 will explain this further.

Prophetism, or the practice of prophecy, constitutes a significant phenomenon within the activities conducted at prayer camps in Ghana. Prophecy is intrinsically linked to healing and deliverance. At prayer camps, the prophetic abilities of the camp leader enable them to divine and diagnose the underlying causes of an individual's issues, such as illness, and to recommend appropriate interventions to remedy the affliction. Asamoah-Gyadu (2015: 11) articulates the relationship between prophecy and healing by asserting that

> healing is related to prophecy because, like divination in the traditional setting, prophecy reveals destinies and the sources of predicaments. Healing in this context encapsulates something more than just the cure of ailments. It includes all those divine interventions made possible by such spiritual disciplines as waiting, fasting, and prayer, through which health and fortunes are restored and deliverance received from one's enemies.

As will be elaborated in the subsequent paragraphs and in Chapter 6, the practice of prophecy bears some resemblance to the practice of *abisa* in Akan indigenous religions. It is through this medium that the prophet or religious functionary is able to reveal and articulate the cause of an individual's problem. Indeed, within African religions, divine healing emerges as the most critical function of prophetic figures. Charismatic individuals who exercise the gifts of the Holy Spirit, particularly in healing and prophecy, are able to captivate their audience, thereby establishing their authority among their supplicants. Notably, the authority associated with prophetic gifting has been cited as a contributing factor to certain abuses linked to healing practices, as this authority often goes unchallenged by supplicants who believe it to be divinely sanctioned (Golo and Benyah 2024; Golo 2024).

Prayer and fasting, indeed, remain the most significant and central activities at prayer camps in Ghana. Visitors to prayer camps engage in fasting in addition to prayers. Fasting is recommended by the prayer camp leader, although not in all cases. Individuals with special needs and problems are always recommended to fast, with the belief that certain issues can only be resolved through fasting and prayers (Mt. 17.21). Family members are sometimes recommended or allowed to fast on behalf of relatives who are unable to fast due to health conditions (Arias et al. 2016; Larbi 2015). During prayer sessions, the prophet or camp leader prays for visitors and performs deliverance to cast out demons or evil spirits thought to be responsible for people's problems. The leaders, who possess the gift of prophecy, are able to prophesy to supplicants by revealing hidden secrets about their lives and conveying God's plan for their situations and what God has in store for them. Individual visitors to prayer camps are also allowed to have their own personal prayer sessions, where they can pray to God in solitude and present their problems for answers or solutions. Specific spots or areas in some prayer camps are designated as special spaces for personalized meetings. These spaces are believed to be saturated with power and anointing for the manifestation of miracles or fast-track answers to people's requests or problems based on the founders' previous experiences at such locations.

Another major activity that takes place at prayer camps is counselling and consultation. I have combined these two activities because they are closely related. In my observations at some prayer camps, what is referred to as counselling is actually consultation. That is, what actually happens during the counselling session is more accurately described as consultation. Counselling is typically provided by the prayer camp leader to offer advice on the issues supplicants bring to the camp in search of a solution. At some camps, the counselling sessions I have observed involve the leader or prophet listening to the supplicants' problems, praying for them and providing guidance or what is commonly known as *akwankyere* in Ghanaian Akan language. As Omenyo and Atiemo (2006: 65) explain, in *akwankyere*, the prophetic leader is expected to provide 'information that is supposed to explain a person's situation and also prescribe solutions'. It is within this context of *akwankyere* that the practice of *abisa* becomes evident (Quayesi-Amakye 2013). In fact, Akan *abisa* has been argued to be similar to *akwankyere* (Ocran 2004). *Abisa* refers to divine consultation and is often used to determine the causes of problems or the outcome of an event. A further exploration of the concept of *abisa* will be provided in subsequent chapters. Individuals who stay at the camp for an extended period of time are offered individual counselling sessions. In the following chapters, I will highlight some of the benefits of the counselling sessions for visitors to prayer camps, particularly individuals who have a history of substance abuse involving narcotics, cannabis and alcohol.

A particular feature worth mentioning regarding prayers at prayer camps is the use of prophylactics or religious substances or materials for healing. At prayer camps in Ghana, there is a strong belief and emphasis on the use of anointed materials or religious objects for healing. These materials include anything ranging from anointing oil, water, herbs or even soil or sand collected from the compound of prayer camps. These materials are believed to be infused with the supernatural grace of God that affects healing to supplicants or whoever such materials are administered upon (Asamoah-Gyadu 2007). Such beliefs and practices bring into perspective Robert Orsi's (1997: 3) account of people's miraculous experiences at a Catholic grotto in Bronx, New York, called Lourdes, where pilgrims who go to the grotto 'bathe in pools fed by Saint Bernadette's miraculous spring, hoping for relief from physical distress' (Orsi 1997: 3). The prayer camps' environment and materials from the camp are believed to be domesticated with such divine presence that brings about healing.

Additionally, Bible studies are a major activity at prayer camps. The goal of organizing a Bible study is to help participants gain a deeper understanding of God's word. Through teachings from the Bible, participants learn about God's purpose for their lives and pray for the fulfilment of those promises. During prayer meetings, camp leaders also preach to participants. The sermons mainly focus on the miraculous work of Jesus Christ and healing stories from the Bible. The purpose of these sermons is to reignite participants' faith and encourage them to believe in God for solutions to their problems.

In some prayer camps, these activities are accompanied by strict moral codes, such as not wearing shoes or using hair extensions. Camp leaders claim that these restrictions were given to them by God through visions to maintain a sacred environment for the Holy Spirit and other divine beings like angels. However, the CoP has prohibited prayer camps under their authority from enforcing such practices, including restrictions on women during their menstrual period, not wearing shoes, kneeling before the leader and designing special chairs exclusively for the leader.[29] The prohibition of women during their menstrual period shows the gendered dynamics within the religious practices of some spiritual churches in Africa. Crumbley (2008) has noted that women, regardless of their ordination status, were systematically excluded from the sanctuary of the Church of Lord Aladura in Nigeria during their menstrual cycle. This practice is often justified by the perception that women in this state are impure and should not come into contact with ceremonial or ritualistic objects (Idumwonyi 2024).

Religious/theological motivation underlying healing practices at prayer camps in Ghana

In the Ghanaian and broader African context, life is perceived as precarious due to the belief in a spiritual realm governed by both benevolent and malevolent forces. The connection between the spiritual and physical realms leads people to attribute the events of their lives to supernatural influences. Consequently, any barriers or obstacles that hinder individuals from realizing their full potential or attaining their desired goals are often attributed to malevolent beings working to undermine God's intended plan for their lives (Akrong 2006). Prolonged and persistent situations such as illness, unemployment, marital challenges, childlessness and difficulties in achieving significant milestones are often interpreted as indicators of malevolent forces at work.

However, Akan Pentecostal Christians maintain the belief that the influence of the devil can be overcome, halted or prevented through the power and sacrificial blood of Jesus Christ (Asamoah-Gyadu 2005). This belief forms a fundamental element of the Akan Pentecostal Christian understanding of salvation, known as *nkwagye* in the Akan Twi language (Larbi 2002: 94). Larbi explains that *nkwagye* is a combination of two words: *nkwa* meaning vital life, vigour, health, happiness and felicity, encapsulating the concept of abundant life or 'life in all its fullness'. *Gye*, on the other hand, holds various meanings but in a salvific context, it conveys notions of rescue, redemption, liberation and deliverance. Therefore, to the Akan Christian, *nkwagye* signifies the 'liberation and preservation of life' and all that it entails (Larbi 2002: 94). Jesus Christ is thus referred to as the *nkwagyefo* (saviour), signifying the one who saves and preserves life. Synonymous terms for *nkwagyefo* include *agyenkwa* (rescuer) and *ogyefo* (redeemer, deliverer). Mercy Oduyoye's (1986: 98) explanation of *agyenkwa* provides valuable insight:

> The Agyenkwa means the one rescues, who holds your life in safety, takes you out of a life-denying situation and places you in a life affirming one. The Rescuer plucks you from a dehumanising ambience and places you in a position where you can grow toward authentic humanity. The Agyenkwa gives you back your life in all its fullness.

Whether used in reference to a divine being or a human being, *agyenkwa* carries the same connotation of deliverance. For example, Larbi (2002: 95) explains that when a person's timely intervention averts a catastrophe or prevents an unfavourable event from occurring, that person can be referred to as *ogyefo* or *agyenkwa* in that specific instance. The *agyenkwa* is always perceived as a powerful person because of his or her ability to save or rescue.

This concept of God and his saving power, demonstrated through his representatives such as prophets in Pentecostal healing camps, is a significant motivation for individuals seeking solutions to their problems at prayer camps in Ghana. It is important to note that this belief in salvation does not undermine the primary understanding of salvation in Pentecostalism, which predominantly refers to the concepts of atonement, forgiveness of sins and reconciliation with God (Larbi 2002). However, Pentecostals emphasize that salvation is not solely about the salvation of one's soul but also encompasses tangible demonstrations of God's goodness in the lives of believers (Prosén 2020). These manifestations include deliverance from sickness, financial breakthroughs, liberation from demonic bondage and success in various aspects of life (Asamoah-Gyadu 2005).[30] Pentecostals anticipate experiencing these manifestations in their present lives while also looking forward to a promise of a brighter future in the afterlife. The subsequent paragraph will explore how this belief system aids individuals in coping with challenges during persistent illness.

When individuals visit a prayer camp seeking answers to their sickness, persistent illnesses, marital problems, business failures, unemployment and protection from perceived enemies, they may experience psychosocial distress, leading to anxiety and depression (Field 1960; Patel et al. 1995). The belief in witchcraft is a domain where the complex interplay of personal misfortune, religious beliefs and cultural values becomes apparent, as evidenced by the works of Field (1960) and Patel et al. (1995). The prophet at the prayer camp serves as a representative of God and is perceived as a 'saviour' who can heal and deliver individuals from various troubles, including witchcraft and illnesses. As a revered figure with a direct connection to God through the Holy Spirit, the prophet prays for and guides supplicants, providing them with spiritual direction to overcome their challenges. For those believed to be affected by evil spirits or demons, a process of healing and deliverance is conducted to counteract the influence of these malevolent entities. In cases where possession is suspected, a deliverance process is undertaken to expel the demon from the afflicted individual's body.

It is important to note that not all diseases brought to the prayer camp result in healing. In such instances, the Pentecostal doctrine of the present and the promise of a better future in the afterlife become significant. That is, the theology of the here and now and better tomorrow hereafter. This theological perspective underscores the concept of hope, which can be understood from two dimensions: hope in the present circumstances and hope in the future, particularly in the context of an improved life beyond the current struggles. Hope in the present time (here and now) is driven by the evidence of miraculous healings witnessed by those seeking help. Individuals who have lost hope due to their enduring illness are inspired to put their trust in God for his healing grace when they witness the tangible impact of God's power in the lives of others who have been healed. Within the healing centres, supplicants place their trust in God through his representative, a prophet believed to possess God's divine power to heal all types of diseases. In this respect, the prophet can be likened to medical doctors who inspire trust in their patients and create optimistic expectations that contribute to their recovery (Porterfield 2005).

Here, John Bowlby's (1969) attachment theory espoused by Lee Kirkpatrick (1992) in the psychology of religion can be applied to this context. In this theory, supernatural beings such as God or God's representatives, like the prophet who acts as a caregiver, serve as attachment figures. The mere knowledge of God's presence and accessibility offers a pathway for religious individuals to approach daily challenges with faith and the belief that God will answer their prayers or provide protection and shelter when faced with danger. This notion reflects *agyenkwa*, as earlier mentioned. In Ghana (and Africa in general), prophets in charge of healing centres are renowned for possessing and demonstrating extraordinary powers that portray them as 'powerful' men of God who have a close connection with God. Consequently, they are capable of identifying ailments, tracing their origins and causes and delivering individuals from their distressing situations (Omenyo 2011). The role and image of the prophet as a healer establish therapeutic pathways that facilitate devotional acts of prayer, leading to the desired outcome of healing (Reynolds 2016). Commenting on the significance of hope in health and healing, Amanda Porterfield (2005: 29) observes that Jesus' ability to heal was influenced by the 'hope and purpose he instilled in his followers and of the sense of community he fostered'. Similarly, the prophet's role as a healer serves as a positive motivation for healing among adherents because there is already an existing expectation for a positive outcome (Reynolds 2016).

The other aspect of hope in healing is deeply rooted in a futuristic perspective (a better life tomorrow). In this particular context, hope can be defined as an optimistic anticipation of a future that is positive and is specifically based on various factors, including mutuality (establishing and maintaining relationships with others), a sense of personal competence, coping abilities, psychological well-being, a sense of purpose and meaning in life and a belief in the realm of what is 'possible' (Miller 1992: 14). For our discussion, it is important to focus on the elements of hope that revolve around finding purpose and meaning in life, as well as having a sense of what is attainable.

Within the realm of Christian theology, the purpose and meaning of life is unveiled through God's plan of salvation and is made manifest through the instructive nature of the parables of the kingdom, particularly as they relate to healing (Miller 1992).[31] One of the unmistakable signs of God's kingdom as evidenced in the ministry of Jesus Christ was his ability to heal. The act of healing the sick performed by the Lord Jesus Christ, his disciples and believers who follow his teachings is a clear indication that the kingdom of God has the power to bring about transformation in a person's present state. Concurrently, it also serves as a testament to the unfailing healing power of God in the everlasting kingdom to come. In his work on *African Pentecostalism and Eschatological Expectations*, Marius Nel (2019) explores the theme of hope in the context of healing and the future kingdom of God. Nel (2019) contends that the kingdom of God has both present and future implications. He argues that the redemptive reign of God involves forgiveness of sins, deliverance from demonic oppression and possession and healing, which serve as signs of the ultimate fulfilment of the kingdom (Nel 2019). Nel (2019: 139) further notes that the concept of 'the kingdom has come' is demonstrated through the healing of the sick and the deliverance of individuals from demonic affliction, but that the kingdom will only be fully realized when Jesus Christ returns and brings salvation to those awaiting his coming (Heb. 9.28). In other words, supernatural interventions such as healing, exorcism and acts of rescue in challenging situations do not signify the complete manifestation of the 'kingdom now' but represent the invasion of the kingdom of God initiated by Christ's incarnation and resurrection, with its ultimate fulfilment anticipated in the near future (Nel 2019: 130).

It is important to note that when individuals do not receive healing for their present bodily illnesses, they maintain hope in the future, where they envision having new bodies free from illness, death and sorrow, as described in Rev. 21.4. For example, among Akan Pentecostal Christians, the expression *Nyame bɛ yɛ* (God will do it or God will come through for me) serves as a means of visualizing hope for a future state of well-being. It provides solace, assuring individuals that God's grace is available and that in due time, God will intervene for them (Rev. 21.4). David Barnard (1995) argues that the experience of hope includes an element of quiet receptivity and surprise – a concept captured by the theological notion of grace. The prospect of the future offers a distinct form of hope, closely associated with the future kingdom. Theologian Jürgen Moltmann (1975) suggests that human beings, as creatures of hope, look not only to the present but also to the future. In the face of difficult and long-lasting illness, the Christian understanding of life on earth as a transitional phase is invoked. Mayo (2016) contends that images of hope also arise from experiences of life as transitional, involving imaginative projections and anticipation of what is to come. Reflecting on the words in Rom. 8.19-23, Nel (2019) argues that believers eagerly await the time when creation itself will be liberated from decay and obtain the freedom of the glory of the children of God. They share in the pain and groaning of labour as they anticipate the redemption of their bodies. Therefore, when science or biomedicine can no longer provide a cure for present illnesses, the hope for a miraculous transformation from sickness to health or from hopelessness to hope becomes a defining feature of the liminal state. This state represents the possibility of transitioning from a diseased body to a healthy one, ultimately leading to the final fulfilment of the kingdom of God.

The motivation behind healing practices at prayer camps in Ghana is rooted in this world-view and beliefs. The healing practices at prayer camps are guided by a strong commitment to trust in God for his healing grace, even when faced with uncertainties. To fully comprehend the reasons why people are drawn to prayer camps in Ghana, it is crucial to understand the culture and religious beliefs and/or theology that sustains their belief system and associated practices.

Prayer camps as cultural religious institutions

One of the crucial aspects to be explored in the discourse surrounding prayer camps in Ghana pertains to their cultural historicity. Prayer camps have emerged as an integral part of the spiritual heritage of the Ghanaian people, encapsulating images of traditional healthcare institutions that trace lineages and knowledge transmission from the past particularly in relation to the traditional methods of healing at traditional healing shrines. Through their healing practices, prayer camps in Ghana emphasize traditional notions and concepts of personhood, health and recovery by effectively integrating these notions with contemporary manifestations of Christian practices.

The immersion of Christianity into Akan cultures by Western European missionary groups encompassed the introduction of biomedicine through the establishment of hospitals and clinics (Walker 2022). Preceding the introduction of biomedicine, the Akan people of the Gold Coast (now Ghana) relied predominantly on indigenous healing systems for medical care (Appiah-Kubi 1981; Twumasi 2005; Mohr 2009). However, the Akan community readily embraced the modern biomedicine system introduced by European missionaries and colonial authorities, while simultaneously engaging in their traditional healing practices. This amalgamation of the two healing systems engendered tensions between Akan converts and the missionary groups. The missionaries perceived the Akan adherence to traditional healing approaches as tantamount to participating in non-Christian religious practices (Mohr 2009).

Despite the resulting tensions, Akan Christian converts continued to seek Akan healing methods as alternative therapies when facing ailments. The Akan Christian converts did not perceive this approach as problematic; instead, they regarded it as a local custom and a form of culturally relative therapy, rather than a competing theology (Mohr 2009). In essence, Akan Christians esteemed the adoption of biomedicine alongside their traditional healing practices as an expression of cultural relativism rather than embracing foreign medical practices. Paul Grant (2020) concisely encapsulates the phenomenon whereby Akan Christians sought healing and empowerment during the era of colonial encounter. Grant (2020) asserts that Akan Christians achieved this by formulating a distinct variant of Christianity that aligned with their specific requirements. This was necessary as the Christian practices they encountered were of foreign origin, prompting them to assimilate the message into their own cultural framework. To address tangible challenges encountered in their daily lives, Akan Christians undertook innovative approaches such as incorporating 'indigenous cosmological framework upon the message, experimenting with Christian ceremonies, buildings, and stories for practical solutions to real-world problems' (Grant 2020: 1).

It seems that the rejection of Akan traditional healing methods by Europeans can be attributed to the prominent role of the *okomfo* (*akomfo* in plural) within the healing system. The *okomfo* holds a central position in the Akan traditional religion and is primarily responsible for the worship of the deities, referred to as *abosom*.[32] The multifaceted role of the *okomfo* includes that of a prophet, priest, healer, orthopaedist, social reformer and exorcist (Ephirim-Donkor 2008). Europeans, however, demonized and stigmatized the Akan traditional religious systems, including their healing practices, as animistic, fetishistic and regressive (Idowu 1973; Busia 1954). The *akomfo* operated from dedicated healing shrines, which served as the setting for various healing rituals. Individuals seeking healing would be directed to these shrines, regardless of their ailments, which could involve mental illnesses as well (Field 1960).

In parallel to the healing shrines, there emerged what are referred to as the 'gardens' of the Twelve Apostles Church, or the spiritual churches commonly known as *Sunsum sorè* in Ghana, as mentioned previously. Baëta (1962: 19) notes that 'every prophet or prophetess has a "Garden" or is attached to one and, except in quite unusual circumstances or emergencies, operates only there'. Baëta also describes other spiritual churches such as the MDCC, which possessed similar healing spaces, such as the 'Nathalomoa Camp' at Mazano, functioning as their primary healing centre. Members of these spiritual churches were explicitly prohibited from seeking assistance from traditional shrines, and those who had already done so were not admitted into the healing centres. Baëta (1962: 135) concisely captures the perspective of the spiritual churches when he writes that 'the "spiritual churches" represent a turning away from these traditional resources of supernatural succour in order that help may be sought, for the same purposes, from the God proclaimed in the Christian evangel'.

However, it is worth noting the underlying continuity between these two healing traditions, as emphasized by Baëta. He argues that since the supplicants' needs and world-views regarding life's challenges remained unchanged, the shift 'from idols to serve a living and true God' does not appear fundamentally different from the customary practice in African religion, where a god or fetish that clearly failed to meet the supplicants' requirements or needs is abandoned in favour of another, believed to be more effective (Baëta 1962: 135). Therefore, the traditional healing shrines were abandoned to some extent in favour of the spiritual churches because supplicants found the latter provided more effective outcomes in dealing with their problems. While the spiritual churches advocated for a departure from traditional religious institutions, their ambivalent nature, which incorporated African religious and cultural customs with Christian teachings and practices, led to their classification as syncretistic by other religious functionaries and scholars (Turner 1967). In fact, both neo-Pentecostals and Western historic mission churches labelled the spiritual churches as syncretic and even condemned certain practices (Kalu 2008; Ayegboyin 2006).

The growth and expansion of Pentecostal/charismatic denominations and renewal movements, including the rise of prayer camps, diminished the influence of the spiritual churches (Asamoah-Gyadu 2005; Atiemo 2006). Prayer camps emerged as a response to the same issues addressed by traditional shrines and spiritual churches, offering members of the Christian community an alternative means to seek solutions without compromising their faith and traditions. This was necessary because the religious and healing practices of the spiritual churches had been discredited by both historic mission churches and the Pentecostal movements.

Members of the mission and Pentecostal churches not only faced stigma for utilizing the services of shrines or spiritual churches but also encountered severe penalties or sanctions (Atiemo 2006).

Meanwhile, historic mission churches failed to provide alternative means to satisfy members' spiritual desires and existential struggles such as health issues.[33] As a result, those who were dissatisfied with their declining health sought spiritual support elsewhere. This perception led some individuals to view mission churches as a dying faith tradition lacking the power of the Holy Spirit to provide experiential aspects of the Christian faith, including healing and deliverance from malevolent spirits (Omenyo 2002). Prayer camps arose from the heightened Pentecostal/charismatic culture and addressed the needs of those who felt frustrated by the challenges of life believed to be caused by evil forces. Prayer camps provided a space and ritual environment to confront these perceived enemies. The emergence of prayer camps serves as evidence of how religious movements respond to new spiritual desires and needs, often arising from social changes within societies. This illustrates the hybridity, continuity and impermanent nature of religious beliefs and practices, while highlighting religion's resilience in meeting people's needs throughout time.

Symbolically, prayer camps can be seen as having significant similarities and cultural resonance with the traditional orthodox healing shrines, anti-witchcraft shrines and indigenous healing cults that emerged in Ghana in the first half of the twentieth century (Debrunner 1961; Parker 2004; Geschiere 1997). In fact, prayer camps have often been described as a reinvention of the old and new healing shrines that focused solely on traditional healing methods to address both the social and psychological effects of mental disorders (Read 2016; Meyer 1999; Field 1960). Scholars who study Ghanaian Pentecostal/charismatic Christianity and theology have identified prayer camps as a Christian variant of the traditional healing shrines. Asamoah-Gyadu (2007: 75) argues that 'prayer camps serve as Christian alternatives to traditional religious shrines'. Onyinah (2012: 203) agrees that 'the prayer camps have replaced the services that the shrines formerly provided for the people'. Additionally, I have also noted the similarities between the traditional healing shrines and the prayer camps (Benyah 2024). Omenyo (2011: 34) has argued that the prophets that emerged within Christianity and were very much associated with the prayer camps attracted large following because 'their respective spectacular manner of ministry … was reminiscent of a traditional priest using Christian resources, thus making them acceptable to both some traditionalists and Christians'.

As sacred places or spaces comparable to traditional religious shrines, prayer camps provide visitors with a sense of cultural significance in their worship services. Apart from the traditional healing shrines, there is also a notable similarity between the camps and the 'garden' operated by the spiritual churches. For example, the garden operated by the Twelve Apostles Church served as a sacred space that functioned as a healing centre or camp where the prophets or prophetess performed rituals, including exorcism, to drive out any perceived demons causing illness.[34] In terms of praxis and ecclesiology, prayer camps represent a significant departure from both earlier spiritual churches and traditional healing shrines. Derived from a tradition of strong synthesis between Christianity and traditional African religion, the spiritual churches adopted and reappropriated traditional healing methods, which have now been reinvented with the emergence of prayer camps (Onyinah 2012; Asamoah-Gyadu 2007).

Therefore, prayer camps help us understand the dynamic relationship between traditional faith healing experiences and the events that have occurred in people's lives over the past six decades in Ghana. This highlights the importance of exploring how Ghana's modern healing traditions, as exemplified in the context of prayer camps, reflect historical trajectories of various healing practices from the past. Cultural elements and historical events that shape attitudes towards healthcare practices are often overlooked in current studies. However, it is essential to conduct a detailed investigation to identify the ways in which historical events and practices have influenced modern forms of healing practices and traditions as observed in Ghana today within the context of prayer camps.

Summary

This chapter has presented a comprehensive overview of the origin and functioning of prayer camps in Ghana. The chapter also highlighted the social and religious factors that contributed to the emergence and proliferation of prayer camps in contemporary Ghanaian Christianity. It explores the various types of prayer camps, their leadership structure, activities and governance.

Generally speaking, prayer camps can be located within the broader narrative of Pentecostal renewal and revival in Ghana. However, their practices and ecclesiology are very much different from other types of Pentecostal churches as they demonstrate a high degree of independence and unique set of features and religious practices that distinctive of other groups or strands of Pentecostal churches or denominations. One crucial aspect that sets prayer camps apart is their cultural and historical context. While their development and expansion in the Ghanaian Christian religious landscape occurred relatively recently in the 1970s and 1980s, their cultural roots can be traced back to the traditional healing shrines that have long existed within the cultural and religious fabric of the country. Prayer camps, as a parallel phenomenon to these traditional shrines, resonate deeply with the Ghanaian population and continue to attract a significant following. This is not to say that prayer camps are same as the traditional shrines, but their style and method of operation is similar to that of the traditional shrines. One reason for the appeal of prayer camps is their ability to address the inherent world views of the people, while another factor is their perceived accessibility and affordability compared to traditional shrines and healthcare facilities (Larbi 2015).

The background information provided in this chapter offers a wider perspective on the issues that will be discussed in the following chapters. It highlights the significance and role of religion in understanding how social and medical conditions, such as mental illness, are addressed within a context where religious beliefs about life and health hold a predominant influence.

In the next chapter, I analyse the role of religion, specifically within the context of prayer camps, as a significant resource for addressing mental health conditions in Ghana. This discussion highlights the gaps in mental health research pertaining to prayer camps in Ghana and identifies two important reasons why these institutions continue to hold significance in the provision of mental healthcare.

Chapter 5

Prayer Camps and Mental Health Research in Ghana: Identifying the Gaps

Religious institutions and their personnel, including clergy, have historically served as significant resources for individuals afflicted with mental health conditions (Mathews 2008; Houston 2004). In Ghana, for instance, Pentecostal clergy have been identified as key figures providing support to individuals with mental health needs (Asamoah et al. 2014; Laugharne and Burns 1999). This is evidenced by the assistance provided by pastor-prophets at prayer camps in Ghana. Globally, clergy engaged in pastoral counselling continue to offer essential support to individuals facing social problems that contribute to stress and mental health challenges (Myers et al. 2024; Jakob et al. 2020). Notably, one of the earliest hospitals established for the treatment of the mentally ill was founded by religious leaders in Jerusalem in 490 CE (Alexander and Selesnick 1966). Indeed, the services provided by religious institutions fill the treatment gap in mental healthcare in many developing countries.

For some individuals grappling with depression and other mental health disorders, interaction with pastors and the communal relationships fostered within church settings provide crucial support in overcoming depressive stressors and anxieties (Lloyd 2023). Particularly in Africa, one of the anticipated roles of a priest or pastor-prophet is that of a healer. Emmanuel Lartey (1986: 75) posits that 'healing, exorcism, divination, diagnosis and the restoration to wholeness of ill or disturbed persons are seen as crucial functions of the priest'. This perspective is rooted in the belief that 'to the traditional African, the most important activity of a priest is the medical one – the ability to diagnose correctly and to prescribe accurate remedies for various diseases'. In Pentecostal communities in Ghana, individuals who are emotionally and psychologically disturbed, and who suffer from various severe forms of mental illness, often seek the assistance of the pastor-prophet to confront their illnesses through prayer (Benyah 2022a; Osafo et al. 2015).

Despite the role that prayer camps play in supporting individuals with mental health challenges, their activities frequently face clinical scrutiny from health professionals and other stakeholders, some of whom perceive the healing activities at these camps as either negative or harmful (Edwards 2014; Human Rights Watch 2012). Such perspectives align with the prevailing attitudes and notions regarding the role of religion in mental healthcare and well-being.

The healing of mental illnesses at prayer camps in Ghana has garnered significant academic attention both within and beyond scholarly circles (Gyimah et al. 2023; Reads 2019; Human Rights Watch 2012). These studies predominantly aim to provide ethnographic accounts of the healing practices associated with mental illness, alongside ethical, clinical, psychological and religious perspectives on the treatment of individuals with mental health conditions at Ghana's prayer camps. While these investigations yield valuable insights into the phenomenon of prayer camps and mental health in Ghana, they often neglect a critical aspect: the reasons why prayer camps continue to serve as a compelling resource for individuals and families seeking to support relatives afflicted by mental health conditions. Considering the discussion on the evolution of prayer camps within Ghanaian Pentecostalism in Chapter 4, this chapter underscores the importance of researching prayer camps and mental health within the Ghanaian context.

In doing so, the chapter first addresses the significance of religion in the provision of mental healthcare in Ghana. This discussion is subsequently contextualized within Ghana's medical pluralistic landscape, with a particular focus on prayer camps. Furthermore, an effort is made to identify existing gaps in mental health research in Ghana, emphasizing that the roles of religion and institutions such as prayer camps have received limited scholarly attention. Additionally, the chapter examines various factors that contribute to the persistent relevance of prayer camps. This examination is framed by an exploration of the unique aspects of the healing practices at prayer camps, which continue to attract individuals while remaining insufficiently investigated.

Religion, a resource or challenge to mental healthcare?

It is incontrovertible that psychiatry has historically adopted a critical or disparaging perspective towards religion. For certain scholars and practitioners, there is a prevailing scepticism regarding the role of religion and spirituality in mental healthcare, dismissing them as mere products of individuals' imagination. They argue that religion holds no scientific validity in the context of mental healthcare (Dein 2018; Crossley 1995). Consequently, the significance of religion in the overall well-being of mental health patients receives minimal consideration, and in cases where it does garner recognition, it is often met with disdain. This gap in acknowledgement is particularly prominent within the realm of mental health specialties, where the separation between healthcare and religion is most pronounced (Koenig 2007). Mental health professionals have historically deemed religion as neurotic and potentially detrimental to sound mental health (Koenig 2007; see also Walach 2021; Sommer 2021). Consequently, religious beliefs tend to be disregarded in the treatment of mental illness by psychiatrists and other mental health professionals. Regrettably, mental health professionals often lack the necessary training to effectively assess factors such as religious beliefs in clinical settings (Rosmarin et al. 2011).

Attempting to exclude religious beliefs from clinical settings creates an aversion to broaching the subject in psychiatric research and practice. This perpetuates the assumption within the field that these aspects are peripheral to human functioning and an incidental concern in treatment (Rosmarin et al. 2011). Rosmarin et al. (2011: 254) argue that existing assessment protocols appear to overlook religious beliefs, and few interventions actively integrate religious and spiritual beliefs into treatment. Simon Dein (2018: 127), an anthropologist and psychiatrist, has remarked that religious beliefs and practices are widely perceived as 'primitive', engendering dependency, inducing guilt, lacking empirical evidence and inherently detrimental to mental health. In certain societies, religious practices associated with health and healing are viewed as irrational, even described as superstitious or magical, and regarded as ineffective approaches to thinking and behaving (McGuire 2008).

Such attitudes towards the role of religion in mental health have often led to scepticism regarding the potential of religion to aid in the recovery of mental health patients. It should be noted that this does not imply the absence of adverse or negative effects of religion and/or spirituality in healthcare. Undeniably, religious beliefs and practices can have both positive and negative implications, and healthcare professionals must be aware of instances where religious beliefs may hinder or conflict with appropriate medical care. Indeed, history reveals numerous instances where religion has been used to justify negative practices, and the restrictive and inflexible nature of religion can impede progress (see Koenig 2007).[1] However, scepticism in the role of religion often results in tensions that give rise to conflict and competition. Conflicts arise from the differing worldviews that inform the practices of both religious healing and biomedicine, which in turn disrupt the well-being of individuals seeking relief. In Ghana, for example, healing spaces have become sites for cultural negotiations, contestations and tensions that are fuelled by interactions between traditional healers, faith healers (particularly those from the Pentecostal or charismatic spectrum and Islam) and modern hospitals (Michael et al. 2021; Read 2019). Consequently, 'conflicting interpretations of disease and competing prescriptions for cure' abound in the medical arena, turning it into an 'adversarial forum'(Sullivan 1989: 3). Curers or healers not only combat disease but also confront each other's opposing views on sickness or health, which are shaped by 'personal development, social events, and cultural history' (Sullivan 1989: 3).

Despite the negative and sometimes detrimental perception of the role of religion in general healthcare and mental health specifically, several studies have highlighted the potential of religion and/or faith-based resources in managing or preventing severe mental disorders (Moreira-Almeida et al. 2021; Janus 2019; Koenig 2018; Schreurs 2001). Indeed, the shift towards more positive perspectives on religious beliefs and practices has demonstrated that religion and its associated practices can exert a beneficial effect on mental health. This conclusion is grounded in the understanding that religion encompasses meaning systems, communities, institutions and practices that may be central to both individual and collective existence. For instance, the aspect of spirituality underscores individual experience and broadens the focus beyond major traditions to incorporate new, emerging and hybrid forms of practice. In other words, religion and spirituality can potentially serve as sources of well-being and resources for coping and healing; however, they can also generate conflicts that may adversely impact mental health, as previously mentioned. These positive accounts of the role of religion are not merely imaginative descriptions but actual experiences of individuals who have witnessed the improvement, assistance or healing of their medical conditions through religion (Olsen 2017; Cabo and Mattson 2019; van Dijk et al. 2014). Indeed, personal claims of positive account of the role of religion in the lives of some individuals cannot be ignored in the face of development and advancement in medical technologies (Peprah et al. 2018).

Since the early 1990s, multiple national and international psychiatric associations, such as the American Psychiatric Association (APA) in 1990 and the World Psychiatric Association (WPA) in 2015, have made efforts to emphasize the importance of recognizing the role of religion in psychiatric practice. These reports and initiatives have been driven by the recognition of how culture and religion and spirituality can impact mental health. Therefore, psychiatrists are urged to consider all factors, including religion and spirituality, that can influence mental health outcomes (Moreira-Almeida et al. 2016). In Ghana, a leading clinical psychologist has emphasized the significance of understanding the belief system and the need for therapists to explore individuals' thoughts, emotions and behaviors in relation to their religious beliefs. This understanding is deemed essential in a context where religious beliefs hold utmost importance for the people. Health professionals are encouraged to find ways to address and integrate aspects of religious world-views into their therapeutic approaches (Sefa-Dede 2014).

At the international level, the WPA and the World Health Organization (WHO) have made efforts to ensure that comprehensive mental healthcare and promotion are grounded in scientific evidence, while also being compassionate and culturally sensitive, taking into account religion, culture and spirituality (Moreira-Almeida et al. 2016). The WPA position statement on religion and spirituality has had broader implications, prompting several national psychiatric associations, including those of South Africa, the UK, Brazil and the United States, among others, to recognize the role of religion and spirituality in psychiatry (Moreira-Almeida et al. 2016). These countries' efforts to fill the gap in mental healthcare by acknowledging the significance of religion and spirituality demonstrate that these aspects are not isolated or esoteric but instead lie at the heart of psychiatry, both conceptually and clinically (Verhagen 2017). Therefore, in psychiatry, 'meaning making, existential issues, including religion and spirituality, are always' present, not only in the lives of patients but also in the way psychiatrists perceive their professional roles (Verhagen 2017: 513). The WPA position statement published in the special issue of the journal *Mental Health, Religion and Culture* contributes significantly by highlighting the importance of religion in psychiatry (Verhagen 2017; Braam 2017; Gray 2017; Dein 2017).

The aforementioned developments regarding the role of religion in psychiatry underscore the significance of religion in mental healthcare. The issue is not whether psychiatrists should adopt the religious orientations of their clients, but rather, it is about recognizing that religious phenomena are central to the daily realities of some clients. In contexts like Ghana, where this is highly relevant, these issues cannot be ignored or marginalized when addressing mental health concerns as found in the context of the prayer camps as well as highlighting the need for clinicians to understand the role of religion and spirituality in providing care in a context where the influence of religion in healthcare is highly pervasive.

Religion and spirituality are not limited to religious or spiritual individuals; instead, they relate to every person facing psychiatric disorders who must grapple with the experience of psychic illness. This experience is fundamentally rooted in the broader understanding of the human person prevalent in cultures where religious and cultural beliefs hold supreme significance in making sense of human behaviour and actions. In contemporary Ghanaian society, the prevalence of faith healing practices in psychiatric care continues to draw attention, partly due to their ability to address the underlying realities embedded in supplicants' world-views. Thus, the practices of healing at prayer camps function as important resource in responding to the needs of supplicants whose world-views or perceived causes of mental illness are multifaceted as explained in the concept of *sunsum yareɛ*. In other words, prayer camps as religious institutions offer support of healing services that are culturally symbolic and meaningful to individuals with mental health challenges.

In the preceding discussion, I referenced the limited number of mental health facilities and mental health professionals available for the provision of mental healthcare in Ghana. The shortage of both healthcare personnel and medical infrastructure significantly contributes to the treatment gap in mental healthcare within the country. The operation of prayer camps and other faith-based organizations in mental healthcare represents a crucial response to the deficit of mental health workers in Ghana and other low- and middle-income countries (WHO 2022, 2006, 2007). Indeed, it is estimated that as many as 80 per cent of individuals in Africa seek traditional and faith-based healing methods to address their healthcare needs (WHO 2002). The practices observed in the context of prayer camps in Ghana align with health-seeking behaviours prevalent across the African continent (Gammelin 2023; LeBeau 2003). In Ghana, in addition to the prayer camps, numerous churches provide spiritual healing that integrates aspects of traditional medicine with Christian beliefs (Asamoah, Osafo and Agyapong 2014). These diverse healing modalities exemplify the pluralistic nature of medical systems in Ghana and simultaneously highlight the efforts undertaken by religious institutions to meet the healthcare needs of their constituents.

Situating prayer camps within Ghana's medically pluralistic society

Ghana has been shown to be one of the most religious countries in sub-Saharan Africa: 71.3 per cent self-identify with Christianity, 19.9 per cent with Islam and 3.2 per cent with traditional and/or indigenous religion, making a total of 94.4 per cent religious affiliations in the country (Ghana Statistical Service 2021).

The medical system in Ghana is characterized by pluralism, indicating the parallel coexistence of indigenous/traditional practices, faith healers (including those from Christianity and Islam) and biomedicine (Roberts 2021; Ayim-Aboagye 2006; Owoahene-Acheampong 1998; Twumasi 2005).[2] As already mentioned, the plurality of belief systems in general, and medical systems in particular, often presents a myriad of healing practices and models that result in differential boundaries, and, at times, suspicion, mistrust and unhealthy competition, which obfuscate or trivialize intended integration and collaboration among practitioners aimed at addressing the well-being of individuals or resolving the shortcomings of each medical category. Mistrust and lack of openness between different healing modalities consequently create a problem of 'theoretical closure'[3] and bifurcate any attempt to find solutions that illuminate an understanding of general problems, such as the articulation of thought and action, individual experience and cultural (and religious) forms and symbols that are fundamental to addressing the health needs of a society that is religiously and culturally diverse (Michael et al. 2021; Comaroff 1981).

In Ghana, the Ghana Health Service (GHS) is the governmental body that regulates the provision of healthcare services across the country. In addition to the GHS, there are various non-state bodies and actors that provide healthcare services to the population, including private healthcare providers and medical centres operated by religious denominations, which fall under the umbrella of the Christian Health Association of Ghana (CHAG). CHAG is an integral part of Ghana's health system and prioritizes mental healthcare. The facilities (hospitals and clinics) operating under the auspices of CHAG are established and managed by religious bodies such as the Catholic Church, Methodist Church Ghana, Presbyterian Church of Ghana and the Church of Pentecost, among others, and they constitute part of the mainstream healthcare service providers. Thus, although these medical institutions are founded by churches, they receive state support and are integrated into the general healthcare system by the GHS, as they operate within the modern scientific and biomedical framework with minimal or no emphasis on the supernatural or metaphysical dimensions of diseases. The establishment of hospitals and clinics can be argued to align with the churches' theological embrace of scientific advancements in the field of medicine. Nonetheless, they also represent a component of the colonial legacies transmitted through European missionary activities and colonial administration (Walker 2022).

Paradoxically, nearly all of the churches mentioned earlier operate prayer camps or healing centres specifically aimed at addressing illnesses or diseases that are perceived to be beyond the curative capabilities of scientific medicine. Consequently, the prayer camps operated by the churches do not function within the frameworks of scientific healing methods. At best, their practices are grounded in biblical teachings and faith healing as demonstrated in the Bible by Jesus Christ. In contrast to hospitals, the healing centres do not perceive the human body merely as an entity affected by pathogens but also as influenced by external forces that cannot be entirely resolved by scientific medicine or detected in medical laboratories.

The establishment and operation of hospitals and prayer centres or camps by churches exemplify their openness to scientific advancement while simultaneously revealing their cultural sensibilities. Thus, they are attuned to the cultural and local realities of their religious constituents and adopt locally and culturally accepted means of addressing their healthcare needs. This also affirms their beliefs in the biblical world-view of supernatural causality, which aligns with local beliefs and theories of disease causation. While prayer camps have become part of the 'informal' health sector, providing healthcare to numerous individuals, particularly those with mental health issues, they do not form part of the mainstream healthcare system nor operate under any central authority, and their services are not sanctioned by any organizations, except for those affiliated with churches.

The Mental Health Authority (MHA) of Ghana, as part of its efforts to integrate mental healthcare into the general healthcare system, has made strides to include mental healthcare as part of primary healthcare in Ghana. This mechanism has been implemented through the MHA decentralization policy – wherein mental health is integrated into primary healthcare at the outpatient department (OPD) level. This approach ensures de-institutionalization, contributing to increased discharges, reduced admissions and the provision of mental health services at the community level. It is at the community level that prayer camps or, more broadly, faith and religion intersect with the services provided by health centres offering mental healthcare to individuals in the communities. At this level, individuals experiment with different healing traditions and seek multiple health pathways based on their interpretations of their illnesses. In a context like Ghana, cultural and religious explanations for illnesses, including mental health issues, are predominantly invoked by affected individuals and their families. Thus, there exists a strong belief in and divine explanation for most health conditions. It is at this point that prayer camps become part of the therapeutic institution's individuals turn to in their quest for solutions to their health conditions. Consequently, prayer camps become integral to the lived experiences of individuals seeking healthcare in a medically pluralistic setting. Therefore, at the community level, the importance of faith healing and/or religion becomes indispensable if efforts to ensure access to mental health services are to be realized.

What renders institutions such as prayer camps particularly significant and influential in Ghana is their provision of hybrid healing ritual practices that amalgamate aspects of traditional healing rituals. In other words, the healing rituals at prayer camps resonate with participants because they incorporate practices that are culturally and religiously meaningful. Prayer camps are also perceived to provide essential social welfare functions that are lacking in a country like Ghana. The major streets of Accra and other cities in Ghana often witness individuals suffering from severe mental health problems roaming unattended. While the MHA and security agencies have occasionally implemented measures to remove such vagrants from the streets, these efforts have proven unsuccessful (Read 2020). The failure of such initiatives can be attributed to the absence of social welfare mechanisms in the country to accommodate these individuals, and prayer camps partially fulfil this role. In Ghana, prayer camps provide various functions, including fostering community belongingness, care, support, compassion and protection, which are frequently deficient in mainstream medical facilities (Benyah 2022).

However, the unquestioned authority of some prayer camp leaders, such as prophets or prophetesses, can also result in unintended consequences stemming from their power and authority as religious figures (Golo 2024). Such power is sometimes misused and abused. For example, there are instances of human rights abuses, forced fasting and chaining, among other issues. While some of these practices may be unintentional, they also illuminate the authority and power wielded by religious figures in addressing societal concerns.

Gaps in prayer camps and mental health research

The popularity of prayer camps in Ghana and the significance of religious and/or spiritual beliefs and practices in addressing mental health issues have been of long-standing interest to scholars in the fields of psychiatry, psychology and anthropology. While several studies indicate that alternative practitioners, such as prophets or prophetesses at prayer camps, are consulted for mental health concerns in Ghana, research on prayer camps remains limited. Existing literature on prayer camps and mental health in Ghana has predominantly emerged from disciplines such as anthropology, psychology and clinical psychology, with a notable absence of major studies from the perspective of religious studies. Only a handful of investigations mainly from anthropology and psychology have attempted to systematically analyse the religious components and their role in mental healthcare in Ghana (Read 2019; Kpobi and Swartz 2018; Yendork et al. 2019; Arias et al. 2016). Consequently, there is a dearth of research examining the impact of ritual, prayer and other aspects of religious experience on mental healthcare in Ghana, and insufficient attention has been paid to the role of religion in mental healthcare. In some instances, religious considerations in seeking mental healthcare are treated with disdain and regarded as somewhat irrational.

Indeed, none of the previous studies have explored the lived experiences of individuals with mental illnesses at prayer camps. The gap in research on mental healthcare in Ghana is further underscored by Yaro et al. (2020) and Read and Doku (2013). Read and Doku (2013: 101) observe that prior studies on mental health in Ghana have demonstrated that 'mental health research in Ghana remains limited in both quantity and quality. In the absence of a comprehensive research record, much is assumed based on scant evidence, and services are heavily influenced by the results of research conducted elsewhere, most often in high-income settings.' The scarcity of research in the domain of mental health in Ghana also contributes to the low levels of awareness regarding mental health among the population.

As already mentioned, recent studies on prayer camps in Ghana describe a sustained belief in malevolent supernatural forces as the cause of most mental illnesses (Arias et al. 2016; Kpobi and Swartz 2018a). Despite responses from some transcultural psychiatrists and anthropologists advocating for the recognition of traditional notions and beliefs about illness in the classification and treatment of mental health issues (Read 2017), a hierarchy of knowledge persists in Ghana (and in a global context) in which 'natural' or biomedical knowledge is deemed superior to 'supernatural' explanations in the theory of disease causation. Although culture and religion have been emphasized as significant factors in psychiatry and mental healthcare (Koenig 2018; Kleinman 1980; Kirmayer and Swartz 2013), much of the existing literature on the subject in Ghana and elsewhere has inadequately addressed these factors.

In Ghana, the low recognition of religion in mental healthcare is evident not only in the literature but also at the institutional level. For instance, while the MHA of Ghana advocates for complementary and holistic mental health by recommending engagement with other stakeholders, such as traditional and faith-based healers, the institution's own policy document, the Mental Health Act (Act 846), does not mention the term 'religion' anywhere in the Act. While one might argue that religion is implied but not explicitly mentioned in the Act, the exclusion of the term cannot be dismissed as a common oversight.

Evidently, Ghana's efforts to establish a Mental Health Act that aligns with the fundamental tenets of global mental health policy directives have been driven by international stakeholders such as the WHO and funded by international donor agencies, including the then UK's Department for International Development (DFID) now referred to as Foreign, Commonwealth and Development Office (FCDO). This necessitated that the drafters of the bill adhere to international provisions for a progressive vision of global mental health standards, which often overlook factors such as religion due to their sensitive nature. As argued by Read (2020: 105), 'Ghana's Mental Health Act is haunted not just by colonial histories of social cleansing … but by psychiatry's own iatrogenic potentiality and the enduring power of hierarchies which mark relationships between the global North and South.'

The consequences of this predicament as a result of these global networks of relationships have been highlighted by Merry (2006), who contends that local stakeholders often find themselves ensnared by the complex relationship arising from their alliance with international donor agencies, balancing the need to appeal to external funders while simultaneously satisfying local communities. Indeed, her concerns resonate with those expressed by Dr Akwasi Osei, former CEO of the MHA in Ghana, who articulates the view that Ghana's Mental Health Act is 'synthesised [and] guided by the WHO, from the mental health laws of many countries with doses of Ghana's own culture. The law was, therefore, uniquely peculiar to Ghana's culture and not a replica of any country's law' (Osei, cited in Read 2020: 120). While this statement is posited amidst concerns to address local initiatives and legislation for providing mental healthcare in Ghana, it undoubtedly reveals the tensions between the global vision of international agencies and local sensibilities, particularly those bordering on culture and religion.

This situation exemplifies the 'clash of cultures' (Taylor 2003) between two 'culturally distinct social worlds' (Merry 2006: 38), with governmental bodies such as the MHA often somewhat hindered in addressing these issues, in part due to the ambiguity produced by their relationship with external or global actors who may frown upon aspects of cultural issues, such as religion, in mental healthcare. Indeed, local political and socio-economic factors cannot be overlooked, especially given that successive governments have defunded mental health sectors, necessitating reliance on external funding. Prayer camps can be regarded as institutions that fulfil the role of culture and religion through their services, stepping in to provide support that state institutions are unable to offer.

Why prayer camps are important stakeholders in mental healthcare

The religious and/or spiritual factors

Needless to say, the defeat of the secularization theory has become evident in the pervasive influence of religion in both the private and public spheres. One area where religion has shown remarkable resilience in everyday life is healing and healthcare (Walker 2022; Hanrieder 2017; Brown 2013; Grills 2009). One of the motivations for this book arose from the desire to explore the usefulness or value of religion in mental healthcare, as evidenced by the healing practices of prayer camps in Ghana. While religion/spirituality is often considered when examining African medical and healing systems (Roberts 2021; Ayinde et al. 2021; Azevedo 2017; Olsen and Sargent 2017; Twumasi 2005), the prayer camp scene in Ghana is unique. As mentioned already, prayer camps have historically emerged as a product of colonial legacies, particularly through Christian missionary activities. Nevertheless, they exemplify a synthesis of traditional therapeutic systems and provide insight into how institutions of domestic and community life influence therapeutic choices.

Emmanuel Akyeampong (2015), a Ghanaian historian, has emphasized that the growth of Islamism and Pentecostal and Charismatic Christianity, with a slight resurgence of African Indigenous Religions, ensures that faith healing will continue to play a central role in the healing landscape of Africa. What is noteworthy in Akyeampong's observation (2015) is that one ongoing challenge in mental healthcare in Africa, for example, is the attempt to clarify the relationship between Pentecostal and indigenous healing (which is primarily spiritual/faith based) and Western psychiatry.[4] Indeed, these different healing modalities present a plurality of medical systems, each with its own array of challenges. And these challenges need to be explored within the context of healing practices within prayer camps.

However, as mentioned earlier, no study, especially from the perspectives of religious studies, has examined the healing practices for individuals who seek support for their mental health conditions in prayer camps in Ghana. This is in light of the recognition by the MHA of Ghana (MHA 2018: 21) that 'culture and religion' are major factors influencing the value society places on mental health, the understanding of causal factors, 'the management of the condition, the degree of stigma and discrimination, access to services, and pathways to care'. It is crucial to investigate the religious factors that drive the prevalence and dominance of prayer camps in Ghana, particularly with regard to the healing of mental illnesses.

The socio-economic and political factors

Several literatures have highlighted the social and political implications of health and healing in Africa (Faleye 2023; Aka et al. 2022; Feierman and Janzen 1994; Falola and Heaton 2006). Historically, prayer camps emerged as both a response to individuals' religious and spiritual needs and a solution to a social problem that Ghana faced in the early 1970s and 1980s due to the impact of structural adjustment programs. In Ghana, for example, the implementation of the 'cash-and-carry' system, resulting from the structural adjustment programme, hindered certain individuals from accessing medical care. Although access to medical care has improved in Ghana due to the implementation of the universal health insurance system and enhancements in medical infrastructure, a significant portion of the population still lacks access to adequate healthcare. Individuals with psychiatric or mental health issues are particularly affected by the absence of or insufficient mental health facilities.

Presently, Ghana has three major psychiatric hospitals, all of which are located in the southern region of the country, leaving the northern sector without direct access to psychiatric institutions. Furthermore, there are four private psychiatric hospitals, with two in Kumasi and two in Accra, both having a total of forty beds (MHA 2018). In an attempt to decentralize mental healthcare and mitigate the challenges associated with accessing psychiatric care, the MHA of Ghana has initiated efforts to establish psychiatric units in teaching hospitals, as well as regional, district and local hospitals and clinics, in order to address the mental health needs of individuals. These hospitals and clinics have added beds to accommodate patients with psychiatric conditions. Additionally, religious institutions such as the Presbyterian Church of Ghana (PCG) and the Roman Catholic Church have contributed to this endeavour. In 2022, the PCG inaugurated the first psychiatric hospital in Bolgatanga in the Upper East Region of Ghana.[5] The Roman Catholic Church also operates rehabilitation centres, including the Damien Centre in Fijai, Western Region; the Mercy Centre in Brafo Yaw, near Cape Coast; the Cheshire Home in Kumasi; the House of St. Francis in Ashaiman, Greater Accra Region; and the Shekinah Day Centre in Tamale, Northern Region, among others (MHA 2018). Moreover, Action Chapel Ghana runs the Compassion Rehabilitation Centre along Prampram Road in the Greater Accra Region (Aning 2019). This is against the over 1,000 prayer camps estimated by the MHA to be operating in Ghana and providing support to mental healthcare in the country.

In addition to the insufficient infrastructure, psychiatry care in Ghana is hindered by limited human resources. As of 2020, there were 39 psychiatrists, 26 psychologists, 2,463 mental health workers, 362 social workers and 6 mental health professionals, including occupational therapists, in both the public and private sectors combined.[6] These numbers are insufficient given the country's population of approximately 31 million (WHO 2022).

The provision of psychotropic medication for individuals with mental health challenges in Ghana is insufficient, posing a significant challenge to the delivery of mental healthcare (Oppong et al. 2016). In certain cases, health professionals take it upon themselves to procure these medications and sell them directly to patients who can afford them, bypassing formal channels (Draicchio 2020). Consequently, the MHA has issued directives to legitimize this practice, encouraging health professionals to engage in the 'buy and sell' of medication to willing patients (Draicchio 2020).[7] This approach undermines the objective of providing mental healthcare free of charge under the health insurance scheme, as outlined in the Mental Health Act of 2012 (Act 846, Section 88). The emergence of such initiatives can be attributed to the frustration caused by the adverse effects of neoliberal capitalist processes of privatization. Mental health hospitals, unable to generate sufficient income, fall victim to these processes, resulting in a return to a 'cash-and-carry' system where individuals seeking mental health treatment in Ghana are required to pay out of pocket (Draicchio 2020).

Indeed, the mental health sector in Ghana has consistently suffered from budget cuts by successive governments. Even in 2023 and 2024, the allocated budget for mental healthcare falls short of 1 per cent of the total expenditure on general healthcare in the country. Furthermore, there are claims that the government does not even disburse the full 1 per cent allocated to hospitals to support their work. In a 2018 documentary on the state of mental health in Ghana, the then director of the MHA lamented that they would only receive approximately 20 per cent of their budgetary requirements by the end of the year, with even this estimate being generous.[8] These ongoing issues have serious implications for the delivery of mental healthcare in Ghana.

The inclination of individuals to seek support for the treatment of their mental health conditions from prayer camps and traditional healers in Ghana has been linked to the insufficient funding and infrastructure (in terms of medical professionals and health facilities) in mental healthcare resulting in a treatment gap. In mental healthcare, the treatment gap refers to the difference between the actual prevalence of a disorder and the proportion of affected individuals who receive treatment. Alternatively, the treatment gap can be represented as the percentage of individuals who need care but do not receive it (Kohn et al. 2004). It is estimated that in Ghana, about 98 per cent of people who need mental healthcare do not get the treatment they need. In other words, there is 98 per cent treatment gap in mental healthcare in Ghana (WHO 2022).

According to the MHA (2018), a considerable number of people with mental health conditions in Ghana resort to seeking assistance from these alternative sources of care such as the faith-based healing centres. While this observation by MHA is somewhat plausible, I hold a contrary view.

I hold the view that the tendency of individuals suffering from mental health conditions and their families to seek solutions at prayer camps is not necessarily influenced by the lack of or inadequate availability of mental healthcare facilities or professionals but rather by the perceived notions underlying the causes of mental illness. Indeed, such arguments suggest that people will cease seeking help at prayer camps or faith-based centres when there is improvement or a sufficient number of facilities to address the needs of individuals with mental health conditions. However, the question that emerges in response to these claims is why individuals in Western countries with advanced medical technologies still engage in faith healing practices (Brown 2013). Therefore, while inadequate infrastructure may be a contributing factor, it does not entirely explain the issue at hand and merely overshadows an important aspect such as culture and religion which play a central role in healthcare seeking for certain individuals (Peprah et al. 2018; Kpobi and Swartz 2019). Other scholars have similarly argued that prayer camps hold significant influence among Ghanaians, and any attempts to establish adequate hospital beds with the aim of redirecting those currently seeking help at healing camps would likely prove futile due to the underlying beliefs associated with mental illness (Ofori-Atta et al. 2018). This argument is aptly summarized by the title of an article on healing centres in Ghana: 'Whether you like it or not people with mental problems are going to go to them' (Ae-Ngibise et al. 2010).

Summary

The discussions presented in this chapter have provided a comprehensive overview of the role of faith-based approaches in supporting the treatment of mental health conditions in Ghana, specifically within the framework of prayer camps. The chapter has also underscored the necessity of directing attention towards institutions such as prayer camps in the discourse surrounding the provision of support for individuals living with mental illnesses. Prayer camps continue to represent a significant institution in the provision of support for these individuals. Although such provisions are not without their excesses, often associated with various forms of faith-based and religious healing practices, they remain an important resource for individuals who are sometimes neglected by the state.

In Ghana, there is a greater number and easier accessibility of prayer camps and faith-based healers compared to mental health professionals. The prevalence of such centres, coupled with the limited number of mental health facilities in the country, indicates that they will continue to be significant institutions, especially given that their operational style and healing practices resonate with the majority of the population. These prevailing factors, among others, render the services provided by prayer camps and other faith-based institutions indispensable in the provision of mental healthcare in Ghana and elsewhere in Africa.

Indeed, the socio-economic and political issues impacting the political economy of healthcare in Ghana, along with their intersections with matters of religion, culture and healing, serve as motivation to explore the emergence of prayer camps as significant institutions in the care of individuals with mental health conditions in Ghana. These socio-economic factors provide a rationale for investigating the utility of religion and culture in the care of individuals with mental health conditions in resource-limited settings, as well as how these factors influence the integration of religion into people's lives amidst developments and advancements in technology.

The ensuing chapters, particularly Chapters 6 and 7, endeavour to establish an empirical foundation for understanding the influence of religion and/or spirituality in the care of individuals with mental health conditions in Ghana.

Chapter 6

PERCEIVED AETIOLOGIES OF MENTAL ILLNESS AND THERAPEUTIC INTERVENTIONS IN PRAYER CAMPS

The discussions in this chapter encapsulate the perspectives articulated by participants regarding their understanding and healing of mental illnesses, derived from interviews conducted at prayer camps. The findings presented here are predominantly based on interviews with patients, their family members, caregivers, prophets and health professionals associated with the prayer camps that were selected for the study.

Caregivers, who constitute a segment of the staff at prayer camps, play a pivotal role in assisting the leaders or prophets with the daily management of the camp, particularly in the care of individuals who have sought healing. This group comprises both male and female caregivers. Their responsibilities encompass the daily management and welfare of the patients, which includes assisting them in taking their prescribed medications, ensuring their nutritional needs are met and aiding those who lack the capacity to bathe due to health conditions. They also play a critical role in the socialization process of patient's post-recovery, prior to their discharge from the camp. The caregivers I interviewed had between twelve and twenty years of experience in the care of individuals with mental illness at the camps. However, they possessed no formal training in psychology or psychiatry. The experiential knowledge and insights they provided were invaluable to the overall findings presented in this chapter and in subsequent chapters.

The patients were individuals with a history of mental illness who had achieved some level of wellness yet continued to reside at the camp. The duration of their stay at the camp varied significantly among individuals. At the time of my visit, some patients had been in residence for a few months, while others had remained for several years. It is also noteworthy that the camps selected for this study operated under different regulations for in-resident patients. While some camps stipulated a maximum stay of four months, others permitted patients to remain until their condition improved. With respect to those camps that imposed a specified duration of stay, there were instances where patients were permitted to remain after the four-month limit had been reached due to the chronic or unstable nature of their mental health conditions. During my visit, some individuals had experienced periods of wellness and had been discharged, only to return to the camp following a relapse. Others had achieved recovery but chose to remain in the camp, as they felt safer and more 'at home' in the supportive environment. Beyond mental health considerations, additional social and political factors such as poverty, stigma and discrimination contributed to the reasons why certain individuals preferred to reside at the camp.

Interviewing individuals who may have a history of mental illness presents both ethical and epistemological challenges. Kim Usher and Collin Holmes (1997) argue that individuals with mental illnesses are perceived as vulnerable research participants, as they are often seen as incapable or less capable of making informed decisions regarding their participation in research studies. However, other studies demonstrate that this perception is not universally applicable (see e.g. Stanley et al. 1981). 'In fact, people with mental illness may wish to take part in a research project despite the paternalistic view of their caregivers, advocates, guardians, or family members' (Liamputtong 2007: 25; see also Usher and Holmes 1997). Stanley et al. (1981) contend that such negative perceptions or labelling of individuals with mental illness tend to compromise their independence in research studies, thereby missing opportunities to partake in research projects that could potentially enhance their health and well-being.

In this study, I opted to interview patients due to their lived experiences of healing at the camp. Consequently, the patients were regarded as 'experiential experts on the subject' under investigation and were therefore 'allowed maximum opportunity to tell their own story' (Smith and Osborn 2015: 31). The patients recounted their profound healing experiences at the camp, experiences that were, for them, as tangible as what modern medicine could offer. In this context, the patients did not employ the term 'healing' merely as a metaphor to articulate their experiences (McGuire 2008; Kirmayer 2004). The articulation of their experiences served to phenomenologically ground the responses within the broader analysis of this study. Thus, the patients' experiences illuminated the methodological approach adopted for this research, facilitating a thorough examination of the efficacy of the healing experiences claimed by the participants. It is widely acknowledged that most studies on religious healing conducted by anthropologists, despite their extensive scope, tend to be merely descriptive in nature, offering little evidence for readers to assess the effectiveness of the claims made by supplicants or the methods and procedures employed (Csordas 1994). The analysis in this chapter and the findings presented in the subsequent chapters not only provide descriptive accounts but also elucidate the experiences of the effects and transformations of religious healing through the testimonies and narratives of supplicants.

Family members or relatives primarily comprised the parents of patients seeking treatment at the camp. All family members residing at the camp were women, predominantly the mothers of individuals suffering from illness. Some of these women were traders who had ceased their commercial activities due to the illness of their dependents, opting to remain at the camp to provide care. Others were engaged in menial jobs to generate the necessary funds for their wards' care. Those who could not afford to take time off work had employed assistants or caregivers at the camp to attend to their relatives while they fulfilled their job responsibilities, visiting the camp regularly to monitor the progress of treatment.

The interviews focused on the history of the patient's illness, coping or management strategies and the usefulness of the coping mechanisms. For example, during interviews, patients were prompted to provide a succinct history of their illness if they could remember, including its onset, the symptoms experienced and their personal interpretations of the situation. They were also encouraged to recount their experiences during their first episode, as much as they could recall. In this context, patients were asked to describe the imagery that arose in their minds regarding their previous circumstances. Questions included inquiries about the experience of being mentally ill and how their illness affected their daily lives in areas such as work and personal relationships.

Additionally, patients were requested to discuss the various therapeutic sources they sought, how they arrived at the prayer camps and the benefits they gained while residing at these facilities. They were also queried regarding what they considered to be the most effective treatment and therapeutic interventions; some of the prompts for this inquiry included attending a hospital, consulting a traditional healer and visiting a prophet at a prayer camp. Inquiries were also made about the successes and failures of each therapeutic intervention they had pursued since the onset of their illness and how these experiences influenced their perceptions of the various healing methodologies.

For other participants, including caregivers and pastor-prophets at the camps, the interview questions centred on their perceptions, understandings and interpretations of the causes of mental illness, alongside their various mechanisms and approaches to addressing it. Inquiries were also made about their experiences in caring for individuals with mental illness and how those experiences informed their professional practices. Furthermore, I explored the nature of the working relationships they had developed with health professionals who were responsible for oversight at the camps. For health professionals, I sought their perspectives on the operations of the prayer camps with respect to the treatment of mental illness and whether these opinions influenced their working relationships with the leaders of the prayer camps.

The findings from interviews conducted with participants at prayer camps indicate that they have a comprehensive understanding of the various factors that may contribute to the development of mental health conditions or illnesses. Participants' responses reveal that, while they occasionally perceive mental health issues as being influenced by supernatural agents, they remain cognizant of the fact that such conditions may also be precipitated by a range of physical or environmental factors. These include poverty, unemployment, the loss of a relative or loved one, car accidents, genetic or biological factors as well as certain diseases.

Mediums for diagnosing the causes of mental illness by pastor-prophets

An interview with staff from prayer camps revealed that significant effort is dedicated to diagnosing individuals sent to the camp for healing, particularly concerning mental illnesses. The prayer camps emphasized that a crucial aspect of this process involves seeking divine insight into the individual's situation through intensive prayer and fasting. It is believed that, through these prayers, God reveals the potential causes of the illness, which staff subsequently communicate to the seekers and their families. A viewpoint articulated by a pastor-prophet during an interview further illustrates his extensive perspective on the mediums used in diagnosing the potential causes of mental health issues:

> When someone is brought to us, we delve deep into the spirit to see what the actual cause of the person's problem is. Sometimes the dead of someone's spouse could result in the person developing a mental health problem. Sometimes a car accident could be a leading cause of someone's mental health condition. A person showing signs of seizure during childhood (epilepsy), with such a person, if no attempt is made to address the problem while growing up, he or she can develop mental health problem in adulthood. A person who has lost his or her money can also cause the person to have a mental health problem.

While the aforementioned quotation illustrates the spectrum of broader understanding regarding the potential causes of mental illnesses, it also highlights the medium through which the pastor-prophets are able to diagnose certain perceived causes that extend beyond biological, natural, social or economic factors. The pastor-prophet states that 'when someone is brought' to them for healing, they 'delve deep into the spirit' to ascertain the underlying cause of the problem. The phrase 'delving deep into the spirit' suggests that the issues presented by their clients at the camp are not easily discernible through mere observation or knowledge of the person's medical history. In such instances, the only means of identifying the cause of the individual's illness is through prayer, with the aid of the Holy Spirit to reveal or diagnose the nature of the affliction. The practice of patients and their families attending prayer camps in search of solutions to health issues, alongside the invocation performed by the pastor-prophet to ascertain the underlying causes of these problems, is analogous to *abisa* (divine consultation). This approach enables the pastor-prophet to determine whether the illness is influenced by supernatural agents. However, according to the pastor-prophet, even in cases where it is discovered that the illness has a supernatural origin, they seldom hasten to make definitive statements about the individual's situation, such as assuming that a witch has caused the person's sickness. This is exemplified in the following statement:

> Sometimes, when we go deep into the spirit, we see that there are spiritual connotations, but we don't subscribe to that wholeheartedly. This is because you can't openly disclose that this person is under the influenced of witchcraft attack or that the person is a witch that is why he or she is sick. In the bible, when a blindman was brought to Jesus, the people wanted to see what exactly was wrong with the person. Whether the condition is as a result of their parents' sins or the sins of the affected person. Jesus never told them what exactly was wrong. He only said this happened so the glory of God would be seen or demonstrated.

From the perspective of the pastor-prophet, illness may occur as a means for the glory of God to be manifested, as illustrated in the biblical accounts of Jesus Christ. The pastor-prophet maintained that attributing an individual's sickness exclusively to witchcraft poses the risk of stigmatization and mistreatment by others. Consequently, there is a necessity for great caution in addressing such sensitive matters upon their discovery. As a result, they exercise considerable care in attributing someone's illness to witchcraft or in accusing individuals of witchcraft:

> Here, we don't accuse anyone of witchcraft. In all our 17 branches in Ghana, we don't encourage witchcraft accusations. Even when someone comes here and we find out that the person is a witch, we don't disclose for people to know. Because when you do that, they will be insulting the person or pointing fingers at them. They will cast insinuation at them. We comfort their souls. We don't want them to be sad in such circumstances ... Even if the person is being disturbed by an evil spirit, we know how to go about such problems. We don't disclose it to people.

The perspective articulated by the pastor-prophet aligns with the discourse presented in Chapter 3 concerning the concept of *sunsum yareɛ*, or spiritual illness. The idea of spiritual illness does not invariably imply an attack by witchcraft; it is somewhat misleading to assert that every ailment attributed to spiritual influences is caused by witchcraft. This is not to suggest that witchcraft influences as articulated by participants are non-existent. The aforementioned quotation indicates that even amidst a strong belief that an individual's illness is caused or influenced by witchcraft, caution is exercised in articulating such ideas due to concerns regarding victimization or the stigmatization of the individual. Additionally, the quotation underscores the significance of an individual's soul (*kra*) to their overall well-being, as discussed in Chapter 1. The perspective of the pastor-prophet demonstrates an awareness of the notion that a distressed soul can potentially impact a person's state of ill health; thus, there is an emphasis on ensuring that nothing is done to exacerbate the emotional distress of individuals seeking healing. In this context, the concept of *ne kra werɛ ahow*, as described in Chapter 1, re-emerges.

Religious/spiritual factors

The interviews revealed that, in addition to perceived witchcraft attacks, there are other circumstances believed to result in mental health disorders or ailments caused by spiritual attacks. These circumstances include the theft of an individual's belongings or property, the desire to acquire money or wealth through occult means and engaging in illicit relationships, among others. The pastor-prophet reflected:

> Sometimes too, the person has gone to steal someone's items or have committed a sin against a fellow or neighbour. Maybe the person has gone for a 'sakawa'

> and has killed someone. When we examine the situation and see that this is the kind of sin he or she has committed, or even had slept with someone's wife or girlfriend and has been cursed. We are able to see all these when they come here.

The perspective articulated by the pastor-prophet aligns with the prevalent Akan belief that individuals are recompensed according to their actions. Consequently, negative behaviour is believed to result in punishment or adverse omens, whereas positive conduct yields blessings. Therefore, an individual's wrongdoing may provoke retribution from the aggrieved party, which can manifest as a spiritual attack, potentially resulting in mental illness. This understanding is consistent with the discussion in Chapter 2 regarding the role of spiritual agency and its implications for mental health. In Akan society, it is believed that individuals who suffer distress due to another's actions – such as infidelity, theft of possessions or other forms of wrongdoing without seeking forgiveness or acknowledging their misdeeds – may face retribution. Such punishment is typically enacted when the offended party consults a *juju* or medicinal practitioner,[1] requesting that they inflict illness, particularly mental illness, on the offender. In Ghana, this viewpoint on the transmission of mental health issues is widely held and corresponds with other disease classifications as examined in the works of Warren (1975) and Konadu (2007).

In addition to this perception, another prevalent notion regarding the origins of mental illness was also evident during the interviews. In Ghana, the term 'sakawa', as referenced by the pastor-prophet, is commonly used to denote cybercrime. Employment challenges and poverty have been identified as significant contributing factors to the prevalence of cyber fraud among Ghanaian youth. Of particular relevance to this discussion is the belief in the role that religious rituals play in cyber fraud in Ghana. Both reported and unreported accounts, alongside various scholarly works, confirm that individuals engaged in cyber fraud often participate in what is termed 'cyber spiritualism'. This concept refers to the utilization of mystical or magical powers and other ritual practices to hypnotize victims into relinquishing their valuables, including money, to the scammers without hesitation (Alhassan and Ridwan 2023; Tade 2013; Whitty 2018; Oduro-Frimpong 2014). However, the process by which scammers acquire or obtain such magical powers to enhance their fraudulent activities is neither simple nor straightforward; strict adherence to ritual protocols is required for success. Reports indicate that individuals who fail to comply with the ritualistic guidelines may risk mental instability. Indeed, Opare-Henaku's (2013: 55) informants identified *sakawa* as one of the potential causes of mental illness as a form of 'spiritual indulgence' whereby deliberate illicit engagement with the spirits could fail and impact the perpetrator's health. As mentioned earlier, since evil actions are believed to have equal and negative reactions, *sakawa* is considered an immoral occult means 'to gain wealth at the expense of others and therefore incur consequences' (Armstrong 2016: 68).

Moreover, the inability of certain individuals to successfully complete the ritual process is sometimes attributed to possessing a light *sunsum* (*sunsum ɔhare*). Those with a light *sunsum* are believed to lack the fortitude required to withstand the challenges posed by the rituals, potentially affecting their vulnerable *sunsum* and leading to madness. Although this notion is not scientifically substantiated, there are numerous anecdotes in Ghana suggesting that some individuals with severe mental illnesses, including psychosis, may have acquired their conditions through such means.[2] The pastor-prophet articulated this belief during the interview as a significant underlying cause of mental illness presented to them for healing. The following statement he shared encapsulates this perspective succinctly:

> Sometimes the person attempted to use occult means to get rich or wealth and when the rituals doesn't go well, they end up getting mad. These are some of the things we see and when we tell them, they don't disprove of them. When people bring their relatives here and we tell them that this is happening to your relative because he or she has done some evil deeds and has resulted in the person suffering or having problems ... sometimes there are others who are able to admit themselves when we tell them. Others too, they are not able to because of the state of their mind, they cannot admit or deny it until the problem is getting worse and they will admit or tell you the truth.

In relation to the aspects of ritual performances and their association with 'madness' and/or mental illnesses, I have discussed in Chapters 3 that within Akan traditional cultures, there exists a strong belief that an individual's failure to accept a calling to serve as a priest of a deity or to perform certain ritual acts expected of them, due to their ancestral lineage and association with that deity, may result in the manifestation of symptoms akin to madness or mental illness. Notably, the symptoms of madness associated with the former context differ significantly from those of madness as a clinical disease. Field (1961) also addresses this distinction.

From the interviews conducted, several caregivers articulated the perspective that some mental illnesses may be induced by an individual's failure to perform sacrifices to a deity, and that such negligence can have repercussions for the entire family. A pastor-prophet shared the following insights:

> In some families, you could see there is some curse in the family. So, for example, I have three kids here who are siblings. They are three siblings. All of them are suffering from mental health problems. One mother, one father. So, we delved deep into the problem. At some point, I went to see my father [the prophet]. He asked me to call the family to come. When they came, we realised that they worshipped a deity. And they are supposed to perform some sacrifice for the deity which they have refused to do. This has resulted in the children getting mad.

In Pentecostal deliverance practices, particularly within the context of the prayer camps, there exists a strong belief that local deities can inflict illnesses, such as mental disorders, upon individuals as punishment for failing to perform specified sacrifices mandated by their covenantal relationship with these deities.

The refusal to engage in such sacrificial practices is perceived to result in a curse that may affect not only the individual but also subsequent generations. Consequently, deliverance practices at prayer camps for individuals experiencing mental illness involve the expulsion or severance of any covenantal bonds between the individual and these deities, with the aim of liberating the person from the influence of such spiritual entities (Asamoah-Gyadu 2004; Banda 2020).

However, within traditional or indigenous Akan cultures and religion, manifestations of symptoms of mental illness from local deities as a result of negligence to perform ritual sacrifices or accept a call as a traditional priest are not typically interpreted as punitive actions stemming from demonic intrusion but are rather seen as sanctions imposed by the gods, intended to draw attention to the necessity for appropriate rituals to restore order and harmony (see also Field 1960). The distinction lies in the perception of deities; in indigenous Akan cultures, deities are regarded as intermediaries between God and humanity, rather than being interpreted as demons, as is often the case in Pentecostal contexts. For example, among the Akan, *Asase Yaa* (the earth deity) is believed to oversee the moral standards of the land, deeming social transgressions such as theft, adultery, incest and other forms of wrongdoing as abominations (Parrinder 1980). Individuals who neglect to offer propitiatory rites to her may experience afflictions manifesting as illness or misfortune (Nkrumah 1992).

What emerges from the preceding discussion is the observation that the attribution of mental illnesses to supernatural causes remains significant. This viewpoint aligns with other findings in mental health research conducted in Ghana (Yendork et al. 2019; Kpobi and Swartz 2018a; Opare-Henaku 2013; Opare-Henaku and Utsey 2017).[3] Throughout the study, various participants who had received treatment at prayer camps and shared their experiences articulated a belief in the supernatural origins of mental illness. As one participant noted:

> I used to hear voices in my ears. When I hear the voice then I feel like I should leave the house to go and sleep somewhere. The voice can be constant. I also see things that are very scary. The voice forcefully asks me to go, and I will take my things and go out. I usually hear the voice at night. So sometimes I go and sleep at the lorry station … I went to the Pantang Hospital, but the doctor only said I had depression. To me I believe this wasn't only physical but spiritual.

Another view shared by a pastor-prophet corroborates the above belief in the supernatural cause of mental illness:

> As black Africans – maybe others don't believe it but even when things become difficult for them to bear – they instead end up turning to God for help. For us, when you come here to do something, you have to believe that there is black power, there is African magic, witchcraft is there. You know those things? We the black people, there are curses too, envy is also there at the workplace – I will cause harm to you because I was there before you came. Why should you come for my position? We Africans, sometimes the home you come from too, no one

> does government work or is educated. If you try to go to school, they can make you go mad. If you try to get work in the public sector or get married, they can make you go mad. If you try to buy a car, designer shoes, and dresses, they'll make you go mad! These are there! For me, what I've seen with my eyes, no one can convince me that madness cannot be influenced or caused by evil forces. And if it is evil spirits that cause people to be mad, we also have to use the Spirit of God to drive the madness away.

The quotations from the respondents indicate a persistent belief that witchcraft, curses, the violation of taboos, spirits or demonic possession are perceived as underlying causes of certain mental illnesses. The views expressed by the participants reflect traditional notions of illness, which are influenced by personal, interpersonal and cultural factors governed by familial, social and cultural contexts.

Social, economic and environmental factors

Despite the perspective suggesting that supernatural evil forces may contribute to mental illnesses, as indicated in the aforementioned quotes, alternative viewpoints expressed by caregivers and patients highlight that social, economic and environmental factors can also play a significant role in the development of mental health issues. In the preceding discussion, the participants noted circumstances such as the loss of a partner, motor vehicle accidents and financial loss as potential factors with mental health implications for the individuals affected. Furthermore, caregivers at prayer camps articulated the belief that personal lifestyle choices, familial disruptions and single parenthood are substantial contributors to the mental health challenges faced by individuals seeking their assistance. One caregiver posited that, for some individuals, mental health difficulties are exacerbated by substance use and alcohol addiction. He contended that many of the individuals treated at their facilities encounter these issues primarily due to the influence of peers in educational settings.

> Some of them come here because they are addicted to alcohol. Some too is wee [marijuana]. Sometimes it is this problem that causes their mental health issues. When you come here, we too we are here to prove to you that what you are in, it won't help you. Some of them go to this problem because of friendship. A lot of them. Some of them were students, you see, but through friendship, hi hi hi, before you realise you are into this habit.

While the caregiver expressed optimism that addiction to the consumption of marijuana and alcohol could lead to the development of mental health issues, he maintained that some individuals attribute these problems to witchcraft. However, the caregiver contended that such issues are not the result of witchcraft but rather stem from personal choices and a lack of self-discipline on the part of the individual. He posited that individuals who lack self-discipline effectively become their own worst enemies, thereby undermining their own lives, and asserted that the root of the problem cannot be attributed to any external forces beyond the individual. He reflected:

> Some of them believe in witchcraft, but sometimes the issue is not about witchcraft. According to us, when we study your issue, sometimes we realise you have been a witch to yourself. You don't discipline yourself. If you don't know, self-discipline is very important. You can get all the things in this world, if you don't have self-discipline, you can lose everything in just a day.

Although the caregiver, on one hand, expressed disapproval of individuals attributing their life problems, which stem from their own behaviours or life choices, to supernatural evil forces, he also articulated views that suggested a somewhat ambiguous stance regarding the potential origins of such problems. This reveals his dualistic world-view concerning the explanations or origins of issues related to life. For instance, he contended that while mental illnesses induced by marijuana use could be ascribed to addictive behaviours, he was quick to add that such addiction might also be influenced by supernatural forces. He thus argued:

> But we study them for some time because some of them smoke. Sometimes you may think that the person is just smoking weed and is normal but *biribi tare akyire*. do you understand? So, if we don't break that the thing and the person goes home, he or she will go back and smoke and the madness come back again.

'Biribi tare akyire', which literally translates to 'something may be behind it', suggests that the addiction to smoking could potentially be influenced by supernatural forces. As already mentioned, the Akan belief posits that physical human actions, such as eating with dirty hands, can lead to illness; however, the explanation for such an ailment is not found in the bacteria that may have caused the individual who ate with dirty hands to become ill but rather in what might have influenced the individual to engage in such behaviour. The answer to this question is almost invariably found in the supernatural. Thus, while this explanation may be viewed as contradictory, it instead demonstrates the pervasiveness of supernatural elements in elucidating the causalities of human affairs within Akan societies.

The perspective that individuals attribute the consequences of their own behaviours to influences of witchcraft can be explained through the Akan theory of causation. Within the context of Akan culture, there are no occurrences that are free from chance; thus, every event in the physical realm is perceived to have some supernatural influence. Consequently, in the context of the caregiver's perspective, individual seeking assistance may believe that some external influence led them to associate with detrimental companions, subsequently resulting in the use of marijuana and drinking of alcohol. Among the Akan, witchcraft is sometimes invoked to account for chronic alcoholism (Appiah-Kubi 1981; Awedoba 2002). Debrunner (1961) posits that individuals addicted to alcohol believe that witches have placed an empty pot in their stomachs, rendering them perpetually unsatisfied with drinking. Adinkrah (2015) echoes Debrunner's sentiments, noting that in Ghana, it is commonly asserted that witches mystically place a large metal container, locally referred to as *grawa* (gallon), into the stomach of the alcoholic to collect the consumed liquor. However, due to the container's enormous size, no quantity of alcohol can satisfy the bewitched individual, resulting in continuous drinking without achieving satiation. Field (1960: 156) supports this notion, asserting that 'drunkards are virtually the only people who ever make direct accusations of witchcraft, and they always blame the witch for making them drunkards'; however, she further argues that they tend to 'blame vaguely rather than pinpointing an individual' (Field 1960: 109). For individuals with substantial economic or social status bewitched with alcoholism, it is believed that they can consume alcohol to the point of depleting their life savings, leading to their economic ruin. This perspective underlies the supernatural explanation of illness and disease. Therefore, while the caregiver's explanation may hold validity when examined within the framework of scientific reasoning – particularly when considering that the consumption of such substances is physiologically detrimental to the individual, partly due to their genetic predispositions or bodily chemistry – it is often the cultural aetiology of illnesses that takes precedence over scientific explanations.

To further underscore his point, the caregiver elaborated that the underlying causes of the mental health issues faced by some young adults are, in part, attributable to dysfunctional family dynamics and the failure of parents to devote adequate time to their children and provide effective counselling. He contended that many parents are career-oriented individuals who spend minimal time with their children due to demanding work schedules, which consequently contributes to the child's engagement in illicit behaviours that ultimately impact their mental health:

> The family, the father, the parents doesn't have the time to tell you all this, you see, because you are student, you just take your money and go. Your parents too they are business people. They don't have your time to sit you down and tell you all these. So, more counselling, some of them they lack it. I can tell you that broken homes are one of the major problems contributing to the cases we handle here on daily basis. Divorce! When there is a divorce, maybe you are the firstborn, the second marriage, there is always a problem. Marriage issues are a lot. If the broken home is there you go to a friend, you follow a friend. Do you get me? If the mother and father stay in the same house doing their own thing together, they watch you not to spoil. But along the way, when the marriage collapses and each of them remarry, what will the middle guy do, he will follow friends. So, majority of them when you study them, it is broken homes that bring about all these problems at the end of day because the parents are not together.

In citing an example to buttress his points, the caregiver further narrated:

> There is one guy here. The mother is alive. One boy, he is doing his masters at the university … he learned how to smoke wee [marijuana] at the University.

> The parents have divorced. For the mother, the boy is the only child, so she decided to invest in her son's education to that level but now the boy became a wee [marijuana] smoker. When the mother told her father about it, he said he does not care. I am told he is married to another woman with three children. So maybe he thinks he doesn't want to have anything to do with the boy. Every month, the mother comes here to visit and provide some money for us to take care of him. Now the boy is doing well so I decided to bring him out of the room so he starts going to church.

However, while the caregiver expressed optimism regarding the implications of broken homes on the well-being and mental health of certain children, he also presented a notable contrast to this scenario. He lamented the phenomenon of affluent families who feel compelled to fulfil every request of their children without hesitation or inquiry into the nature of the lifestyles their children have been leading. According to him, some parents, in their desire to indulge their children by meeting all their needs without appropriate oversight, may inadvertently foster habits that could adversely affect their children's mental health. He contended:

> Sometimes too, it is not a broken home, but the parents pamper their children. Maybe the person is the only child of the parent. They pamper them a lot and forget to discipline them and that too can bring a lot of problems, you see. In some cases, the child ends up picking some habits that are not good. A woman came here yesterday to visit the son. I have one boy here. They are two siblings, a boy and a girl. The boy is a nurse, but he has become addicted to alcohol. He really drinks a lot. A government worker, by 6:30am he would be drinking alcohol. Now he is here with us.

The caregiver, in substantiating his claim, further pointed out that some individuals currently seeking healing and solutions for their mental health issues at the camp were children of prominent individuals in the country, including a Member of Parliament.

> Some of them are coming from rich homes. They are here. Even we have some Member of Parliament [MP], the son is here. MP, MP's son is here because of how they pamper them from the beginning, you see. Sometimes is not everything you have to give to the child they ask you. We don't raise children like that. But the problem is that sometimes, they want to feel at home, they want them to feel good.

The interviews conducted also demonstrate that the family generates yet another nostalgic moment for the individual seeking healing at the camp. Ironically, some of the individuals seeking help believe that their parents are the source of their mental health issues. Consequently, due to this perception, some individuals do not wish to see their parents while at the camp. The caregiver shared:

> Some of them their parents come here once in every month. We also monitor the situation because there are some of them who gets very angry when they see their parents. When the sickness comes, some of them believes that their mothers are behind the cause of the sickness, so he or she doesn't want to see the mother's or the father's face. With such people, we stop their parents from coming here until we see that they are better. When they come back to themselves, we allow the parents to come over and visit.

From the discussions conducted during the interviews, the aforementioned perception articulated by the caregiver regarding the attitudes of individuals seeking assistance towards their parents can be interpreted from two perspectives. The first potential explanation may be that patients may feel irked by their parents' inability to provide them with the requisite security, discipline and care, which could have contributed to their current predicament. The second plausible factor relates to the widespread belief among the Akan that only a kin member within one's family possesses the capacity to cause harm, engendering the notion that their illness may have resulted from their parents' purported witchcraft. While these perspectives were not explored in depth, the prevailing accounts of analogous situations and the narratives provided by caregivers suggest that the two factors in question are indeed plausible.

In addition to the aforementioned factors, the interviewees also illuminated that some causes of mental illness may have been exacerbated by economic circumstances, such as unemployment or the failure of a business. Although an interviewee could not establish any direct linkages, the accounts presented imply that the collapse of a son's business may have contributed to his mental health condition.

> It's been a while the sickness started. Is about 12 years now. He wasn't with me when it started. He was somewhere working, and the person brought him to me. He was into trading but someone, but someone stole his goods. So, a friend introduced him to some business. He was travelling with the friend to go to neighbouring countries to buy goods, and they come to sell … I was there one day, and the friend brought him to me that my son is suffering from a mental health problem … we have been to many places including the hospital before coming here. When we came here too, the people from Ankarful came for him and later they brought him back.

While the interviewee was uncertain about the cause of the illness, the statement 'we have been to many places' illustrates the dilemma surrounding the origins of the son's mental health condition. The ambiguity regarding the cause of the illness accounts for numerous decisions to resort to different therapeutic modalities when illness arises (Gammelin 2023; Lebeau 2003). This also reveals, on several occasions, the various narratives or interpretations of the ailment (Read 2017; Janzen 1992). The mother's decision to seek a solution at a prayer camp after several unsuccessful attempts at a hospital suggests that she has assumed the illness may potentially be caused by a supernatural agent. However, the narrative provided regarding the son's business trajectory indicates that his illness might have been triggered by stress and depression resulting from the theft of his goods or unsuccessful business ventures. This explanation aligns with other research findings concerning the causes of mental illnesses in Ghana (Sulemana et al., 2021; Canavan et al. 2013) and is also corroborated by the views expressed by the pastor-prophet in the earlier account, which posits that the loss of a job or the theft of someone's money could lead to mental health issues. This discussion also resonates with the themes presented in Chapter 2 regarding social and spiritual agency and its implications for mental health.

Biological/natural factors

Additionally, family members who articulated their perspectives concerning the circumstances of their relative's seeking assistance at the prayer camps offered valuable context regarding their relatives' illnesses. The interviews revealed that the underlying causes of certain mental health issues may be genetic or hereditary or by other biological factors. One participant noted that their daughter's illness commenced following the birth of her sixth child, while another attributed the ailment to hereditary factors or as a familial disease. The woman whose daughter had experienced a mental health issue after childbirth conveyed the following:

> I am here with my daughter. She has given birth to 6 children. She is here with me now. The sickness started just after she gave birth to her sixth child. So I sent her to some place, but she didn't stay, and she came back. It was a prayer centre. We have also gone to several hospitals. And someone told us to come here. So it was just Saturday that we came here.

While articulating her concerns, the daughter, who had been admitted to the prayer camp, arrived at the location of the interview and began to speak aloud to herself without provocation while attempting to escape from the camp, with some prayer camp staff striving to prevent her from fleeing. In the Ghanaian Akan language, her behaviour might be described as '*basa basa*', which indicates signs of 'madnesses' or a severe form of psychosis. However, without prior knowledge of her medical history, I could not ascertain the precise nature of her issue. Nonetheless, the account provided by her mother suggested that the daughter's condition could potentially align with what is medically referred to as puerperal psychosis (PP). PP is a mental health condition that develops in women following childbirth (Glover et al. 2014; Stewart et al. 2019). For some women, postpartum experiences, such as baby blues, may occur after delivery; however, these are expected to last between twenty-four and forty-eight hours (Heron et al. 2008; Lewin 2006). If the symptoms persist beyond two weeks, they can escalate into severe mental health conditions, including PP. A discussion with my informants, who are medical professionals, revealed that several factors, including stressful life events such as marital tension, relinquishing careers, fluctuations in pregnancy hormones and pre-existing mental illness, could potentially contribute to the development of PP. For instance, women with a history of bipolar disorder have been identified as particularly vulnerable (Brockington 1996). Other contributing factors include socio-economic circumstances and complications associated with pregnancy and delivery (Nager et al. 2005).

As previously mentioned, while it is not possible to determine definitively whether the situation described earlier is indeed PP, the context surrounding the illness, as narrated by the patient's mother, could be categorized as biological. The leaders of the prayer camp could not provide further insights, as they were awaiting the arrival of medical staff who visit the camp to attend to the patient. Of particular interest in this discussion is the emphasis on the biological factors underlying some of the mental health issues presented to prayer camps for healing. Another individual who was also receiving treatment at the prayer camp shared the following:

> Hmmm, I really don't know what to say but sometimes I have a feeling that this is a family problem because of past experiences in the family. You see, my aunty who is my mum's sibling had an issue like that. And then my cousin too and here I am. But I believe in God everything will be fine. You can see that now I am okay. Before, I couldn't have talk to you. I think I'm better.

For this individual, the mental health issue was perceived as a hereditary condition due to the presence of mental illnesses within the family history. This perspective aligns with other findings regarding the perceived causes of mental illness in Ghana (Gyamfi et al., 2022). In the Akan context, this familial trajectory of illness may be classified as *yadeafo*, which is understood as a form of generational curse, as highlighted in Chapter 4. However, it may also be regarded as a hereditary condition that is predominantly biological or genetically induced. A nurse who had worked in collaboration with a prayer camp for seven years collaborated this:

> A lot of them. Several instances but you will see that this is a clear schizophrenic, is a clear bipolar disorder. Is a clear depression. Because when we are taking your history we realise, I was attending to twins, same twins, identical twins with schizophrenia in the same prayer camp. So upon history taking their immediate father was a patient. So, this is more like hereditary … so there are cases you see this is clear psychiatric disorder.

It is important to note that at prayer camps in Ghana, illnesses, including mental health issues, whether perceived to be of natural or supernatural origin, are met with a strong belief in God as the ultimate healer. Consequently, individuals often seek divine intervention through prayer for the healing of their ailments. Such decisions do not necessarily imply that the illness for which an individual is seeking healing at the prayer camp is believed to be caused by supernatural malevolent forces.

Choice of therapeutic interventions

The factors presented earlier constitute part of the existential issues encountered by prayer camp leaders, as articulated by individuals seeking assistance at prayer camp facilities. Indeed, the perceived cause(s) of mental illness significantly contribute to a sense of uncertainty and dilemma in efforts to secure support for leading a 'normal' life. Research indicates that individuals' perceptions of illnesses, their beliefs regarding these conditions and their explanations for their causes directly influence the options they consider when seeking redress or solutions (Lynch and Medin 2006). Consequently, individuals may exhibit distrust towards the potency or efficacy of treatment options that do not align with their beliefs, perceiving such treatments as inherently less satisfactory (Kucharski and Piot 2014; Taylor 2003; Godin and Kok 1996).

Thus, while I will discuss the effectiveness of healing mental illnesses at prayer camps in the subsequent chapter, it is pertinent to note here that one reason individuals living with mental illness may resort to prayer camps for assistance is the belief that the underlying cause of their condition – particularly if perceived to be of a supernatural nature – cannot be addressed within conventional hospital settings. Therefore, the selection of therapeutic interventions is largely informed by the explanatory models or interpretations that participants and their families ascribe to the illness. However, it is also crucial to emphasize that some individuals intentionally seek divine intervention for healing, even when they are confident that their ailments are not spiritually influenced or caused. The following quotations illustrate how some participants expressed the belief that their mental health issues were supernaturally instigated, leading them to view prayer camps as a viable alternative for remedying their circumstances:

> My sickness was spiritual. If they had taken me to the asylum, then I don't believe I would have recovered. I was forever going to be in a state of illness because when they brought me here, no one gave me an injection or medicine. It was only prayer and the water they fetch from the cocoa farm (*cocoa ase nsuo*) and bathe me with that made me receive my healing. My hair and beard had developed dreadlocks while roaming about in Tema and Accra … when I first came here, they took pictures of me. So, when I had my recovery, I realised that although the asylum is good, it doesn't help other people because if it is a spiritual attack like mine, there is no way the asylum can deal with it because you don't need those injections they give there. What you need is prayers!

In the aforementioned quotation, the patient asserts that his illness originated from a spiritual source. Consequently, he believes that he would not have experienced recovery had he been admitted to a hospital for treatment. Although the claim that he would not have received healing in a hospital setting cannot be substantiated, it nonetheless underscores the patient's deeply held conviction in the efficacy of divine intervention to cure his ailment. The patient reports suffering from mental illness for several years, during which he wandered the streets of

Accra and Tema, leading to the development of matted hair. This imagery is likely to resonate with individuals familiar with the sight of those living with severe mental health disorders in major urban centres in Ghana, such as Accra, Takoradi and Kumasi. According to this patient, he experienced healing on the first day of his arrival at the camp when a prophet prayed for him after he was taken there by some friends. His experience leads him to conclude that while psychiatric hospitals may be beneficial for some, individuals with conditions similar to his own would achieve relief solely through spiritual healing at a prayer camp.

Another patient who also affirmed the importance of prayer to her healing remarked:

> My daughter and sister brought me here. Since I came here, the voices I used to hear have suddenly ceased. I've been here for three months. They said they would discharge me after Easter, but I have told them I want to stay a bit longer. The camp has really helped my situation a lot, especially through prayer.

For this patient, the prayers offered for her at the camp resulted in the cessation of the voices she had been experiencing. In a previous citation from the interview, she articulated that the voice she heard compelled her to leave her home and seek refuge in public transport stations. She also reported witnessing distressing phenomena and expressed that the voices were so forceful that they instructed her to gather her belongings and depart her home. Despite having visited the hospital multiple times, where medical professionals diagnosed her with depression, the voices persisted, leading to her prolonged absence from home and aimless wandering in the streets. She asserted that the prayers at the camp constituted her sole form of intervention. The pertinent question that arises from this participant's response, as well as from others who may present similar claims, is how prayers may contribute to the cessation of hearing voices.

The phenomenon of voice hearing, particularly among individuals with mental illnesses such as psychosis, has been investigated in Ghana, India and the United States by Luhrmann et al. (2015). A notable finding from their study was that half of the participants interviewed in Accra, Ghana, reported that the voices they encountered were positive (Luhrmann et al. 2015). While this is not intended to undermine their findings, it raises intriguing questions regarding the participants' claims of positivity about these voices. If the voices were indeed positive, one might anticipate that this positivity would manifest as a degree of orderliness, controlled behaviour or positive outcomes in their lives, potentially alleviating the need for hospitalization, as was the case for some participants in the study.

What I wish to convey is that experiences of hearing voices among participants exhibiting signs of mental illness are predominantly negative, often depriving individuals of a peaceful or stable state of mind. Thus, in contrast to the experiences articulated by Christians, who assert that God speaks to them without harm, some of the voices reported in these contexts do not confer positive outcomes. Furthermore, these voices, frequently associated with familial or spiritual entities such as ancestors or demons, often compel individuals to engage in behaviours that are detrimental or contrary to normative conduct, akin to the experiences reported by the aforementioned participant and also evidenced in the claims made by some of the participants in the study conducted by Luhrmann et al. (2015). This perspective contradicts the assertion made by Luhrmann et al. (2015) that participants find the voices to be comprehensible or enjoyable. In such circumstances, attending a prayer camp can serve as a means of addressing and dismantling the source of these voices, thereby liberating the individual from an unstructured or chaotic existence.

As reflected in the account of the participant earlier, the voices she hears have ceased following her engagement in the healing process at the prayer camp, resulting in considerable improvement compared to her previous experiences. It is important to highlight the disappearance of the symptoms associated with the voice hearing. In religious healing rituals, efficacy is often derived from emic accounts of experiences that elucidate the mechanisms at work (Kirmayer 2004). Frequently, narratives of healing are predicated on ontological world-views that recognize specific forms of efficacy, which are linked to definitions and the assignment of agency, causality and outcomes. Thus, 'the effectiveness of a healing practice is embedded in a larger cultural system that identifies different types of malady or affliction and prescribes appropriate interventions' (Kirmayer 2004: 43). Similar to the biological sciences, each medical or healing taxonomy possesses its methodologies for establishing the efficacy of healing; within the context of Pentecostal healing experiences, the disappearance of previously encountered or reported symptoms signifies the occurrence of healing and the resultant freedom of the individual. Here, as affirmed by Kirmayer (2004), the success of the healing intervention can be deemed effective on the grounds that the afflicted individual has recuperated, with recovery assessed based on enhanced functionality or diminished symptoms and suffering. So, here, the participant claim that she is feeling better after the prayers can be termed effective since her symptoms of hearing voices before the healing process has diminished.

One of the caregivers expressed the importance of the prayer camps in helping people deal with their mental illnesses:

> Indeed, the prayer camps help a lot … When you come to the prayer camp, we have our prophet there. The first welcome is to go and see him. He will pray for you and give you some directions (*akwankyere*). After three days he will ask you to bring the person back and through that the healing takes place. Sometimes he will also say God has done his part so take the person to the hospital for medical attention. When that is done, everything is balanced.

Another caregiver also reflected:

> When we pray at night from 12 to 3am, we pray against curses, ask for forgiveness of sins, we also pray and ask God for his mercies for them and take them out of such situations. Sometimes too, you could see that some of them their minds have been taken and hidden somewhere. We also pray that

wherever their minds have been removed and tied, the Holy Ghost should go there and untie them.

In the first quotation, the caregiver specifically expresses the view that while prayer is good in addressing the problem of mental illness, they also combine it with or resort to biomedicine when necessary. Going to the hospital in the aforementioned quotation means using therapeutic interventions other than those found at the prayer camp. This becomes important especially when the sickness persists after periods of fasting, prayer and directions from the prophet.

The perspective articulated by the other caregiver further reinforces the concept of spiritual causation, as well as the theory that illness is deeply embedded in local ontologies. It suggests that hospitals often lack the knowledge related to divination and the means to effectively treat certain diseases. For example, the expression indicating that an individual's mind has been taken and hidden elsewhere implies a belief in witchcraft as a possible cause of mental illness. The notion is that a witch can spiritually remove an individual's mind, leading to an inability to think rationally or behave in a manner deemed normal, thereby resulting in mental instability. It is believed that the witch can hide the individual's mind in a coven or pot, often situated under a tree or at a location where witches convene for their nocturnal activities (Debrunner 1961). The integration of prayer with medical treatment, as advocated by caregivers, parallels the findings of Auli Vähäkangas (2012) and Carl Sundberg (2020) in their respective studies on healing practices in Tanzania and Congo. Such treatment aims to provide patients with a holistic approach to healing, which hospitals are perceived to be unable to offer. In certain regions of Africa, 'traditional medicine' and faith healing have been incorporated into the broader healthcare system and redefined as a novel framework of scientific knowledge to enhance the development of biomedicine and healthcare, as well as to support the advancement of modern scientific expertise (Meincke 2015).

As is reflected in the quotations, the healing process used at these prayer camps may include long periods of fasting, confession and other spiritual activities that aim to hasten the individual's recovery and well-being. Faith healing, as typified in Pentecostalism and evidenced at the prayer camps, has been categorized as more holistic and all-encompassing. The view is that the biomedical scientist-physician is a curer rather than a healer. The biomedical model or approach to medical care is seen as one that distances itself from the holistic psychological, emotional and spiritual disturbances associated with disease (McGuire 2008). The title of a book by the Ghanaian author, Appiah-Kubi (1981) – *Man Cures – God Heals* – captures this succinctly.

Prayer camps and local ontologies/world-views

From the earlier perceived causes of mental illnesses, healing and treatment practices offered at the prayer camps are embedded in local meaning systems, cultural symbols and language that resonate with the general Ghanaian Akan world-view.

A healing ritual at a prayer camp is generally viewed as having the ability to offer holistic cleansing and fostering personal transformation by invocations of God through Jesus Christ and the power of the Holy Spirit (Atiemo 2017; 1994). Healing rituals at prayer camps also reassure or symbolize to the wider community that a person is no longer potentially dangerous because the vestiges of mental illness and associated evil powers have been destroyed or removed. As others have noted, 'Healing practices are embedded in local meaning systems that give them part of their social value and potential efficacy' (Kirmayer and Swartz 2013: 48).

As the aforementioned quotations show, causal explanations for mental illness are often found in spiritual curses, breaking of taboos, offending a third party, or a deity, among other examples. It is within this framework of non-material illness causation that mental illness primarily finds its interpretation and meaning in Ghana and other parts of Africa. As such, mental illness is not only explained, at times, in biological and physiological terms but also, and perhaps more importantly, ingrained with supernatural undercurrents. This understanding of illness causation has also 'continued into Pentecostal Christianity and the Ghanaian Christian's understanding of illness is cast in the framework of the traditional interpretation' (Atiemo 2017: 267). In an African or more particularly the Ghanaian Pentecostal context, healing and health are recast in this traditional framework of understanding and the two – healing and health – are believed to be intimately 'connected to social behaviour, moral conduct, and spiritual forces' (Clarke 2014: 71; Asamoah et al. 2014). Thus, Pentecostal explanations, theory of illness causation and healing reverberate with many 'African, Asian cultures and Latin American cultures that envision health as depending on the right relationships with the natural and spiritual worlds' (Brown 2011: 7; see also Hatala and Waldram 2016).

The dilemma between the two domains of potential causative factors, between the material and spiritual, determines and regulates how patients and family members negotiate their healing journeys in an attempt to find solutions to or in the management of a chronic condition, especially sicknesses in the realm of mental health that may defy methods of 'Western' scientific treatment. In this sense, Read (2017: 172) observed that the practice of 'trying out' medications from the hospital in the form of 'pills or injections is as much part of the process of identifying a spiritual illness as consultations with healers or pastors' since 'the success or failure of biomedicine is an important empirical marker of the cause and nature of illness'.

After repeated forms of treatment have proved futile, including a visit to the psychiatric hospitals, patients and family members can resort to prayer camps to alleviate persistent suffering in the face of a chronic condition and its frequent fluctuations. As already mentioned, the resort to prayer camps does not suggest a disbelief in biomedical science but rather an additional resource to deal with the uncertainty of the nature and cause of the illness. Again, as Read (2017) observed, almost all the people she met during her fieldwork in Ghana had agreed to having visited the psychiatric hospitals in search of a cure. This is not different from what I encountered at the prayer camps I visited in Ghana. What is at stake, however, is that the pluralistic nature of the belief systems fashions the 'intracultural diversity and medical systems that are manipulated by patients according to the principles that go beyond traditional definitions of cultural specificity' (Jacobson-Widding and Westerlund 1989: 9).

My respondents' responses show a continuous trajectory from Ghanaians' approach to seeking healing for mental illnesses as described by Field (1960). The difference is the healing space or context from which the healing is sought and the religious functionaries involved. The prayer camps differ from the indigenous healing cults or shrines Field (1960) describes, though they share some affinities and cultural resonances in terms of the understanding and interpretation of mental illness as having a potential supernatural origin or being spiritually instigated. The prayer camps replaced the old healing shrines and provided an escape for their visitors from the severe sanctions, criticisms and stigma that accompanied visits to the shrines by new converts or 'born-again' Christians. As already mentioned, the healing shrines were discredited and demonized by the joint forces of Christian preaching dominated by a pronounced Pentecostal/charismatic culture (Atiemo 2006; Kalu 2008).

At prayer camps the practice of *akwankyere* (direction) is similar to the act of *abisa* as practiced in Akan traditional healing shrines. These two terminologies or concepts may thus differ in theory but not in practice. *Akwankyere* at prayer camps involves elements of consultation. It is through the consultation that the prophet diagnoses the problem or cause of an illness and prescribes appropriate solutions or directions (*akwankyere*) to remediate the situation. As already emphasized, people resort to warding off evil spirits after all initial attempts to find a cure (including biomedicine) or solution to sickness prove futile, and through *abisa* they find that the problem has a supernatural origin (Benyah 2024; Onyinah 2012). My research participants also regularly reported having first tried other solutions before visiting the prayer camps. Caregivers mentioned that for some of their clients the prayer camp was their 'last stop' after consulting several other healing sources, including going to a psychiatric hospital:

> They believe that God is the solution to everything that is why they come here. There are some of them who will even come here for prayers after they are discharged from the hospital before they will go back to their houses … Some of them went through fetish and at the end of the day no results before coming here. We have to know all these things, so we just don't take you in like that. Someone like that came here few days ago but now she is doing well … they sent her to fetish priest somewhere and they mark mark her body and put in some concoction … when you go to these places, they sometimes ask you to buy things like sheep, fowl, and so on and when it doesn't go well as expected before they bring it to God. Here becomes the last stop. You see. So we are on it.

At prayer camps supplicants or individuals with problems consult the prophet, who is believed to be endowed with the supernatural ability to diagnose and prescribe solutions to their problems. In the previous quotations, the pastor-prophets mentioned that they 'delve' into the spirit when an individual is brought to them for healing. As indicated earlier, delving into the spirit suggests the idea of prognostication to find out the cause of the illness. A caregiver who had spent eleven years working in one of the prayer camps narrated that a family visited the prayer camp with a problem of mental health involving a member of the family. When they arrived at the camp, the prophet after consultation informed the family that the problem was spiritual and had come about as a result of a covenant relationship between the family and a certain deity. However, the individual also showed symptoms of psychosis. To deal with the problem, the pastor-prophet gave them some directions which involved both spiritual and medical aspects:

> So, the prophet gave them *akwankyere* (directions) to follow. Through that the problem is gone. All the family came here to do waiting [fasting and prayers]. They did 21 days of fasting. All the family members. After that, we gave them medications. After the medical treatment, they are okay. This is just one case example regarding a family with such issues. There are multiple cases like that. I have handled such issues with about four of five people at this place. Some of them are still here as we talk.

The example narrated by the caregiver above shows how some of the prayer camps combine both faith healing and biomedicine in the care of individuals who patronize their services. While this approach may not be representative across various prayer camps, it shows the openness of prayer camp leaders and the effort being made by the health professionals to engage biomedicine in the care and treatment of persons with a mental health issue. This effort has been highlighted in other research on faith-based healing and mental health in Ghana (Ofori-Atta et al. 2018; Arias et al. 2016). The openness of prayer camp leaders to engage biomedicine in the treatment of persons living with a mental illness shows that the believe in evil spirits may function as an explanatory term and not as a single diagnostic category. This is very expressive of the Akan dualistic world-view of both natural and supernatural factors in the explanation of illnesses.

Within the context of the prayer camps, the practice of *akwankyere* and consultation which usually occurs in the realm of prophetic revelation may resembles traditional forms of *akom*, despite some notable differences. In the traditional method it is the *akomfo* (the priests) that are possessed and thereby give a prognostication and directions for the cure of the sickness. In the context of the prayer camps, it is the clients or the patients who sometimes become possessed and report the cause of the disease. Yet the role of the prophet in this process must not be downplayed. As Onyinah (2012) points out, it is the presence of the prophet and 'his diagnostic ability that make *abisa* (divination) possible'. Some prophets can also diagnose the problem through their prophetic gifts as people who are gifted with discerning spirits and word of knowledge (1 Cor. 12) and the ability to see beyond the physical realm (Asamoah-Gyadu 2015).

Regarding the healing of mental illnesses at prayer camps, *akwankyere* works as a kind of divination in which the prophet employs diagnostic tools to determine the cause of the illness and ward off the supposed antagonistic evil spirits or demons associated with it through prayer and fasting. Healing and ritual praxis at the prayer camps are suffused with features that delineate an affinity with traditional Akan world-views. In other words, discourses on health and healing suggest both continuity and rupture with African indigenous cosmologies. Indeed, healing has become important in Ghanaian Christianity because it was important in the traditional culture. Within the Akan context, medicine is closely associated with religion because it is the possession of the Divine Healer (i.e., God) who dispenses it through the agency of the divinities and other spirit beings who in turn make the knowledge available to priests, pastor-prophets and medicine men and women (Quarcoopome 1987). This religious and ritualistic approach to healing takes care of the spiritual causes of illness, for, as Appiah-Kubi (1981: 90) aptly observes, 'the belief in evil forces as a cause of misfortune and of disease is part of the African answer to the existence of evil in the world'. Kalu (2008: 264) has argued that the 'Pentecostal theology of health and healing recognizes that coping practices are mediated by the surrounding culture, worldview, symbolic systems, and healing myths'. Kirmayer and Swartz (2013: 48) asserts that 'ritual healing is part of larger religious and sociomoral systems that cannot be simply replaced with psychiatric practices, because, even if symptoms are treated successfully, the existential meanings of the illness and the patient's social predicament are not addressed'. Social predicaments may include the traditional or societal view of illnesses as demonically influenced, with which hospitals cannot deal but are believed to be tackled through deliverance rituals at prayer camps.

As previously mentioned, the approach to sickness and healing employed at prayer camps and in other Pentecostal streams of Christianity or churches corresponds to familiar cultural and religious world-views, values and perceptions. The prophets have become the Christian equivalents of traditional priests and diviners, and despite their resort to a Christian ethos or Christian beliefs, they very much reflect 'ways in which religious mediations occur within primal societies in Africa' (Asamoah-Gyadu 2015: 86). Onyinah (2012: 203) surmises that 'prayer camps have replaced the services that the shrines formerly provided for the people'. Read (2016) has also noted the similarity of Field's (1960) healing shrines to the more recent growth of Pentecostal prayer camps, with the old minor gods now equated with the 'demons' of Christianity and with a new power of healing through prayer restricted to the God of the Christians (Meyer 1999). Prayer camps can thus be argued to be a reinvention of the shrines and healing cults that emerged in the twentieth century in Ghana. People visit the camps to discover the supernatural causes of their problems and afflictions, find out their future and seek protection.

Summary

This chapter has examined the perceived notions regarding the causes of mental illness as articulated by participants at prayer camps in Ghana. The findings indicate that, while supernatural beliefs play a prominent role in explaining the potential causes of mental illness, other factors, including environmental, social and biological influences, are also acknowledged. It is noteworthy that these findings align with previously conducted studies on mental health in Ghana. However, it is essential to emphasize that some studies tend to prioritize supernatural dimensions over other potential factors, such as biological and social influences, as discussed in this analysis. The findings demonstrate the willingness of prayer camp leaders, staff, patients and their families to consider a broad spectrum of causes of mental illness.

Furthermore, the discussion has identified the methods by which pastor-prophets at prayer camps diagnose illness, as well as the types of therapeutic interventions employed once diagnoses are made. The discussions have reaffirmed that the views expressed by participants regarding the potential causes of mental illness, along with the approaches employed in addressing it, reflect continuities with local Akan ontologies and world-views concerning health and healing. While the chapter has illustrated that the explanations provided for the causes of mental illness influence the choice of therapeutic interventions, it is crucial to note that not all illnesses, including mental health conditions, are cured or healed at prayer camps. Individuals seeking support in these settings are aware of this reality and continue to place their trust in God, maintaining hope for an illness-free future.

The next chapter examines how the environment of prayer camps functions as a space for managing social distress and the stigma associated with mental illness within the Ghanaian context.

Chapter 7

HEALING AND THE MANAGEMENT OF CHRONIC MENTAL ILLNESSES IN PRAYER CAMPS

In Ghana, mental illness is culturally and socially perceived as a chronic condition. Among the Akan, a prevalent saying or proverb states, *ɔbɔdamfuɔ se ne dam kɔ a, na ɛnyɛ deɛ ɔde hunahuna mmɔfra*, which literally translates to 'if a lunatic claims to have been cured of lunacy, traces of lunacy that can frighten children often remain'. In other words, 'if a person decides to desist from a well-formed habit, many a time, traces of the habit, at least enough to frighten, remain' (Amfo et al. 2018: 4). This proverb illustrates the chronicity of mental illnesses in the minds of individuals, particularly within Akan communities in Ghana, and defines the extent to which these views are socially integrated. Individuals are acutely aware of their interactions or relationships with those who have a history of mental health issues, driven by a fear of rekindling past negative disorders at the slightest provocation (Amfo et al. 2018). Cultural idioms such as this elucidate the sustained cycle and the production of mutually reinforcing negative behaviours directed towards a person living with a mental health issue, whether current or historical. These negative attitudes towards person with a mental illness in Ghana adversely impact their daily routines and functionality – individually, socially and economically. Indeed, it has been well established that individuals living with mental illnesses encounter different forms of stigma, discrimination and exclusion.

Drawing from these perspectives, this chapter offers an in-depth discussion on the management of chronic mental illnesses in Ghana. The discourse centres on how participants utilize spiritual and faith-based resources, as well as the strategies available at prayer camps, as coping mechanisms for navigating the daily dilemmas and uncertainties associated with chronic mental illnesses in Ghana. It also examines how these approaches contribute to maintaining and sustaining hope amid chronicity. In doing so, this chapter makes a significant contribution to the understanding of the role and utilization of faith-based resources in promoting wellness for a person living with a mental illness, particularly those in the Global South.

Within this context, this chapter highlights both the individual and social roles played by religious organizations such as prayer camps in facilitating the management of chronic mental illnesses in Ghana. It also explores how faith-based resources are harnessed in the pursuit of wellness and wholeness. Although chronic illnesses have received considerable attention in global healthcare (WHO 2005), far less focus has been placed on the role of religious institutions that can support this work. Indeed, a decade and a half ago, Koenig (2005: 113) argued that 'although the use of religion to help cope with stress is well established, less is known about how religious belief and activity are related to severe, persistent mental illness[es]' and possibly other chronic health issues in general (Roger and Hatala 2017). Consequently, this examination does not seek to uncritically evaluate or romanticize the role of faith-based resources in the management of chronic conditions, such as mental illnesses, but rather aims to uncover and outline the potential contributions and local cultural significance of prayer camps, as well as how such religious or faith-based resources serve as aspects of hope and wellness amidst uncertainty and chronicity.

To achieve this objective, patients at prayer camps were asked in the interviews to talk about their satisfaction with their current condition and the reasons for their feelings. They were asked to compare their lives prior to becoming ill with their current state. Patients were also requested to assess any changes observed since arriving at the prayer camp and to identify factors contributing to those changes, if any. Additionally, inquiries were made about the attitudes of individuals towards them both within the camp and externally. Patients were questioned on whether they would consider returning to the camp after discharge and if they would recommend it to others. In some instances, when discussing their treatment experiences at the camp, some patients expressed positive feedback, while others did not. Attempts were made to explore further the perspectives of those who held differing views on their treatment. This involved speaking with caregivers regarding the treatment of patients in the camps, revealing a range of opinions on the nature of care provided. The quality of treatment appeared to vary significantly depending on the patient's willingness to engage with the recommended treatment process, severity of the illness and the limitations posed by financial constraints especially for patients whose condition required additional medical care and attention but lacked the financial means to support treatment and even their daily subsistence at the camp.

Prior to conducting the study, reviews were made of existing literature and reports regarding prayer camps, which documented instances of patient abuse. Consequently, the questions aimed to investigate the validity of claims made in previous studies regarding the infringement of patients' rights within these settings.[1]

Furthermore, patients were asked to reflect on their thoughts, feelings, experiences and the meanings they ascribed to practices such as counselling, Bible studies, fasting and prayers engaged in at the camps. These questions were pivotal in assessing the effectiveness of these practices in facilitating their recovery. Moreover, they aimed to re-examine certain pre-existing assertions made by stakeholders and in some literature regarding the fasting and prayers undertaken by individuals at the camps, which have been claimed to be inconsequential or lacking in improving the lives of those who patronize these establishments (see Edwards 2014; Human Rights Watch 2012).

Healing and deliverance for individuals seeking solution to mental illnesses

All mental illnesses, whether perceived as being caused by supernatural, medical or biological factors, undergo a healing and deliverance process when individuals experiencing mental health issues are sent to prayer camps for treatment. Healing prayers for individuals with mental illness at prayer camps are interventionist prayers offered on behalf of the supplicants by the pastor-prophet or caregiver. These prayers aim to liberate the individual from any malevolent spirits, demons, ancestral chains, curses or witchcraft associated with the illness, particularly when such conditions are attributed to supernatural influences. Moreover, even for medically diagnosed mental illnesses, it is believed that healing or a cure can be attained through the divine healing power of God.

At the prayer camps selected for this study, deliverance sessions are organized on Wednesdays and Thursdays for individuals seeking healing and treatment for mental illnesses. In one of the prayer camps, the caregiver disclosed that every Wednesday, patients seeking treatment are directed to the prophet for prayers. Additionally, some patients are required to participate in the general deliverance session held on Thursdays for all visitors to the prayer camp. Beyond these designated days, the caregiver noted that the prophets also visit the sanatorium when they receive specific revelations or directives from God to pray for particular individuals:

> We select those who behave well for deliverance service on Thursdays. And on Wednesday too, we take some of them to the prophet. The prophet prays for them, break any curse and witchcraft spirit and sometimes will give you *akwankyɛrɛ* (directions). Sometimes too the prophets come to the sanatoriums when he receives a revelation from God to come and pray for someone. Not all the time but once a while. But every Wednesday we take some of them to him. Those who can control themselves.

In the context of healing and deliverance, the objective is to dispel any perceived malevolent entities, ancestral chains and curses believed to be the underlying causes of an individual's illness. Consequently, prayer directed against witches and other diagnosed spirit agents deemed responsible for the affliction serves as a means to facilitate release or freedom for the individual experiencing distress. By expelling the demons associated with the sickness, the individual is thought to attain liberation and regain their health (Mohr 2013; Asamoah-Gyadu 2005).

Based on observations and interviews, deliverance sessions for individuals exhibiting aggressive behaviours can manifest in various forms. At one particular prayer camp, healing and deliverance for individuals living with severe mental illnesses with restricted mobility occur between midnight and 1.30 am. The prophet and his assistants conduct these sessions at the sanatoriums. The healing sessions commence with the singing of healing songs and the playing of drums. The music begins slowly and increases in intensity as the session progresses. The prophet noted that the purpose of the music is to calm the individual and capture their attention, thereby facilitating focused prayer. After approximately thirty minutes of music, the prophet and his prayer warriors engage in fervent prayers, interceding for the patients and beseeching God to heal them and to break any curses or remove demons associated with their illnesses. At another prayer camp, the prayer sessions occur from midnight to 3 am, where only caregivers convene in the courtyard in front of the sanatoriums on a daily basis. One caregiver indicated that the prayers are intended to seek forgiveness and to intercede on behalf of those who are unable to pray due to their health conditions. He asserted:

> Every day we come here to pray for them from 12am to 3am midnight. The four of us. The staff members. Because is not everyone that can pray. Some of them are mentally not sound so they cannot pray. So, we intercede for them. So, if they have committed any sins, God can forgive him or her.

In Ghanaian Pentecostal healing and deliverance praxis, sin is consistently perceived as intrinsically linked to illness. Consequently, the concept of deliverance transcends the mere expulsion of malevolent spirits; it also encompasses the liberation of individuals from the shackles of sin (Asamoah-Gyadu 2005). For instance, if an individual's mental illness is deemed attributable to a sin they have committed, the individual is mandated to confess and seek forgiveness, thereby enabling God to absolve their sins and lift any associated curse, which facilitates restoration and healing.

Indeed, the repudiation of sin and evil as sources of suffering, alongside the invocation of the healing power of the Holy Spirit in addressing such sins and evils, correlates with indigenous African perspectives on healing methodologies. At Akan shrines, the act of confessing sins and seeking forgiveness is referred to as *nteteho*, and it serves as the sole means through which healing can occur if the ill individual or patient has offended someone. These themes are also predominant in the work of the African Independent Churches (AICs) and/or the *sunsum soré* (spiritual churches) which integrate indigenous healing practices with Christian moral rectitude. Pobee (2001: 51) emphasizes that

> healing is to search for the power of God and the goodwill of other spirit-beings who, so to speak, under God administer various aspects of life and health. This mentality has seeped into the church. There is an AIC in Kumasi, Ashanti called 'Christ Power Church'. That name is eloquent of the power of Christ which that church enshrines and therefore, as the channel for effective cures.

He further argues that 'this African mentality requires that for effective healing clinical medicine, psychology and pastoral counselling must be in one bag. Healing must be composite, multidisciplinary and interdisciplinary' (Pobee 2001: 59). In other words, in the pursuit of healing and wholeness, it is essential to address aspects of human life that affect personal relationships, as well as emotional, psychological and social well-being. Practices such as seeking forgiveness for one's sins and restoring relationships form part of pastoral counselling, which yields psychological benefits and support for the affected parties.

With the exception of a few cases, healing prayers for patients at the selected camps during the observed period were not particularly assertive. Patients who were deemed violent were confined and prayed for by their caregivers until they exhibited signs of improvement, at which point they were released into open space within the camp. According to one of the caregivers at the prayer camp, the intercessory prayers for patients have yielded significant results, thereby demonstrating the efficacy of divine healing at work within the camp. He reflected:

> Here, sometimes, God descend in some mysterious ways. The way the angels come and heal them, it will surprise you when you see it. If the person gets well, sometimes God will reveal to you that this particular person, today when you go to work, go and discharge him or her because the person is okay. So, when you go and you begin to have a conversation with the person, you will see that the person's speech is clear. So you can release such a person and begin to observe him or her.

The caregiver's assertion reflects a belief in the workings of angels, visions and dreams, particularly within the context of prayer camps. The belief in the role of angels is also significant in the practice of *sunsum soré* (Asamoah-Gyadu 2005). Angels are regarded as supernatural entities that are believed to descend at night, saturating the atmosphere of prayer camps to facilitate healing for individuals seeking healing. Indeed, the presence of the divine has been recounted in various literatures as one of the reasons individuals with diverse afflictions attend prayer camps in search of help (Asamoah-Gyadu 2007; van Dijk 1997; Daswani 2015). For those experiencing mental illness, it is this divine presence that is thought to bring transformation and liberate individuals from the influence of malevolent beings believed to be responsible for their condition.

It is essential to acknowledge and reiterate the view that healing and deliverance practices at prayer camps illuminate both the ruptures and continuities within African religio-cultural world-views particularly regarding the world-views associated with the causes of illness and the process deployed to remedy the affliction. I have noted elsewhere how the healing and deliverance practices at prayer camps exhibit similarities and approaches, for instance, with traditional healing shrines and spiritual churches, as well as the contests surrounding these practices (Benyah 2024).

Management of stigma, discrimination and exclusion

Social stigma, discrimination and exclusion frequently constitute the daily lived experiences of individuals with mental health issues (Mehta and Thornicroft 2013). In Ghana, both social, religious and cultural norms associated with the belief that mental illness could be caused by supernatural forces have been identified as part of the factors that impel discriminatory practices against persons living with a mental illness (Mfoafo-M'Carthy and Grischow 2021). These manifestations of social suffering significantly exacerbate the challenges faced by individuals living with chronic mental health conditions in Ghana. Participants reported that prayer camps assist individuals with mental health conditions in coping with stigma, discrimination and exclusion by fostering a sense of community characterized by 'brothers and sisters'. Many caregivers and patients articulated how the prayer camp provides social support and serves as a source of hope and restoration:

> You see, no one walks to the pharmacy shop and says I want to buy a drug or medicine that causes mental illness. What has happened to them can happen to any individual or person. We live together with them as brothers and sisters. That's why for many of them, after they have recovered, they don't want to go home … we don't discriminate against them.

The notion of living 'together with them as brothers and sisters' signifies the close-knit relationships established between caregivers and patients. At some of the camps visited, caregivers engage in open interactions with patients. The relationship between caregivers and individuals residing at the camp transcends the conventional roles of patient and client, evolving instead into friendships and familial bonds. For some patients, these interactions facilitate the management of anxieties, bolster their confidence, restore a sense of agency and assist them in deriving meaning from their lives.

Interviews with participants further indicate that stigma, discrimination and exclusion are predominantly experienced outside the camp, within the home, community and even at the workplace. Such experiences render life unbearable and can exacerbate their mental health conditions. As one participant conveyed:

> You see, sometimes when they see you coming, they want to hide themselves. It is as if you are no longer a human being. It is very depressing. It worsens your case because you feel lonely, and you begin to think about rejection and now maybe you feel like even committing suicide because no one wants you around him or her.

Another participant echoed a similar sentiment:

> As for mental illness like the one I went through, the problem here is the stigma. Both the family, society, friends, and loved ones all think you are not useful any longer. I lost my relationship. I lost my job.

In numerous respects, individuals experiencing mental illness and other chronic conditions are frequently rendered hopeless and marginalized by their families or communities due to the complexities associated with treatment and caregiving (Stanford and McAlister 2008). Furthermore, mental health practitioners and family members who become exasperated with these difficulties and the daily responsibilities of care often relinquish their efforts in the healthcare and management of the affected individual (Mattingly et al. 2011). Indeed, in several cases observed, families and communities demonstrated a reluctance to accept or associate with the individual due to prevailing stigma:

> Some of them leave here, and their families are not ready to accept them. Then they will return to the camp. Even when the person is showing signs of wellness, the community will be pointing fingers at him. 'Oh, this man, he was insane.' So, many people don't get closer to them. Then they have to return to where they will welcome him or her. Because you see, when the thing happened, he would sometimes break car windscreens, walk naked in his or her neighbourhood and so forth. When you tell them the person is healed or better, some people don't really believe it. So, the person will come back and say that when I went home, I wasn't received. Then we would have to accept him or her back. That's the kind of problem we are in now.

Despite the significant challenges associated with caring for individuals with chronic mental health conditions, the prayer camps provide an enabling, supportive environment and sacred community essential for restoring hope amidst the ongoing fluctuations in individuals' conditions. They function as 'informal health sectors' (Mattingly et al. 2011) with minimal or no support from relevant health authorities or government agencies in Ghana. In response to this challenge, a leader of one of the prayer camps remarked:

> That has been our biggest challenge, but that is the essence of we being a Christian organisation. You can't just throw them out there. Interestingly enough, there are also some who would not even like to go because they feel more comfortable here. We help them through different socialisation processes as well.

In affirming the support provided by the prayer camp in addressing stigma and exclusion, a participant noted:

> I feel very good staying here. I have been here for three years now. The people here live and relate with me as family. When I even go home, they still think I am mad, and people don't want to associate with me. Here too, no one will point fingers at you or something. My family members even hardly come here to visit me. But I am hoping and trusting God that everything will be fine. I owe the camp leader every gratitude. They have been very supportive and have shown concern and care to me, and I now feel a sense of belongingness.

The circumstances within the camp contrast markedly with those external to it. Within the camp, patients receive care and respect, fostering an environment in which they experience a sense of belonging and support as integral members of a community. This expression of affection alleviates individual distress, anxiety and disappointment frequently associated with chronic conditions and mental illness. It also enhances interpersonal relationships and one's connection with the divine, while contributing to the accumulation of religious and social capital essential for their recovery. Ultimately, the camps impart to patients a sense of meaning and personal value that counteracts the segregation, discrimination and fragmentation prevalent in Ghanaian society outside the camp.

Prayer camps and the management of chronic mental illnesses

The narratives and experiences delineated in this chapter elucidate the ways in which prayer camps in Ghana can assist certain individuals with chronic mental illnesses in managing their anxieties, recurrent or persistent behaviours and the challenges associated with social stigma and discrimination, as well as the dilemmas and uncertainties surrounding beliefs, causes and treatments pertaining to the chronic aspects of their mental health conditions (Benyah 2024; 2022). While biological factors are acknowledged, the influence of religious and spiritual beliefs related to mental illness is noteworthy; consequently, faith-based approaches and spiritual resources are frequently employed to alleviate and address the experiences of illness. The interventions discussed in this chapter exemplify the positive contributions that prayer camps can make in helping individuals with chronic mental health conditions navigate their circumstances – through personal strategies, community-based approaches and the sacred dimensions intrinsic to the prayer camps that may foster improved mental well-being.

Despite the necessity for critical engagement and discourse surrounding potential human rights abuses at these camps, it is important to recognize that this issue does not pertain universally to all prayer camps. Similarly, Arias et al. (2016) indicated that certain prayer camps 'emphatically rejected' any form of corporal punishment or abuse. For instance, the practice of chaining is not uniformly applied, and attempts to generalize claims regarding such practices inevitably lead to oversimplification of the operations of the camps. This study demonstrates that not all prayer camps are implicated in human rights violations, and it is unjust to categorize their activities uniformly, as some studies appear to do. Such generalizations may inhibit the mental health and research communities from recognizing the potentially beneficial and supportive roles that prayer camps can play in the lives of individuals suffering from chronic mental illness.

The concept of the camp as a sacred space for healing and deliverance provides a significant context for the reconstruction of new identities. The camps remain, in a sense, nature sanctuaries where patients lacking hope or a sense of security within the broader society find solace and cope with their illnesses, thereby fostering overall wellness (Seymour 2016). Individuals with a history of substance abuse report that fasting and prayer, alongside motivational messages from their caregivers, have facilitated reflection on their lives, enabled them to find meaning amidst challenges and prompted a transformation away from their previous behaviours and self-defeating practices (Mustain and Helminiak 2015). This notably underscores the various ways in which the camps serve as crucial faith-based resources for assisting individuals in managing their chronic conditions. The religious and spiritual practices conducted within the camp enhance coping mechanisms and provide social support that nurtures optimism and hope in times of crisis. Participants assert that their stay at the camp aids in managing their fears, recurrent behaviours and lifestyle choices that contribute to regression, thereby undermining any potential for restoration. These findings align with other studies that demonstrate the critical role of religion and spirituality in managing chronic conditions, including mental health issues (Garrett 2002; Gojer et al. 2018; Koenig 2005; Park 2016). Koenig (2018: 164), for example, argues that many mental health patients utilize religious beliefs and practices to manage stress, seeking comfort, meaning, control and social support. Additionally, other researchers have indicated that faith-based and/or spiritual practices serve as coping mechanisms in health-related challenges, promoting an overall positive outlook on life (Hank and Schaan 2008).

Although scholars have been critical of the influence of malevolent forces and the role or effectiveness of religion and spirituality in addressing the challenges of mental illness (Edwards 2014; Krause 2015), I contend that questions regarding whether illness could be influenced or caused by supernatural evil forces are not of paramount importance. Instead, a careful and thoughtful evaluation of people's theories of causation regarding illness is instrumental in developing culturally and socially embedded approaches that are likely to provide holistic clinical measures to address health-related issues (Kirmayer and Swartz 2013). The significant issue is that belief in such forces exists and is widely held in many African communities and societies, and even pervasively in certain Western countries or subgroups (Stanford and McAlister 2008). The findings presented herein indicate a considerable trust and confidence among participants in the ability of prayer camps to provide the necessary interventions for managing and restoring hope and wellness amidst chronic uncertainties, especially in situations where scientific medicine is unable to help or where families are unable to cope with their loved ones any longer. The findings also illustrate how individuals' causal explanations and beliefs regarding illness influence their decision-making behaviour concerning treatment (Yendork et al. 2017; 2019).

There was a general consensus among the participants interviewed regarding the capacity of the prayer camps to facilitate meaningful relationships concerning care, networking and social support. Patients at the camp frequently expressed the sentiment that they felt more loved, protected and cared for there than at home. In addition to providing housing and basic material needs, this environment assists individuals in managing their chronic conditions and related challenges associated with mental illness, such as counselling, medication or treatment regimens. The findings demonstrate how the caregivers at the camps comprehend the predicaments faced by those with mental illness and how they function as social mechanisms that are crucial in fostering resilience, building confidence and mitigating the detrimental consequences of chronic conditions. The structural arrangements at the camp, in which caregivers freely interact and socialize with patients, contribute to enhancing the patients' confidence and creating a safe and supportive environment conducive to healing and wellness. They also ensure love and care, which are essential components in managing distress (Ammerman 2013; Turner 1969).

A critical aspect of the overarching issue concerning the provision of mental health services in Ghana is financial constraint. The challenge of insufficient funding to deliver care to individuals with mental health needs impacts not only the families of those affected but also the state institutions mandated to provide such services. As previously noted, mental health hospitals in Ghana face significant defunding. This circumstance has compelled medical professionals to impose charges for psychotropic medications that should ostensibly be available at no cost. Consequently, this situation has rendered access to healthcare services in hospitals relatively expensive. In such circumstances, patients and their families rely on alternative sources, such as prayer camps, to manage prolonged illnesses, which imposes additional social and financial burdens. My interaction with family members, caregivers and patients also revealed that the cost involved in seeking treatment at a psychiatric hospital is one reason some resort to prayer camps for the required care and assistance.

Current circumstances means that medical treatment at a psychiatric hospital can be prohibitively expensive and beyond the means of the average Ghanaian citizen who is economically disadvantaged. As Kalu (2008: 263) argues, 'The popularity of divine healing in Africa arises from the poverty in the communities that are plagued by the collapse of [the] healthcare delivery system.' In this context, a prayer camp becomes an alternative. Although patients at some of the camps I visited were required to pay a monthly fee for their subsistence, this was more affordable and accessible than treatment at a psychiatric hospital. This aligns with Gammelin's (2018) observation that in Tanzania, although biomedical care is theoretically accessible to all, not everyone can afford it due to their financial circumstances. Some caregivers explained that the responsibility of caring for the mentally ill was largely shifted to the leaders or authorities of the camp, as most patients were unable to afford the fees being charged. However, these socio-economic issues do not negate the premium placed on the spiritual root cause of mental illness, as it was found that individuals with high socio-economic status who could afford the costs of hospital treatment were also brought to the camp. This included the children of university lecturers, Members of Parliament and ministers of state, revealing the significant role and pervasive influence of religion in matters of illness and healthcare.

Joining faith healing and biomedicine in the management of mental illness

A significant concern regarding mental illness in Ghana pertains to the ways in which individuals patronize Pentecostal healing camps and traditional shrines in their pursuit of treatment for mental disorders. While practitioners and healthcare professionals often view the services provided by these religious entities as complementary – and, at times, beneficial in expediting the recovery process of patients – they maintain a critical stance and express scepticism towards the efficacy of traditional and faith healers.

In a recent webinar held on 29 July 2022, organized by the Mental Health Authority of Ghana on the topic 'Schizophrenia: Balancing Our Beliefs and Appropriate Knowledge to Manage the Condition',[2] panellists comprising a clinical psychologist and a psychotherapist shared their insights regarding the beliefs that patients manifest when grappling with schizophrenia. Their responses highlighted that patients and their families frequently attribute the onset of schizophrenia to supernatural malevolent forces, a phenomenon the panellists attribute to the pervasive influence of cultural beliefs surrounding mental illness.

Despite their openness to complementary approaches that incorporate both biomedicine and religious resources, the panellists identified religion and belief systems as potential barriers to effective mental healthcare. Notable statements made during the webinar, such as references to a 'lack of understanding of the disease' and assertions that there exists 'real treatment for the disease', somewhat, reflected their discomfort with the tendency of patients and families to seek assistance from traditional and faith healers. These remarks further underscore their level of mistrust towards such resources. Moreover, the statements somehow show a dismissiveness and ambiguity regarding the integration of traditional and faith-based approaches as supplementary resources in providing effective mental healthcare, a practice recommended by the Mental Health Act (Act 846) of Ghana. Furthermore, this scenario maybe an example of the projection of colonial conceptions of mental illness onto the local context, failing to acknowledge the complexities in the interpretation of mental illness shaped by diverse cultural contexts and understandings.

While I am not attempting to romanticize traditional and faith-based approaches to addressing mental health issues in Ghana, the current situation reflects the suspicion and disbelief that individuals hold regarding the overall efficacy of such resources in mental healthcare. When cultural and religious beliefs are perceived as obstacles to the treatment of mental illnesses, psychotherapists may engage in psychological interventions such as the application of cognitive behavioural therapy (CBT), which aim to reconstruct some of the negative thoughts or world-views that patients possess about their mental health conditions. Clinicians can take the time to study the cultural context in which they operate, gaining an understanding of the 'common-sense' interpretations of mental illness, thereby enabling them to meet patients halfway during treatment. This may assist clinicians in adopting appropriate forms of psychotherapy.

In his recent book, *Psychopathology and Religion: Structural Convergences between Mental Disorders and Religion*, Damian Janus, a Polish psychotherapist, advocates for the adoption of the 'hermeneutics of disorders' to unpack the often ambiguous conceptualizations of mental disorders that lead to various interpretations and meanings surrounding mental illnesses. According to Janus (2019), this phenomenological approach provides a 'non-reductionist' perspective on mental disorders, in contrast to the reductionist emphasis of the biomedical model of disease. In his own practice, Janus argues that this method enables him to observe the lived experiences of patients, and by 'empathizing' with their narratives, he is able to intuitively extract information that, he contends, 'makes it possible to synthesise the information and reach a conclusion that would not be available in a purely rational way of thinking' (Janus 2019: 14). Such an approach, he asserts, alters the understanding of mental illnesses and consequently impacts the nature of the physician's or therapist's interactions with patients (Janus 2019), which 'has serious consequences in the preferred treatment method, ways of informing and cooperating with patients' families … perhaps most importantly dealing with patients' (Janus 2019: 7). A nuanced perspective that integrates diverse causal and healing epistemologies will significantly contribute to ensuring holistic and comprehensive treatment interventions. Therefore, an understanding of this healing landscape equips clinicians with the tools necessary to engage meaningfully in therapeutic processes.

In discussing the significance of religious beliefs and traditions for therapy in Ghana, Araba Sefa-Dede, a renowned Ghanaian clinical psychologist, has recommended to psychiatrists and clinical psychologists to

> understand the belief system and to be willing to explore the individual thoughts, emotions, and behaviours concerning it … This is essential within a belief system where only the religious is highlighted. However, it is possible and essential that this expertise be integrated into the original belief system in order that there is consonance between some aspect of the religious worldview and the help being offered. (Sefa-Dede 2001: 3, cited in Amoah 2014: 217)

Sefa-Dede's recommendations align with those of Kirmayer (2004: 34), who asserts that clinicians require an

> understanding of these healing practices in order to consider their implications for biomedical treatment. Some practices directly challenge the assumptions of biomedicine; others may conflict with prescribed treatments. At the same time, healing traditions offer important resources for patients. Practitioners able to work in concert with these complementary medical systems and resources of healing will be better able to serve their patients.

It can be argued that, given that much of the Ghanaian world-view favours interpretations associated with supernatural realities, knowledge of such interpretative approaches serves as a valuable tool for those working in this context. Primarily, efforts to employ a culturally adapted version of CBT by clinicians or health professionals would be beneficial in addressing some of the challenges faced by clients seeking assistance (Naeem et al. 2023). This is particularly important due to the diverse social and cultural backgrounds that impart differing meanings to mental illness.

Summary

The qualitative data presented in this chapter highlight the role played by faith-based resources in the healing and management of chronic mental illnesses in Ghana. In a political and economic environment that is relatively deficient in medical practitioners in the fields of psychiatry and mental healthcare, treatment facilities and adequate funding (Ofori-Atta et al. 2010), prayer camps in Ghana have emerged as alternative sources of hope, care and support. The prayer camps are situated as borderlands of mental healthcare in this context, holding individual, social and religious significance (Mattingly et al. 2011). While much of the current patronage of prayer camps by individuals living with mental illness can be attributed to the lack of or inadequate infrastructure to support mental healthcare delivery, a closer examination of supplicants' views or decisions to seek support at religious facilities such as prayer camps reveals otherwise.

Specifically, the recourse to prayer camps for the healing of mental illnesses is not solely due to inadequate facilities for mental healthcare. Rather, individuals patronize these centres because of the underlying world-views associated with mental illness and the belief in the power of God to heal diseases. As demonstrated in the participants' responses in Chapter 6, mental illness is believed to be caused by multiple factors, including spiritual, social, environmental, economic and biological influences, among others. Individuals who visit prayer camps believe that even in cases where the illness is not perceived to be influenced or caused by supernatural forces, they still trust in the power of God to heal such ailments. Thus, the healing rituals at the prayer camps are perceived as holistic and provide individuals with the opportunity to seek total well-being that transforms the soul, mind and spirit. Indeed, the communal nature of the healing process offers participants a form of social support and belonging that is essential for recovery.

The issues discussed in this chapter offer clinicians and health professionals working in the area of mental healthcare in Ghana the opportunity to reflect broadly on the importance of having a comprehensive understanding of the role of religion and culture in mental healthcare in Ghana. This understanding is vital due to the extensive role and impact of religion and culture in the lives of Ghanaians in articulating their views on mental illnesses. A comprehensive understanding of the religious and cultural landscape would not only assist clinicians and health professionals in developing cultural competence and humility in the care of their patients but would also aid in adopting the necessary treatment options or strategies to achieve results that would be beneficial to those seeking help as well as to the health professionals themselves. Furthermore, an understanding of the religious and cultural landscape regarding beliefs about mental illness will foster self-awareness in therapists concerning their own belief systems and inform the appropriate pathways to care.

The next chapter examines the reasons why prayer camps are sometimes regarded as alternatives to seeking medical care in hospitals or clinics by families and individuals experiencing mental illness in Ghana.

Chapter 8

WHY PRAYER CAMPS ARE SOMETIMES ALTERNATIVES TO PSYCHIATRIC HOSPITALS

As previously noted, prayer camps play a vital role in providing a ritual context for individuals facing a variety of challenges and ailments who seek spiritual remedies or solutions to their issues (Larbi 2015; Onyinah 2012; Arias et al. 2016). With limited state resources allocated to psychiatry and mental healthcare, alongside a lack of support and commitment from successive governments to prioritize mental health within the general healthcare system, prayer camps have served as 'healing homes' or substitutes for mental health hospitals. Despite their attempts to address the shortcomings arising from the shortage of specialists and government defunding of the sector, prayer camps have faced substantial criticism for some of their practices and methods of healing (Selby 2011).

Previous studies have documented troubling practices such as chaining, forced fasting and the appalling conditions in which patients are detained (Edwards 2014; Carey 2015; Arias et al. 2016). There is widespread public awareness of forms of abuse that occur within certain prayer camps in Ghana. The global media has also highlighted perceived violations of patients' human rights at some prayer camps in Ghana and beyond (Benyah and Sjö 2024; BBC 2018; Carey 2015). Some literature and media reports have contended that the government and state authorities should shut down these camps, arguing that they do not promote the healing or well-being of mental health patients. Critics assert that the practices of some camps result in various forms of victimization and the devaluation of patients, producing self-regressive narratives that undermine any potential for restoration (Edwards 2014; Human Rights Watch 2012). Nevertheless, despite these criticisms and negative perceptions, prayer camps continue to exert considerable public influence and receive goodwill from the populace (Ae-Ngibise et al. 2010).

The central question this chapter seeks to address is: Why do research participants perceive the healing rituals at prayer camps as valid and adequate alternatives to medical treatment in hospitals or clinics? In the subsequent discussion, I examine several reasons why prayer camps remain an alternative to both state-owned and private hospitals and clinics for individuals living with a mental illness and their families in search of therapeutic intervention. In undertaking this exploration, the chapter reiterates some of the underlying world-views or perceived causes of mental illnesses as articulated in Chapter 6. Furthermore, the chapter reinforces how the practices and understandings of health and healing found at prayer camps are framed within traditional interpretations and identifies plausible factors that have contributed to both the religious and public significance of prayer camps in the support of mental healthcare in Ghana.

To achieve the objective outlined in this chapter, the discourse initially explores the narratives of participants in navigating Ghana's medical pluralistic landscape. As presented in Chapter 6, the accounts provided by individuals seeking assistance for their ailments in Ghana oscillate between medical technologies, including hospital diagnoses, faith-based healing and traditional healing practices. Individuals engage with a spectrum of Western, traditional and faith healing therapies to alleviate their symptoms. In essence, the movement across various healing paradigms is often significantly influenced by the outcomes of treatments. This chapter elucidates some of the assertions made by patients regarding their perspectives on why they consider prayer camp services to be a viable alternative to hospital care in certain circumstances. As the ensuing discussion will demonstrate, while patients do not dismiss hospitals or clinics as vital components of healthcare, they perceive these institutions as lacking capacity in addressing specific dimensions of health-related issues. The discourse elucidates participants' views on the perceived sacredness of the prayer camps' environment, the spiritual and physical resources employed in addressing chronic mental health challenges, the holistic approach to healing and the capacity of prayer camp services to mitigate the stigma associated with mental illness. This chapter presents participants' accounts of their experiences in light of these themes and additionally offers perspectives on the effectiveness of healing at prayer camps in Ghana.

Negotiating medical pluralism: A tale of two camps

A significant theme that emerges from my conversations with patients at prayer camps in Ghana, who are seeking support for their mental health, is that nearly all individuals I spoke with had visited a hospital prior to attending the camp. Only a few had not sought hospital care, primarily due to either a lack of financial resources or a strong conviction that their illness was influenced by spiritual factors, rendering hospital medicine irrelevant. The narratives of individuals navigating different healing modalities in search of remedies for their ailments illuminate the dilemmas and uncertainties surrounding the diagnosis and treatment of mental illnesses. Additionally, these narratives reflect the pluralistic medical landscape in which participants reside, highlighting how each medical domain shapes therapeutic decisions and interventions.

While the concept of medical plurality offers patients a variety of choices and potentially a more holistic approach to healthcare and healing, it also underscores the competitive nature of the medical arena, as evidenced by patients' stories regarding the effectiveness of various camps – whether traditional medicine, faith-based healing or biomedicine. My participants noted that while hospitals can be beneficial depending on the nature of the illness, they firmly believe that prayer camps provide something that hospitals cannot, particularly when the illness is perceived as spiritual or related to the individual's soul or spirit. As a patient articulated, if the illness is spiritual, 'all you need is prayers and not injections'. For some patients, if the illness has a supernatural origin or is the result of a disrupted relationship, the resolution to their problems can only be found through consultation with a pastor-prophet who can diagnose the issue or provide context for reconciling the broken relationship to enhance health and well-being. This perspective aligns with views expressed by a participant in LeBeau's (2003: 81) work:

> I usually only go to a healer when the illness is not clear to the Western doctor or when it is other things like madness, craziness, or bad luck. For a Western doctor you go for any pain, flus, and sicknesses that are clear. You go to traditional healers for any ... complicated illnesses which are not clear for the Western doctor.

Within the African and more particularly the Ghanaian context, the options for alternative treatments are contingent upon the perceived underlying cause of the symptoms. The Akan people of Ghana possess an intricate classification of diseases based on the circumstances of the 'illness situation', which, in my experience, significantly influences the therapeutic choices made by patients and their families.

It is significant to note that narratives provided by patients in navigating the multifaceted arena of medical pluralism to address their healthcare needs are frequently interwoven with perspectives from physicians trained in Western scientific medicine. According to the patients and caregivers interviewed, some physicians, motivated by curiosity, would recommend that they seek assistance from alternative sources outside the hospital after conventional treatments had repeatedly failed and signs of recovery were absent. A caregiver conveyed:

> Let me tell you something, I can tell you that the cases we handle here, about 80% of the solution to the problem comes from the prayer camp. In fact, the medical doctors who really know God very well, when he or she critically observes the situation, they can say no, take this to the prayer camp. This hospital ... that place, they often refer people here. I can tell you there are some things it is only prayer that can deal with it and there is nothing wrong if you find out it is only prayer that can help your situation, and you resort to it.

While certain physicians may be reticent to acknowledge these claims due to professional ethics and standards, the narratives illustrate the dialectical relationship, methodologies of diagnostic trial and error and treatment and interaction among diverse agencies in negotiating a highly heterogeneous landscape of medical therapy, each with competing assertions of efficacy. Furthermore, it is essential to highlight that existing records reveal an interactive and discursive boundary established between medical practitioners and traditional healers in the Akan town of Techiman, located in the Bono region. According to

Konadu (2019), in Techiman, medical personnel and doctors who recognized, to some degree, their shortcomings in specific areas of practice were not averse to consulting healers, particularly in domains where the latter were perceived to be more effectively decisive, notably concerning psychiatric illnesses.

For instance, Konadu (2019) reports from a documented film in which Dr Willem Boere acknowledged, stating, 'The more total approach of the indigenous healer to illness is probably best reflected in the treatment of psychiatric diseases and psychosomatic diseases ... Usually, when these illnesses occur, I advise the patient also, besides drug treatment, to consult a traditional healer.' Sr. Mary Ann Tregoning of the Holy Family Hospital similarly remarked, 'For quite a while now we've referred patients to them that have psychiatric illnesses ... [We] have known for a long time that [healers] are [also] very skilful in fractures' (Konadu 2019: 189). Konadu (2019) also recounts that the esteemed traditional healer Kofi Donkor, reportedly at the conclusion of the film, articulated that 'previously, the doctors did not understand what we were doing. But now they work with us. The doctors find that there may be a sickness of a spiritual nature that they cannot cure, and they will send that patient to us for treatment', a sentiment echoed by Dr Boere, who stated, 'I think it is better in the long run to cooperate with the healers than to fight them' (Konadu 2019: 189). Indeed, a letter written by the Chief Psychiatrist of the Accra Psychiatric Hospital in 2002 requesting for a permission to allow some health personnel from abroad to visit a prayer camp to observe the spiritual healing of diseases in Ghana echoes similar sentiment: 'We have much heard of your wonderful performance of healing of diseases that, sometimes cannot be healed by the scientific methods in hospitals. Having considered some spiritual healing centres in the Central, Eastern, Northern and Greater Accra Regions, we decided to involve and use your centre (church for this gracious work.'[1]

In numerous respects, this illustrates the narratives the exist between faith-based healers, traditional healers and medical professionals in Ghana. And it also reflects in the ongoing collaboration between mental health professionals and prayer camps in Ghana (Gureje et al. 2020). Despite the hierarchical and perceived superiority of biomedicine over other medical therapies, such initiatives demonstrate the efforts of medical practitioners to acknowledge the existence of multiple medical traditions within specific societies. Additionally, they strive to establish a framework wherein patients may select therapies they consider beneficial, while concurrently providing a context for the delineation of roles among various forms of medical practice. This approach does not compromise the ongoing negotiation within the therapeutic continuum that encompasses both biomedicine and faith healing.

The environment and sacred context of the prayer camps

Since the patients and camp leaders primarily attributed the cause of mental illness to supernatural agents, the prayer camp, as a religious space, was consequently perceived to offer the spiritual context and resources necessary for recovery.

Participants believed not only in the manifestation of a divine spiritual presence through prayers for faith healing but also that materials sourced from the sacred ground of the camp were endowed with a sacred quality and supernatural potency that embodied the presence of God for healing and restoration.

According to one pastor interviewed, the narrative surrounding the establishment of the camp fostered a belief that it was a unique space ordained by God, revealed to the prophet and leader of the camp through a vision. One leader recounted, 'In that vision, God gave him a complete picture of this place. It was a complete bush, far away from everywhere. But God gave him the picture of everything.' The pastor elaborated that the prophet received this divine vision while fasting and praying at a prayer camp in a different region, following personal crises and unsuccessful attempts to reside outside Ghana. The leaders' personal account of the prayer camp portrayed it as a sacred place distinctly separated from its surroundings, imbued with religious significance and meaning, particularly pertaining to the divine for those who frequent it (Thiessen and McAlpine 2013).

The presence of ecclesiastical structures and the observance of daily religious practices and social interactions foster both horizontal and vertical relationships among individuals, as well as between humanity and the divine or spiritual realm. In essence, one of the reasons the prayer camp is regarded as a 'sacred place' is due to its perceived role as a meeting point between heaven and earth – a nexus between God and humanity. The renaming of buildings with biblical names or images of divine beings for individuals with severe forms of mental illness draws attention to the healing power of the divine (Kilde 2008). A pastor-prophet reflected:

> Another person's faith could also be augmented by such images. Because there are some people when they are worshipping or praying, they want to see the image of Jesus, they want to see the cross. When they see such things, it is like they have seen God, and they can talk to God about their problems. It works for some people. So everyone has their own faith and beliefs when it comes these things.

Cocoa ase nsuo, as referenced by one respondent in the previous quotations in Chapter 6, literally translates to the water beneath the cocoa tree. This term refers to a small river located on the banks of one of the camps. According to one pastor interviewed, the prophet at one of the camps received a revelation from God to utilize this water for healing and other purposes as directed by the Holy Spirit. In relation to mental illness and other ailments, the *cocoa ase nsuo* is perceived to aid wellness and recovery, owing to its associated sacramental value and therapeutic or ritualistic potential in facilitating healing and transformation – similar to a sensorial healing process (Hatala and Waldram 2016).

Patrons at the camp collected water from the stream using their bottles and containers, as they believed that the stream was imbued with divine presence to facilitate healing. Camp leaders informed me that numerous visitors have shared remarkable testimonies regarding the miraculous and efficacious nature of the water. Indeed, Asamoah-Gyadu (2007) has previously highlighted the experiences of pilgrims at prayer centres and healing camps in Ghana, where they collect sand, leaves from trees and gallons of water, which they believe possess miraculous healing powers. As previously mentioned, this religious experience involving the use of water from a sacred site for healing is akin to Robert Orsi's (1997) account of individuals' miraculous experiences at a Catholic grotto in the Bronx, New York, known as Lourdes. At this location, pilgrims 'bathe in pools fed by Saint Bernadette's miraculous spring, hoping for relief from physical distress' (Orsi 1997: 3). According to Orsi (1997), the benefits of the miraculous and efficacious water extend beyond the immediate visitors to the grotto; distant relatives and family members who are unable to visit Lourdes also partake in this experience through those who retrieve the water and send it to them.

This discussion also aligns with T. M. Luhrmann's (2020) work, *How God Becomes Real*. In chapter 7 of this book, Luhrmann elucidates how the invisibility of God or the divine is rendered tangible through various sensory capacities and practices that bring the divine into being. Luhrmann posits that one way an individual knows that their prayers have been answered is through the sensation of a divine being or spirit becoming palpable. She articulates that 'what it means for gods and spirits to feel real is that humans feel a responsiveness, an aliveness – and this places them into a relationship that changes the humans' (Luhrmann 2020: 157). I argue that the materials or religious substances collected by patrons function as mediums or points of contact through which the presence of the divine is experienced. These substances transform and bridge the abstract notion of God, enabling the faithful to feel a connection to the divine and fostering the belief that their prayers are heard and answered for the healing of ailments such as mental illnesses.

In addition, there exists a prevailing consensus among patrons and visitors at the camp that the vicinity of the cocoa tree fosters a sense of connection to nature during periods of meditation and prayer. Interviews with participants indicated that individuals who pray in the area beneath the cocoa tree have experienced numerous miracles and significant breakthroughs in their lives, as well as in their healing journeys. Furthermore, one could contend that the spatial configuration, topography and geography of some of the healing camps itself offer therapeutic benefits to visitors, patients or worshippers. Many participants reported that the tranquil atmosphere, combined with the cooler temperatures resulting from the elevated terrain or mountainous surroundings and the natural environment, tends to mitigate stress and anxiety, which are widely recognized facets of healing and well-being (Hatala et al. 2020; Wood et al. 2017). This environment also aids individuals in coping with pain, thereby contributing positively to their health and wellness (Seymour 2016). These represent some of the potentially beneficial aspects of the prayer camps that previous studies have inadequately acknowledged or highlighted (Carey 2015; Edwards 2014).

Spiritual and physical resources in dealing with mental illness

Patients also utilize both spiritual and physical resources available at the prayer camps to derive strength and construct meaning amidst the challenges posed by mental illness. These spiritual resources encompass healing rituals, exorcisms aimed at expelling perceived evil spirits often associated with witchcraft, 'all-night' prayers, dawn prayer sessions, Bible studies, counselling services and fasting. Fasting and prayer are considered prerequisites for healing, and individuals seeking any form of recovery at the camps are encouraged to engage in a specified fasting period, which may range from three to forty days, contingent upon the severity of the illness and health status. In the context of Pentecostal and charismatic traditions, which are prevalent in the prayer camps, fasting is a widely practised custom. However, various studies and human rights reports indicate that, in some instances, fasting may be imposed upon mentally ill individuals at prayer camps in Ghana (Arias et al. 2016). Although instances of such coercion may occur, this assertion is not universally applicable across all camps in Ghana. The following quote from a pastor-prophet at one of the selected camps illustrates that not all patients are required to fast:

> Here, we do not permit patients to undergo a period of fasting because the individual is already fatigued and unwell. There is a saying that *deɛ wo abrɛ no, hɔn haw no* [translated as you don't stress anyone who is already tired or going through stress]. The individual is already exhausted. If you impose additional burdens on him or her without exercising caution, the results could be detrimental. To ask this individual to fast. When you do that, you are putting extra burden on the person.

This finding, along with my own experiences, suggests that the assertion regarding the coercion of fasting may stem from a misinterpretation by observers who assess these practices from a secular standpoint, without an appreciation of the religious context within which these activities occur. Many of the respondents I interviewed expressed positive sentiments regarding the role of fasting in their lives and its contribution to their recovery, mental health and overall wellness. As noted in the aforementioned quotation, individuals who are ill and significantly weakened are not permitted to undertake fasting. For such individuals, their relatives, who are committed to supporting their wellness and healing process, may remain at the camp and fast on their behalf, should they wish to do so. Indeed, during their observations of fasting practices at prayer camps, Arias et al. (2016: 9) noted that 'fasting was viewed as not necessary for all patients' and that 'camp staff only encouraged patients without serious mental illnesses to fast, encouraging relatives or pastors to fast in the place of those unable to fast themselves'. Notwithstanding these discussions, many participants in this study reported a positive and fulfilling experience associated with their fasting, a finding corroborated by other studies (Cabo and Mattson 2019; Zhang et al. 2015).

Counselling services are also provided to all individuals who present at the camp with issues related to mental illness and other ailments. These services are administered by the prophet, and based on the nature of the issue, a referral is often made to a mental health specialist or hospital for further evaluation. In such instances, following consultations with specialists at the hospital, patients are typically referred back to the camp to receive further assistance through prayer, alongside the ongoing administration of Western medicine. In Chapter 6, I mentioned a situation where a family was given a direction by the prophet to fast twenty-one days for the healing of their relative. In this case, the individual reported experiencing symptoms of psychosis. The manifestation of such symptoms caused distress within the entire family, who sought healing solutions for their relative at the camp. Upon arrival at the camp, the prophet recommended that they fast after diagnosing the issue. However, as the individual continued to display signs of discomfort, prayer alone was deemed insufficient. Consequently, the prophet referred them to a hospital, where, following medical intervention, the individual began to exhibit signs of recovery. This example highlights how some healing camps are integrating biomedicine with faith-based healing to provide support for individuals facing mental health challenges. In instances where spiritual causal factors are excluded, the spiritual resources available at the camp are still perceived as beneficial, offering existential, social, emotional support and contributing to overall patient wellness.

The camp also frequently offers Bible study sessions aimed at fostering and reinforcing the faith of participants to facilitate additional support and healing. In a Christian context, the 'Word of God' is employed to motivate individuals, instil hope and provide comfort for their emotional and psychological needs, assisting them in finding positive interpretations of challenging experiences. As outlined by both participants and caregivers, various Christian scriptures, such as Phil. 4.4, 7, 8, 13 and 19, are routinely utilized, read and contemplated when addressing issues of anxiety and depression, along with other conditions present within the camps. These spiritual resources are often characterized as offering 'therapeutic' benefits, imparting meaning that alleviates anxieties and emotional distress associated with chronic mental health conditions. For some patients, these practices have also facilitated a closer relationship with God and encouraged increased prayer for 'breakthroughs' in their journey towards healing and wellness. One individual reflected: 'The Bible studies and all meetings are helpful. Sometimes you hear the stories of other people during church service, and that gives you hope.' For others, the knowledge gained from the Word of God has played a transformative role in their lives, aiding their recovery from chronic mental illness, habits and behaviours contributing to mental health issues, including addiction and substance abuse:

> Essentially, it has been about the kind of advice and the spiritual activities we engage ourselves in at this place. My caregiver sometimes calls, sits me down, and talks to me. He will ask me to sit beside him, and he will give me plenty of advice using the scriptures. He will ask me to compare myself to the other people. Then I will realise that the difference is now better as a result of me being at this place … I have been here before. But I went home and went back to my old ways, so I came back again. I have spent like one year now and I haven't gone back home again. I am here all the time.

As outlined, the spiritual activities at the camp facilitated the recovery of many individuals from chronic habits such as smoking, drinking and substance abuse, while also providing a sense of deeper meaning and a feeling of wellness amid their chronic conditions.

In one of the interviews, a medical practitioner who has collaborated with a prayer camp noted that one area in which the role of prayer camps has been particularly significant in the management of mental health issues is in addressing behavioural disorders associated with practices such as smoking, substance addiction and alcoholism. According to her observations, when individuals are admitted to the prayer camps, they are deprived of the opportunity and freedom to engage in these detrimental habits, while the activities in which they participate at the camp contribute to their transformation. She argued:

> A particular area I have seen much improvement regarding treatment of mental health issues at the prayer camps are mental health problems that is associated with some behavioural factors such as smoking, alcoholism, and abuse of hard substances. When they come there, they are not able to engage in such practices and that helps in the long run.

Additionally, the medical practitioner indicated that another aspect in which the prayer camp has been beneficial to individuals seeking assistance for their mental illnesses is the sermons or preachings encountered during worship services at the prayer camps. A specific area highlighted by her is the impact of sermons on individuals experiencing the hearing of voices. According to the medical practitioner, individuals with such challenges, particularly those who hear negative voices, find motivation and strength in the messages they receive, which can psychologically empower them to withstand the adverse effects or consequences of these voices. She conveyed:

> There are instances some will say, I have been hearing voices. The voice tells them this person wants to harm me. Do you get it. But when they go to church, the sermon is about no one can harm you. Is at the back of their mind. So even if the voice is coming, some have positive attitude towards it and not be afraid. Do you get it. All of us do have such ill feelings sometimes that something bad may happen. So the moment they hear the man of God speaking that touches their heart, in a way it influences them. So that is what I will say about some cases been spiritual and healed.

In Chapter 6, I analyse briefly the phenomenon of voice hearing reported by certain participants seeking assistance at a prayer camp, as well as the efficacy of the prayer camp in addressing such issues. Notably, while these experiences are frequently observed among patients diagnosed with schizophrenia, some individuals interpret them as supernatural occurrences, often attributing them to the influence of spiritual entities, as highlighted in the work of Luhrmann et al. (2015). Within the context of prayer camps, in addition to deliverance prayers aimed at dispelling negative auditory hallucinations, the perspective of the medical practitioner, as quoted earlier, suggests that not only do deliverance prayers aid in mitigating such experiences, but also the preaching of sermons or the messages patients encounter at worship services provide intrinsic psychological benefits. These benefits appear to empower individuals experiencing these phenomena, enabling them to resist the influences of the voices, thereby contributing positively to their overall well-being and health outcomes.

In terms of physical resources, the prayer camps offer a conducive environment by providing rooms or dormitories to accommodate patients. By a conducive atmosphere, I refer to the provision of a suitable environment that is free from setbacks that could hinder the recovery of patients and instead assists them in coping with their circumstances. However, the living conditions, particularly regarding accommodation, may not meet the ideal standards one might envision or desire for their homes. Most prayer camps in Ghana face financial limitations, which hampers their ability to provide adequate hostel facilities for their visitors. Nonetheless, there are camps, particularly those utilized for the purpose of this study, that have managed to provide suitable forms of dormitories and hostel accommodations for their patients and visitors. Consequently, it is essential to recognize that there exists variation in living conditions across the diverse prayer camps in Ghana (Arias et al. 2016).

Although patients are required to pay a nominal fee for their daily subsistence, this presents challenges for many who are unable to pay due to financial constraints. One caregiver articulated the following concerns:

> To tell you the truth, here the patients only pay a little amount of money for their care and support. Most of the things are coming from papa [prophet and leader of the camp]. Because for some of them, they just bring the person here and they will not come back here again. We feed them both morning and evening. So, if we don't have anything with us, we just go to him and say old man (prophet) things are not going well ooo. Then he knows we are out of food items … we use some to also pay for the utility bills.

He further elaborated:

> For the patients, some are willing to pay the monthly charge of 200 cedis. However, for most of them, their condition has been there for long [chronicity] and they have spent a lot of money searching for cures or solution at different places. By the time they come here, they have nothing left to contribute to their upkeep and welfare while here. Everything now depends on us!

In expressing similar concerns, another pastor-prophet reported:

> We don't charge anyone for the healing services we perform. We use our own resources in taking care of the patients. We don't take anything from you. Anyone who will say when I came here, they took this amount from me, then know that the person just wants to disgrace us.

The caregiver and prophet's efforts in providing essential material facilities have significantly contributed to alleviating the stress and frustrations often experienced by individuals with chronic mental illness in Ghana. In this context, the provision of shelter, care, love and support cultivates a sense of community among patients, which further aids their wellness and healing journeys. Many patients shared their experiences regarding such resources, with one stating, 'My family don't bring me anything here, but I eat and I'm okay. Gradually, I am becoming better. I feel like I'm home. For me, I even want to live here and not go anywhere again.' Another individual remarked, 'The support we are receiving here is amazing. For me, it has helped me forget about many things that were not helping my condition.' Furthermore, another respondent reflected on the relationships and community fostered in the camps:

> What is really important to me is that you have people here you can look up to. Our leader especially gives us some hope. We see others being prayed for getting their healing. It all helps us to have faith and pray more. It helps us to get closer to God in anticipation.

Despite the potential scarcity of material resources, the shared experience and profound spiritual relationships characterized by care and trust have universally enhanced patients' connection with God, feelings of support, community integration, belonging and overall wellness, as they are surrounded by others who share similar beliefs and faith in a supportive, positive and uplifting environment.

Prayer camps provide holistic approach to healing

Previous research (Opare-Henaku 2013; Kyei et al. 2014; Kpobi and Swartz 2018b) and responses from my informants provide an answer to the question of why people turn to prayer camps: the healing they provide resonates with their underlying religio-cultural beliefs. As shown in the views shared by participants, mental illness in Ghana is often attributed to external and supernatural evil forces such as witchcraft and *juju*. Patients and their families therefore often view hospitals as lacking the ability to offer the necessary diagnostic or divinatory tools to establish the causes, consequences and remedy of afflictions. However, prayer camps are believed to provide a ritual context in which individuals suffering from mental health disorders undergo a period of fasting and prayer and with the help of the prophet ward off any antagonistic spirit associated with the illness. The prophet or leader of the camp, who is believed to be endowed with the Holy Spirit, can communicate with the spiritual world and offer solutions to remedy the situation. The prophet can thus divine the 'why' of the supplicant's complaints. He can also understand his clients' needs from cultural, religious, social and psychological perspectives, a need which is completely absent in hospitals or biomedical care (see also Ayim-Aboagye 2006; Appiah-Kubi 1981).

There are also general prayers that serve as interventionist strategies to seek healing from the power of the Holy Spirit for other forms of illnesses that are not associated with any supernatural entities. Thus, not all illnesses are attributed to the devil, but even in situations where they are not, the participants still see the need to rely on God's grace and providence for 'total' healing. In such situations prayers are said over prescribed medications before they are taken or administered (Krause 2012). As one prayer camp pastor reflected, 'Even the medicines, if you don't pray over them, won't work. Even some of the doctors who really know God very well – when they examine the situation, and he thinks there is more to it than being physical – will say send him or her to the prayer camp.'

Additionally, participants were of the view that hospitals cannot provide a solution to problems of a spiritual origin. For one patient, for example, although 'the asylum [mental hospital] is good, it doesn't help … because if it is a spiritual attack … there is no way the asylum can deal with it because you don't need those injections they give there'. For this respondent prayer was the only antidote to his sickness, which he claimed was spiritual. Another caregiver argued that

> if the sickness has a spiritual origin, no medication can deal with it. If evil spiritual entities can cause illness in people, then we also need the power of God and the Holy Spirit to drive that demon out so that the person can have his or her healing. Because you can't use medicine. No, that won't help!

Healing is also framed in a theological narrative about the essence and existence of the human person. For example, a different caregiver asked:

> Why is it that when someone purchases a vehicle, and it gets spoilt, they send it to the mechanic and not a different place? You see. So as a human being, when you are sick, it is God that created us, so you send it to the creator who is the source of life. We believe in the medicine all right, but even those who practise medicine, it is God that gave them the knowledge and wisdom. If God doesn't give you that, you can't [have it].

The views shared by the respondents corroborate Brown's (2011: 8) argument that most Pentecostals do not reject modern medicine, but 'they do insist that God is able to heal even when medicine is unable to help'. Similarly, Yong (2011: 6) notes that 'Pentecostals have always negotiated the tension between a robust belief in faith healing that repudiated medical technology entirely and the belief that faith healing and the use of medicine were indeed compatible'.

Furthermore, prayer camps have remained an alternative because of the stigma attached to seeking treatment at a psychiatric hospital and because people feel that the care provided in medical hospitals is not holistic. Some respondents argued that when people or even family members see them visiting the psychiatric hospital, they always assume they have a mental problem, and they hurriedly categorize them as 'mad people' or people who are 'insane'. In Ghana the stigma attached to seeking treatment at a psychiatric hospital not only concerns patients but also professionals who work in such institutions or the field of medicine (Buertey et al. 2020). Such labelling sometimes prevents patients seeking hospital treatment. However, those who still seek hospital treatment also find the care they receive to be non-holistic or incomplete. Indeed, some of the patients I encountered at the prayer camps claimed to have visited the hospital before going to the camp. When asked why, they shared the view that it was God who had given them the total healing they were seeking because He is the source of life and the master or the ultimate healer.

A personal conversation with pastors, caregivers, and patients suggests that a healing ritual at a prayer camp is believed to have the ability to offer holistic cleansing and foster personal transformation through invocations of God through Jesus Christ and the power of the Holy Spirit. The healing at the camp is thus seen as all-encompassing and more transformative than Western medicine. The prayer camps serve as a community and a support system that aids in patients' healing. There is a relationship between the patients and the community that affects their healing and social positioning. This finding supports the argument of the sociologist Meredith McGuire (1985: 272) that 'because western medicine is focused on the curing of "disease" rather than on the healing of illness, the provision of meaning is privatized and undermined'. In contrast with religious forms of healing, she argues that 'religious rituals and symbols may impart a similar sense of empowerment to those who believe in them. This symbolic empowerment may indeed have concrete physical and psychological effects', thereby raising the sick person's hope and reducing their social predicaments (McGuire 1985: 274).

Unlike hospital treatment, the healing practices at prayer camps offer protection to patients and enhance their reintegration into society. As already observed, seeking treatment at a psychiatric hospital contributes to patients' stigmatization and reduces their self-confidence. However, a prayer camp is seen as a place of prayer, a community of faith where believers, Christians and non-Christians,[2] gather to seek the face of God for the redemption of their problems. The camps help diminish a pattern of behaviour or an illusion the patients may have had in the aftermath of their hospital treatment. At the prayer camp the relationship that is developed between the patients and the community removes any fear that lurks in the personality traits of the patients regarding their social positioning after hospital treatment. Through exorcism, healing and deliverance rituals the individual is believed to be redeemed and purified. This increases their confidence, builds social capital and enhances their reintegration and social positioning. Grimes's (2000) statement 'Cured, you are fixed; healed, you are reconnected' captures this point appropriately. This is supported by the view that 'Christian healing can be distinguished from other forms of religious healing in its appeal to Christ as the transcendent source of healing and prime symbol of personal and social integration' and that 'Christian healing situates people in community and establishes expectations and relationships' (Porterfield 2005: 9).

The effectiveness of healing of mental illnesses at prayer camps

A recurring question that I commonly receive from individuals during discussions about this study at conferences, seminars or in one-on-one interactions pertains to my belief in the claims regarding the healing of mental illnesses by patients at prayer camps.

Referring to claims of religious healing, these inquiries are not unexpected. Such inquiries have been at the centre of scrutiny by researchers and scholars in anthropology and religious studies, particularly those focusing on religious healing. Notable among these are the anthropologist Thomas J. Csordas and Ogbu Kalu, a Nigerian historian of religion and scholar of Pentecostalism in Africa. Csordas (1994), in his book *The Sacred Self: A Cultural Phenomenology of Charismatic Healing*, sets the framework of the study in the introduction by posing the following questions: 'How does religious healing work, if indeed it does? What is the nature of its therapeutic efficacy? What is actually being healed by the performances of … medicine man, or the faith healer?' (Csordas 1994: 1). Kalu (2008: 263), discussing the discourses surrounding the efficacy of healing among Pentecostals, poses similar questions: 'What exactly do the churches mean by healing? Can healing always occur? Can healing occur without physical cure? Are the claims sustainable or fraudulent?'

Both scholars, in their attempts to address these questions, limit the discussion to the religious communities they have studied, focusing on what constitutes healing, how it is understood and the modalities employed in determining or establishing its efficacy. For instance, Csordas (1994: 2) observes that 'it has become commonplace to observe that efficacy is contingent on the nature of problems addressed by different forms of healing, how those problems are defined in cultural practice, and what counts in cultural terms as their successful resolution'. As already mentioned, the transcultural psychiatrist Kirmayer has also examined the problem of efficacy in healing. He argues that 'the effectiveness of a healing practice is embedded in a larger cultural system that identifies types of malady or affliction and prescribes appropriate interventions'. Consequently, 'evaluations of outcome are always made with reference to specific problem definitions, hierarchies of values, and contextual frames' (Kirmayer 2004: 43). Kirmayer notes that the effectiveness of a particular healing modality can be assessed against a variety of different outcomes, which also raises epistemological, ethical and aesthetic concerns. Epistemological concerns centre on how one can ascertain that a healing practice is effective, whereas ethical and aesthetic values pertain to what constitutes a positive change, improvement, health or well-being.

Just as the concepts of causality and patterns of thought differ from person to person or culture to culture, what constitutes a good outcome may also vary (Kirmayer 2004). As he posits, 'What counts as a good outcome may range from change in a discrete behavior viewed as troublesome, or improved "quality of life", to the restoration of harmony between body, social order, and the cosmos' (Kirmayer 2004: 42). For example, as discussed in Chapter 6 and in this chapter, for an individual who has attended a prayer camp, the effectiveness of their healing may be attributed to their newfound ability to sleep peacefully at night, free from previous visions of torment by an unknown person in dreams or the experience of hearing voices while asleep. Although these outcomes could be self-confirming, they are deemed a positive outcome since the individual's issue has been resolved. Among indigenous healers, for example, Konadu (2007: 92) notes that the claim to effectiveness of a healing procedure is usually determined or affirmed by the patients. The confirmation by the patient 'to perform a task that their illness prevented prior the prescribed treatment' is an important marker in establishing an effectiveness of a particular medicine or a healing procedure.

Similarly, health professionals may employ different criteria and definitions regarding what constitutes a successful outcome. Thus, in addressing the question of the effectiveness of religious healing, it is imperative to consider how individuals define their illness both culturally and socially, as well as what is deemed effective in addressing the perceived causes. Consequently, attention must be directed towards understanding why individuals pursue specific methods of healing when unwell and how effective these healing methods are perceived to be. Importantly, it is crucial to ascertain what constitutes an effective method in counteracting the presumed or defined causes of illness. Erica Bourguignon (1976) assessed the effectiveness of religious healing, positing that a key question to ask when evaluating any form of religious healing is: 'How is healing related to diagnosis in a specific case, or more generally, to the diagnostic categories or nosological systems employed in a given culture? In other words, what is to be understood by illness?' (Bourguignon 1976: 5). According to her, these questions are fundamental, particularly in contexts where religious healing has demonstrated considerable efficacy, with 'much evidence to show that religious healing is successful and efficacious in the view of its clientele' (Bourguignon 1976: 18).

Further investigation into some of the inquiries posed by individuals interested in my work reveals that, more often than not, such questions arise from an ill-informed perspective or are intentionally crafted to undermine or cast doubt on a particular religious or social framework regarding what is significant to them, particularly when they juxtapose such practices with the advancements in scientific and technological knowledge within their own social contexts. Under such circumstances, the question arises: Why do individuals continue to believe in and resort to these practices in a modern environment characterized by scientific advancement? Indeed, similar inquiries appear to have guided a recent research project concerning the activities of prayer camps in Ghana, resulting in some international non-governmental organizations producing a critical report on the prayer camps (Human Rights Watch 2012).

Additionally, independent writers and human rights organizations have raised critiques regarding the effectiveness of prayer camps in addressing mental health issues (Goldstone 2017; Edward 2014). While some of these concerns may warrant legitimate attention,[3] a broader examination of the report reveals a significant misunderstanding of the phenomenon under scrutiny or reflects a similar error by adopting the perspectives of their predominantly Western donors, thereby perpetuating a colonialist imperative by imposing their values onto another culture or society and expecting individuals to conform to particular practices as they would in their own contexts. Mohr (2013: 40) reports a comparable situation involving Roman Catholic missionaries in East Africa, who 'systematically misrepresented African religion and culture in the missionary press, embellishing African misery and savagery in order to increase their funding by patrons troubled by these images'. Similarly, Atiemo (2014) observes that contemporary assessments and critiques of prayer camps by human rights organizations predominantly reflect the privileges of the Global North, often neglecting the local and cultural nuances inherent in the discourses surrounding the care of individuals with mental illness.[4]

Summary

Despite the ongoing public support and promotion of biomedical care by both state and non-state institutions, religious entities involved in medical care and treatment, such as prayer camps, continue to enjoy significant popularity among the population in Ghana. On one hand, the phenomenon of medical pluralism reveals competing therapeutic approaches within a religiously plural and culturally diverse context; on the other hand, it offers individuals the opportunity to explore various pathways of care that align with their social, cultural and religious worldviews, thereby facilitating holistic well-being. As demonstrated in the discussion, prayer camps in Ghana attract substantial patronage due to the beliefs held by individuals regarding their ability to address aspects of illness that they perceive hospitals fail to adequately resolve. This does not imply a lack of faith in the hospitals' capacity to cure illness; rather, it suggests that the methods of treatment employed by hospitals do not always resonate with their medical conditions as defined by their cultural, social and religious experiences. For instance, individuals who visit prayer camps perceive these spaces as providing the ritual context or environment necessary to address the perceived symptoms of their illnesses, which are distinct from those offered by hospitals. As illustrated in this chapter, the environment of prayer camps is believed to be imbued with divine presence, along with communal and social support systems that assist patients in addressing both the social and spiritual dimensions of their afflictions.

While not every illness presented at the prayer camps results in healing, patients believe that this space aids them in confronting the stigma associated with their conditions. Therefore, I argue that prayer camps will remain significant for the foreseeable future, even in the presence of adequate resources to establish psychiatric hospitals, due to the religious and cultural beliefs and the desire for wholeness that encompass both the spiritual and physical aspects of healing in the lives of Ghanaians. This phenomenon arises not from a rejection of biomedical care but from the conviction that biomedicine cannot always provide solutions to certain health issues or conditions, particularly those perceived to be influenced by unseen malevolent forces, broken social relationships and emotional illnesses that affect the soul and spirit of the affected individual.

The next chapter advances the discourse by examining the integration of spiritual and/or religious healing with biomedical care to provide holistic healthcare and well-being for the Ghanaian population.

Chapter 9

TOWARDS EFFECTIVE INTERSECTORAL COLLABORATION AND DECOLONIZING OF PSYCHIATRY

The preceding discussion, alongside other related studies on traditional and faith healing (TFH) and mental health in Ghana, has elucidated the influence of religion – specifically within the context of prayer camps – and culture on mental health. It particularly emphasizes how these two phenomena affect help-seeking behaviours among individuals seeking support for mental health issues. A noteworthy aspect of the discourses concerning the interplay between faith-based healing and biomedicine in mental healthcare in Ghana is the advocacy for collaboration between these two distinct medical paradigms. It is important to recognize that this call for collaboration is not a novel concept. Prior studies, such as those conducted by Konadu (2019) and Kpobi and Swartz (2019), have documented earlier instances of such collaborative efforts. Indeed, an earlier initiative worth mentioning in the context of collaboration between healthcare systems in Ghana is the establishment of the Ghana Psychic and Traditional Healing Association (GPTHA) by the inaugural president of the Republic of Ghana, Dr Kwame Nkrumah. Through this association, Nkrumah sought to implement a mechanism aimed at creating a holistic healthcare system in Ghana by modernizing, promoting and integrating traditional medicine within the broader healthcare framework. The formation of this association constituted an integral part of Nkrumah's agenda to advance and modernize traditional medicine while incorporating Western medical practices as part of his Africanization strategy to reconstruct colonial medicine following independence (Adu-Gyamfi and Anderson 2022).

Recent appeals for collaboration between TFH and biomedical practitioners have underscored the potential benefits of such integrative approaches in medical care, particularly concerning mental health (Gureje et al. 2020). Nonetheless, it is essential to acknowledge the challenges inherent in these initiatives. Notable among these challenges are a pervasive lack of trust between biomedical practitioners and TFH, which is rooted in post-colonial legacies and presents significant conceptual and methodological issues; insufficient engagement or exclusion of individuals with lived experiences of mental illness; financial limitations; a dearth of qualified medical personnel; competition for scarce resources; and ethical dilemmas in care (Kpobi et al. 2024; Read et al. 2023; van der Watt et al. 2017).

Despite these obstacles, some progress has been achieved through the implementation of various programmes (Kpobi et al. 2024; Ben-Zeev 2018; Ben-Zeev at al. 2024; Gureje 2020). However, these ongoing challenges raise fundamental questions regarding current strategies to foster and enhance collaboration and intersectoral partnerships between faith healers and biomedical practitioners. For instance, to what extent have the current initiatives rolled out by the Mental Health Authority (MHA) and non-governmental organizations (NGOs), and independent researchers, involved cultural and religious experts in the design and formulation of programmes aimed at addressing issues of distrust? What effective methodologies have been established to evaluate faith-based and traditional healing practices? Are there existing models to assess the efficacy of faith healing when integrated with biomedicine, which may illuminate whether patients experience better or worse outcomes compared to those receiving strictly positivistic or biomedical care? To what extent are human rights activists prepared to adopt local strategies while implementing global perspectives to address human rights concerns emerging from the treatment of people at prayer camps, for example?

While this chapter does not aim to provide definitive answers to these questions, it offers insights into existing collaborative efforts and outlines potential pathways to strengthen and enhance the effectiveness of partnerships between biomedical practitioners and faith healers, particularly prayer camps in Ghana. The discussions presented herein are informed by the findings of this study, in conjunction with personal reflections on the relevant literature in the field. It should be noted that my perspective is primarily that of a scholar in religious studies and may not encompass the concerns raised by other disciplines analysing these issues.

Collaboration between prayer camps and health centres

As previously noted, it is essential to recognize that researchers examining the interplay between religion, culture and mental health in Ghana and beyond have consistently advocated for collaboration between TFH and practitioners of biomedicine. Several of these recommendations highlight the necessity for training for healers and emphasize the importance of cultural sensitivity and responsiveness among clinicians. Indeed, in Ghana, concerted efforts have been undertaken by the MHA and NGOs to train healers as part of the initiative to support the implementation of the Mental Health Act. An example is the work done by the Ghana *Somubi Dwumadie* (Ghana Participation Programme) in partnership with other agencies such as Basic Needs, MHA and other international collaborators to address mental health issues in Ghana.[1]

During my fieldwork in Ghana, I observed that one of the prevailing practices at the prayer camps involves collaboration between these camps and mental health professionals operating in the districts where the camps are situated. This collaboration afforded the opportunity for certain camps I visited to integrate both prayer and biomedicine in the care of individuals with mental health issues. However, one of the camps included in the study did not endorse the use of biomedicine and relied exclusively on their belief in the method of divine healing. Conversations with some of the health professionals revealed that they viewed this collaboration as a positive development, as it enabled them to monitor the conditions of certain patients at the camp and to administer medication and injections when necessary. One of the caregivers corroborated the efforts of health professionals when he asserted:

> Although we pray for some of them when they bring them here, the prayers don't calm the person immediately. In such situations, we call on the nurse to give some injections, so it calms the person down for some time. If not, we get tired because of the violent and aggressiveness of the person. Some of them can even break and open the metal gates. They hurt other colleagues sometimes. At that point, you need the nurse to be around to support you to do whatever you have to do.

The aforementioned quotation underscores the significance that prayer camp staff attribute to their collaboration with biomedical practitioners, while simultaneously revealing their recognition of the limitations inherent in their approaches to addressing certain challenges encountered in the provision of care. For instance, at this camp, the discontinuation of chaining – following education and training by health professionals – has rendered the restraint of aggressive patients increasingly difficult, necessitating reliance on conventional biomedicine to manage such issues. This situation illustrates the impacts of collaboration in ceasing chaining and enhancing the lives of individuals seeking care at prayer camps. Consequently, for the prayer camps, such collaboration aids in addressing some deficiencies and providing solutions to the latent functions of healing practices within these sites.

The partnership between the camps and healthcare centres constitutes a component of the decentralization agenda of the MHA of Ghana. As already mentioned, one of the primary objectives of enacting the Mental Health Act in 2012 was to decentralize mental healthcare in Ghana. This objective included the de-institutionalization of mental health services in favour of a community-based approach. This strategy encompassed collaboration with TFH (including prayer camps and Islamic healers) throughout the country, who reportedly oversee a substantial proportion of individuals afflicted with mental health disorders in Ghana (MHA 2018). The decentralization agenda also aligns with the objectives of the World Health Organization's (WHO's) mental health policy and the Global Health Movement for Mental Health established in the 2000s (Read, Adiibokah and Nyame 2009). Indeed, decentralization has been a pivotal factor in health policies in Ghana since the 1980s, following the recommendations of the 1978 WHO Conference in Alma-Ata, USSR, in September of that year. This event not only gave rise to the concept of primary health care (PHC) but also, and most importantly, advocated for the incorporation of indigenous healers within national healthcare systems in the developing world (Senah et al. 2001).

Current collaboration at the intersection of biomedicine and spiritual care for mental health patients in Ghana suggests a promising new relationship between biomedical care and prayer camps. This may afford opportunities for clinicians or healthcare professionals to cultivate cultural competence within their practice. Indeed, as other studies have indicated, the application or adaptation of cultural models can assist clinicians in navigating complexities and frustrations, often transforming these challenges into motivation for enhanced care (Kirmayer et al. 2003). Overall, such collaboration enhances the awareness of cultural issues among biomedical practitioners in mental healthcare and fosters corresponding clinical skills, ultimately aiding biomedical practitioners in developing respect and strengthening intra- and inter-personal relationships necessary for sustaining collaborative efforts (Kpobi et al. 2024). The recommendation by Kirmayer et al. (2003: 145) that 'clinicians need training in working with interpreters and culture brokers' aligns with my initial inquiry regarding how existing programmes in Ghana aimed at addressing some of the challenges in collaboration between biomedical practitioners and faith healers have incorporated individuals with expertise in culture, religion and medicine.

Impact of the collaboration between prayer camp and mental health professionals

Impact on prayer camp staff

A very careful observation of the current landscape of healing practices at prayer camps in Ghana, particularly concerning individuals seeking support for mental health issues, reveals that significant work remains to be done in addressing the challenges identified in earlier studies. In other words, despite concerted efforts to implement programmes aimed at addressing issues associated with TFH, the situation does not appear to be improving, necessitating a sustained commitment and motivation from various stakeholders, including both state and non-state actors, to enhance overall conditions. Nevertheless, despite the existing challenges and the shortcomings of current frameworks designed to address some deficiencies in prayer camp practices, certain findings from this study suggest potential for future improvement, provided that current efforts are maintained and sustained. For example, some prayer camp caregivers reported that collaboration with mental health professionals has positively transformed their personal behaviours and attitudes towards care, which has, in turn, led to improved health outcomes for their patients. One caregiver reflected:

> The collaboration has really helped a lot especially me. That time I have quick temper. You see. I don't mind. Before the collaboration if you misbehave, I will

> slap you right now. If you misbehave, I will beat you. But before they finished that programme, they made me consider the fact that they are sick. So now I have calmed down. I have cooled down for them. That is the impact of the programme. At first, I easily get angry at everything. I didn't know that they don't reason like me. Anything, I will just yell at you. Now, I have stopped and relate with them well. Even out of the relationship you will see the person get wells. So, to me per se, it really helped me.

For this caregiver, the collaboration has substantially transformed his approach to the treatment and management of the patients under his care at the camp. He notes that this change in attitude towards his patients has led to enhanced health outcomes and recovery for those in his care. Furthermore, it has positively affected his emotional state, mitigating feelings of anger that were detrimental to his overall well-being. Another caregiver, reflecting on the impact of an educational programme focused on human rights, emphasized the necessity of discontinuing the practice of restraining patients who are seeking healing activities at the camp:

> I wish such programmes will continue because as a person you always have to learn. It is good that you get knowledge about certain things. You see at first, we will chain you. We will remove the chain when you are going to have your bathe. But when you return, we put you in chains again. But now we have stopped chaining. You see we have obtained new knowledge regarding that. At first when they brought the idea, we didn't understand them. You may think it will be difficult for you to adapt but now is cool. At first, I said how is this going to work, but when they gave us the education on how to go about it and we came into consensus with them it was nice.

A pastor-prophet also mentioned:

> Here, we longer put people into chains since we started collaborating with the authorities. You see the structures here, the authorities helped us to put them up. The funds got finished so we have not managed to complete them, but I can say that it has helped us a lot. We no longer put anyone in chains here. The nurse come here from time to time, but he says the medicine doesn't come nowadays so his visit hasn't been regular these days.

From the aforementioned quotations, the training received has facilitated the discontinuation of the chaining of patients. As evidenced in the narrative, the transition away from chaining was not an easy adaptation; however, through education, new knowledge regarding various methods of patient restraint has been acquired, thereby alleviating some of the difficulties associated with their work. As revealed by another pastor-prophet, a state agency, through the support of several international donors, has helped their prayer camp receive funding to construct buildings to accommodate patients seeking care at the camp. This initiative, according to the pastor-prophet, has significantly aided the camp in ceasing the chaining of individuals seeking treatment. Other caregivers reiterated that through education, they have learned essential practices, including the importance of wearing gloves and how to assist in administering oral medications, among others. One caregiver expressed enthusiasm regarding the impact of education through collaboration, stating, 'Education will really help us, and it makes you happy even with the work. We need more education and training like that to add to the spiritual aspects.' This finding aligns with the findings of other studies that have shown the openness or desire to collaborate (Gureje 2020; Kpobi et al. 2024; Read 2019)

While this change in attitudes through education presents a positive outlook for the operations and activities of prayer camps, other studies have posited that training alone may not be sufficient for effecting long-term changes in certain practices (Ventevogel 1996). This recognition necessitates that stakeholders evaluate educational programmes and training strategies to ensure they are more bidirectional rather than unidirectional (i.e. 'from medical "expert" to healers, rather than a mutual learning process'), which is the format that most current interventions appear to adopt (Read et al. 2023: 145). A bidirectional approach may help to mitigate some of the suspicion, mistrust, scepticism and power dynamics that have been identified as significant obstacles to collaboration (Ae-Ngibise et al. 2010; Kpobi et al. 2024; Kpobi and Swartz 2018c).

In this regard, this study argues that the collaboration between prayer camps and biomedical care should not merely be perceived as a potentiality but rather as a key strategy in addressing a critical healthcare challenge within a pluralistic medical economy. Finding common ground in reconciling differences in the interpretation, meaning and treatment of illness is essential for devising solutions to existing problems, such as chaining and other practices that are detrimental to individuals seeking treatment at both healing camps and some treatment centres. As previously mentioned, the integration of spiritual care and biomedicine is not detrimental; rather, it serves as a complementary mechanism within a holistic healthcare environment. Both modalities are often desirable to patients (Kpobi et al. 2024; Gureje 2020).

Impact on health professionals

Although this study did not initially aim to focus on the experiences of biomedical practitioners collaborating with prayer camp staff, their inclusion became pertinent during fieldwork. One of the biomedical practitioners interviewed had spent a period of seven years working in collaboration with a prayer camp. She expressed a positive view of the camp and indicated how it has contributed to her development of cultural responsiveness and enhanced her approach to work. According to her, her observations of the experiences of individuals at the camp have led her to adopt a more open approach to treatment. She expressed concern that while some patients respond to treatment, particularly with medication, others do not, even when attempts are made to modify their medication. In such situations, she argues that the only recourse is for the patient to resort to prayer alongside medication:

> There are instances you will do whatever the patient will not respond to treatment. So sometimes we make calls to actually make changes of medication for the patient. Sometimes it works when there is a change in medication. Sometimes too you just realise the case is just chronic especially depressive cases. Depressive cases take a longer time for you to see the effect you want to see. In some cases, you will see is the same and you just have to allow the prayers to go on.

According to her, in situations where medication fails to be effective, the cultural and religious interpretation that the illness may be influenced by supernatural forces becomes pertinent. Consequently, patients, with the support of their family members, are allowed to undergo their deliverance procedures. Allowing the patient to engage in the healing process through prayer is particularly significant, especially when the patient believes that their afflictions are spiritually caused. She argued that this may help satisfy their religious convictions and perspectives regarding the illness, as well as assist in addressing the bodily and social realities of the condition for a positive health outcome alongside biomedical treatment. Indeed, John Bennet and Jon Rohde (2008), in their essay titled 'Hospitals and Clinics', recommend that healthcare workers in Africa seek a middle ground by integrating traditional treatment methods and world-views into hospital or clinic settings. They argue that 'the strong belief systems of most Africans make careful study of local healers and working partnerships a key strategy for good healthcare. At a minimum, health workers must know and respect local language, beliefs, and practices if they are to succeed' (Bennet and Rohde 2008: 538). Such collaborations have been noted to ensure an effective, ethical and value-laden relationship that contributes to the overall well-being of patients (Read 2019; Arias et al. 2016).

Research has demonstrated that situations where biomedical practitioners fail to collaborate often lead to chaos, with patients bearing the brunt of such confrontations (Taylor 2003; Fadiman 1997; Kleinman 1980). Indeed, these conflicts typically arise from cultural differences and divergent 'explanatory models' attributed to illness and what is considered effective or ineffective treatment. In the article 'The Story Catches You and You Fall Down', Janelle S. Taylor (2003) reflects on the tragic case of a young Hmong girl, as narrated in *The Spirit Catches You* by Anne Fadiman. Taylor (2003) highlights how the uncompromising stance of an American-trained physician at a hospital in Merced, California, regarding the 'explanatory model' of epilepsy (as influenced by a divine spirit) presented by the parents of the young girl named Lia Lee, resulted in catastrophic consequences for the four-year-old girl. Recounting the destructive effects of the situation on both the girl and her family, Taylor (2003) argues that a compromise on the part of the physician could have facilitated effective cross-cultural communication, potentially preventing the subsequent comatose state that befell the young girl. As she argues, this situation exemplified a clash or 'collision of cultures' that produced detrimental effects on the child's health. Therefore, Taylor (2003) underscores the importance and necessity of 'cultural competence' in medical practice, emphasizing the need for physicians and healthcare practitioners to be trained to understand 'cultural differences' within their field. This promotes cultural sensitivity, as evidenced in the experiences of the aforementioned nurse, and encourages the adoption of mediation and negotiation strategies by healthcare professionals, resulting in overall effective medical care and the prevention of negative health outcomes for patients.

In Ghana, for instance, many of the tensions or opposing views between prayer camps and international human rights organizations, as well as some health professionals, can be attributed to a lack of proper understanding of the complexities of cross-cultural medicine, ineffective communication and differences in the context of healing and medicine concerning the 'explanatory models' of the causes of mental illness.

Impact on lived experiences of people living with mental illness

Although some participants demonstrated nonadherence to biomedical care, they maintained a positive perspective regarding the efficacy of biomedicine, as evidenced by the case of a participant previously cited in Chapter 6. Several participants articulated a favourable view of the integration of biomedicine into their overall well-being and health outcomes. Some participants contended that the combination of prayer and medication has contributed to the enhancement of their condition. For instance, one participant noted that while the medication prescribed for her was beneficial in alleviating some of her symptoms, it did not completely eliminate them. She reported that she had been visiting the hospital for approximately five years until someone recommended the prayer camp. However, she indicated that her condition had significantly improved since she began attending the prayer camp while continuing her medication. She reflected:

> I have been going to the … hospital for five years now. At some other time, I will see things are a bit okay but then it start getting worse again. This has been happening for 5 years now until someone asked me to come. I can say that things are okay compared to my previous situation … I have been here for 2 months now and I'm hoping everything will be fine.

One of the primary domains in which participants reported positive outcomes was among individuals whose mental health conditions were exacerbated by behavioural factors such as smoking and alcohol consumption. In certain cases, excessive alcohol intake and smoking have contributed to the development of dissociative disorders, characterized by loss of identity, disruptions in memory, altered self-perceptions and impaired behavioural controls, as well as multiple personality disorders. For these individuals, the medication administered at the camp proved effective in alleviating anxiety and addressing bodily dysfunction resulting from substance abuse. In addition to medication, participants expressed optimism regarding their stay at the camp, attributing their improvements in well-being and health outcomes to prayer and counselling. For example, one participant indicated:

> You know something maybe if I was not here, I would have been somewhere doing my own things. You know what I mean right. But staying here has really helped me. Now I can say that I am gradually overcoming all the things I found it hard to overcome. We go to church, they prayer to us. We do bible studies and the counselling too. I have been taking my medications. They both help me at the same time. So is good. With all that has happened I didn't even consider myself as important. I loss several jobs and that has started affecting the way I think and everything. Now is good as you can see.

For this participant, although the medication had aided him in managing specific challenges stemming from alcohol abuse, he expressed a positive perspective on his experience at the camp, perceiving it as a contributor to his overall well-being.

While some individuals expressed affirmative views regarding adherence to both prayer and medication, others did not share this sentiment. For those who opposed this dual approach, the primary rationale was their belief that there was no justification for receiving injections or medications when their issues were diagnosed by the prophet as entirely spiritual. Conversely, other participants who had been concurrently taking medication and receiving prayers found that their conditions had not improved to the extent they had anticipated, resulting in feelings of dissatisfaction and a desire for discharge from the camp. Unfortunately, the circumstances of these participants did not allow for further investigation. Nonetheless, this indicates that not all individuals receiving treatment at the prayer camps were content with their care, irrespective of whether it was biomedical or spiritual.

The experiences of individuals who do not achieve recovery despite receiving treatment – be it spiritual, biomedical or a combination of both – illuminate the fluctuations commonly associated with mental illnesses. While some individuals may recover, occasionally without medication, it is evident that not everyone will have the same experience. For some of these individuals, the environment of the prayer camp becomes a space to find solace amidst the persistent nature of their illness. Consequently, the impact can be realized not solely in the tangible outcomes of their conditions but also in the resilience cultivated to emotionally withstand the devastating effects that often accompany chronic or persistent mental illnesses. In certain cases, it is this resilience that generates both social and spiritual capital, which in turn enhances their transformation and restoration to a state of normalcy.

Challenges to collaboration

In addition to several challenges already highlighted in previous studies, I would like to address three additional challenges identified during the course of this study.

Interactions with health professionals collaborating with prayer camps revealed that the staff at these camps had not received training in obtaining a patient's medical history upon their arrival. For instance, they were inadequately informed about the timing of the patient's initial episode, among other pertinent factors. This lack of training created significant challenges, as healthcare providers often did not possess the necessary information to administer appropriate treatment during emergency situations and frequently lacked the resources to transport patients to healthcare facilities. It was suggested that basic training would enable camp staff to accurately record patients' medical histories, which would also assist in tracking the number of patients entering and exiting the camp. The health professional argued that the provision of such records by prayer camp staff would enhance their collaboration with the camp, as it would supply them with essential information regarding the patients. As part of her recommendations to address this issue, the medical practitioner advocated for the introduction of a folder system at the camp to help mitigate these challenges. She asserted:

> When I was working there, there are things I wished, or I always urge that the government will help us initiate. The folder was one aspect. Then maybe a card to monitor their treatment. I'm sure currently in Ghana … so if the government regulate it, then some of the things happening at this place in Eastern or Central region could be repeated elsewhere.

Additionally, the medical practitioner raised concerns regarding the format of the reporting system employed by the Ghana Health Service. She indicated that while the Ghana Health Service mandates the submission of a monthly report detailing activities in relation to their collaboration with prayer camps, the current format of the reporting system restricts their ability to provide a comprehensive account, thereby limiting the opportunity to present critical aspects of their engagement with prayer camps. This issue could be ameliorated by adequately equipping medical practitioners collaborating with prayer camps to submit comprehensive reports to the appropriate department of the Ghana Health Service, thereby ensuring that they remain well-informed and can devise strategies and mechanisms to enhance their collaboration with prayer camps and the delivery of mental healthcare services through the community support system.

Although the challenge posed by entrenched religious beliefs in supernatural explanations for illnesses has been emphasized, particularly in studies conducted by Arias et al. (2016), I would like to reiterate this issue here. As previously noted, one of the camps selected for this study did not endorse the use of medication for the treatment of ailments. This belief, which has been associated with certain Pentecostal movements in Ghana, obstructs the possibility of collaboration. Consequently, such entrenched positions hinder a progressive approach to healthcare that has the potential to address the needs of the populations they aim to serve.

Decolonizing psychiatry and mental health

Several scholars in the field of global mental health, including Heaton (2020), Fernando (2014), Mills (2014), Hickling (2020, 2021) and Ratele (2019), have underscored the necessity of decolonizing perspectives on mental health, particularly within post-colonial contexts. This imperative has become increasingly urgent due to the tendency for the universal application of health systems, especially in mental healthcare, which frequently do not function effectively in settings different from those in which these modalities were developed. For instance, there are prevalent assumptions that Euro-American categories and concepts have universal applicability, combined with a reliance on evidence-based interventions derived from Euro-American models and research. Although efforts have been made to address these discrepancies through the development of *DSM-5*, the cultural complexity and ambiguity, alongside the dynamics of interpretation, the varied manifestations of symptoms of illness and the evolving nature of mental illness influenced by diverse environmental factors, continue to create intricate narratives surrounding the diagnosis and treatment of mental health conditions.

Furthermore, while previous studies advocating for collaboration between biomedical practitioners and TFH have identified tensions arising from post-colonial legacies and differences in conceptual frameworks and interpretations, it appears that none of the existing studies conducted in Ghana have explicitly called for the decolonization of mental health as a component of collaborative efforts. Although decolonial perspectives on mental healthcare may be perceived by some as a means of totalizing and reifying cultural experiences and narratives, they actually advocate for the recognition of local cosmologies within the complex global narratives of care and support. I contend that a decolonial approach would be significant in addressing and alleviating some of the obstacles currently identified as hindrances to collaboration. In fact, there exists a tendency or high risk of perpetuating the problems we observe today as impediments to collaboration if a decolonial approach to the practice of psychiatry and mental healthcare is disregarded, particularly in contexts such as Ghana and other African nations.

Indeed, recent historical scholarship on the evolution of post-colonial psychiatry in Africa has underscored how colonial psychiatry propagated ideas and ideologies that had far-reaching implications for all aspects of life for colonized individuals (Heaton 2018, 2013; Zadowsky 1999). Given the pervasive influence of colonial psychiatry and its role in reinforcing social order, including health and medicine for colonized populations, it is unsurprising that many historians of post-colonial psychiatry have sought to revise our understanding of both colonialism and the social history of medicine through their examinations of colonial psychiatry concerning indigenous populations in Africa from the early nineteenth century to the decolonization period (Kilroy-Marac 2019; Pringle 2019; Linstrum 2016; Keller 2001). These studies not only address the colonial construction of psychiatry but also seek to investigate the processes of change that have occurred in the aftermath of colonialism. In doing so, the literature complicates the discourses surrounding the colonial approach to the treatment of mental illness in relation to African traditional frameworks.

Mapping prayer camps in decolonial discourses on psychiatry

Prayer camps, as Christian religious institutions, embody inherent ambiguities within post-colonial discourses regarding mental health in Ghana. This ambiguity stems from the view that Christianity was initially imposed during the colonial era, disseminating largely through the establishment of educational institutions, healthcare facilities and other similar establishments. As discussed in Chapter 4, missionaries encountered challenges in accepting Akan converts who sought recourse to traditional medicine for health-related issues. The dichotomy between Christianity and traditional or indigenous medicine was notably exemplified by the colonial administration's denigration of Akan traditions. Such denigration has persisted within certain Ghanaian Christian groups, where traditional or indigenous religions and their associated practices – such as Akan shrines and the roles of priests and priestesses – are frequently characterized as manifestations of malevolent forces, thus regarded as demonic and 'primitive'. Furthermore, the Pentecostal movement, from which the prayer camps originate, has demonstrated a pronounced aversion to traditional religions, often demonizing indigenous cultures and religious practices while striving to reform these systems by eliminating practices considered outdated and obstructive to progress in contemporary society (Kalu 2008; Meyer 1999; Piot 2010).

Despite the existing tensions between the Pentecostal movement and traditional cultures, numerous scholars in Pentecostal and charismatic studies argue that the success of Pentecostalism, wherever it has thrived, can be attributed to the appropriation of primal world-views (Premawardhana 2018; Kalu 2008; Omenyo 2002; Cox 2001). As previously discussed, similarities can be identified between Pentecostals and the early African Indigenous Churches (AICs) regarding healing practices, as emphasized by Omenyo (2014). Healing, broadly understood within the Pentecostal tradition and within the context of prayer camps in Ghana, can be framed within indigenous world-views. Consequently, while a case may be made regarding the tension between Christianity and traditional religions, there exists a persistent reality of indigenous cultural world-views manifesting within the practices of prayer camps, particularly in relation to healing. Indeed, it is this framework of understanding and significance attributed to healing that renders the healing practices at prayer camps in Ghana appealing to the general public, as they address issues rooted in the cosmological and/or indigenous world-views of the people. The socio-cultural web of meanings associated with illness, as understood through indigenous knowledge systems, coupled with the diverse healing approaches and practices employed at prayer camps, aligns with Ghanaian cultural and therapeutic paradigms. Both Pentecostalism and indigenous knowledge systems conceptualize healing as encompassing liberation from attacks and oppression by demonic and malevolent forces (Benyah 2024). This aspect has been inadequately addressed in numerous studies that focus on healing and mental health in Ghana.

Therefore, while prayer camps may be perceived as conflicting with traditional religious practices, a thorough critical evaluation reveals that they are, in fact, a reinvention of traditional healing practices (Asamoah-Gyadu 2007; Onyinah 2012). This evolution presents an opportunity rather than a challenge within post-colonial approaches to mental healthcare. Since the views and approaches to healing are largely similar but occur in different healing settings with distinct religious functionaries, they provide a potential framework for intervention programmes that amalgamate both healing traditions into a unified approach to addressing mental health issues. I acknowledge that while this may appear straightforward in theory, it is considerably more complex in practice.

Within post-colonial discourses, the primary concerns centre on how the two religious institutions can be equipped and retooled – whether through education, training or enhanced resource capacity – to effectively address mental health challenges, as both institutions engage with cultural, religious and traditional realities and utilize language that resonates with the community. This is exemplified by the discussion on mental illness as *sunsum yareɛ* in Chapter 3, alongside other local linguistic interpretations that resist straightforward comprehension within universal frameworks, thereby creating epistemic challenges in mental healthcare. Nonetheless, prayer camps and indigenous healers navigate these challenges proficiently.

The observation concerning the social control exerted by prayer camps among the Ghanaian populace is substantiated by the research of Ae-Ngibise et al. (2010). Ae-Ngibise et al. (2010) investigated the factors contributing to the widespread appeal of TFHs in Ghana, further identifying the forces that could facilitate a seamless 'bi-sectorial partnership' or impede the relationship between faith healers and biomedical care providers for mental health patients. Their findings indicated that TFHs resonate significantly with respondents, as these practices align with their cultural explanatory models of disease aetiology and are simultaneously more available, accessible and affordable in comparison to other treatment options, such as biomedical care. In Chapter 6, I examined how the causal narratives surrounding mental illnesses in Ghana are intrinsically linked to local ontologies. One key inference drawn was that the Pentecostal understanding and interpretation of illness are reframed within the traditional Akan paradigm. In other words, it is feasible to map Pentecostal healing discourses onto indigenous or traditional world-views. To fully comprehend the systems of healing and the behaviours of individuals in seeking healthcare, it is imperative to consider foundational cultural nosology[2] and specific cultural explanations or causal attributions that confer legitimacy to particular forms of health and healing practices within a designated cultural milieu.

It is well established that colonialism has had a profound impact on African medicine by providing solutions to health problems faced by Africans. However, colonial ideologies, methodologies and systems of medical practice and health administration ensured that access to preferred treatment was not universally available (Heaton 2018). Consequently, the indigenous health systems that existed prior to colonialism 'continued to compete effectively with biomedicine for the trust and care of African patients' (Heaton 2018: 315). Indeed, the African reception of European medicine varied considerably depending on the context. Scholars have grappled with and continue to engage with this dimension of medical history by examining the political, social, technological and professional aspects of medical taxonomy, particularly in the field of psychiatry.

Research in transcultural psychiatry, medical anthropology and the social history of psychiatry in Africa has illuminated the complex and often conflicting relationships between biomedicine and traditional healing systems in mental health care (Pringle 2019; Heaton 2018; Mohr 2013). This is particularly evident in the ways narratives surrounding African psychiatry have been constructed. Matthew H. Heaton (2020), for example, notes that the history of psychiatry in Africa is intricately linked to the processes of European colonialism and imperialist ideologies. He observes that a limited but coherent historiography has effectively demonstrated how European conceptions of mental illness and their associated treatment methods were entangled with 'racist and paternalistic ideologies of European imperialism in the early twentieth century' (Heaton 2020: 82). One of the initiatives to address this concern is articulated by Heaton (2013) in his work *Black Skin, White Coats*, wherein he suggests that Nigerian psychiatrists, for instance, positioned themselves as 'gatekeepers who negotiated and blurred the boundaries between indigenous/colonised and Western/colonial knowledge bases and power structures' (2013: 15).[3]

To reinvigorate the narrative, African scholars who began writing during the colonial and post-colonial eras faced the challenge of not only deconstructing the Eurocentric paradigm that governed the historiography of African healing systems and medicine but also training African physicians to address the medical needs of their communities (Heaton 2018). In Nigeria, for instance, Heaton (2020) posits that one approach adopted to decolonize mental health was led by indigenous Nigerian psychiatrists who pursued a nationalist agenda aimed at reconstructing colonial knowledge and practices surrounding mental health. A parallel example can be observed in Ghana, particularly in the case of Emmanuel B. Forster, who was the first African psychiatrist to practise in the country with a similar vision (Read and Doku 2013). This agenda facilitated the implementation of culturally sensitive methods of research and practice. The objective of these African writers and practitioners was to reconstruct or reformulate the corpus of ideas, technologies and theories that had been undermined by the colonial intelligentsia or to revive ethnoscience or philosophy. However, it is notable that African scholars appeared to have adopted 'an approach similar to the North American or Western European one: that science and religion are at one level rigorously separate domains, while at another level [they] all struggle with zones of tension and interpretation' (Feierman and Janzen 2011: 244). Such tensions arose from the fact that many early African-trained psychologists were educated in the West, where they were influenced by certain ideologies of Western science. This often presented challenges in reconciling their previously held traditional beliefs with those of medical science. Indeed, 'one cannot maintain that there is a common field of medicine but rather that there are parallel medical worlds that compete, overlap, and clash' (Vähäkangas 2015: 5). What post-colonial African writers and scholars sought to achieve was to provide a mechanism or synthesis of ideas within a broader scientific-religious field characterized by diverse perspectives, aimed at integrating traditional knowledge systems of healing and medicine with those of biomedicine (Feierman and Janzen 2011).

Following this consensus, one persistent challenge has been the processes necessary to ensure a mutual integration of a healthcare system that incorporates traditional knowledge systems of healing alongside biomedicine as articulated by previous studies on collaboration between biomedical practitioners and TFH for mental healthcare. Feierman and Janzen (2011: 244) acknowledge this challenge, arguing that numerous scholars in Africa have reflected on the broader context and responded by attempting to 'forge an original and characteristically African synthesis of science and religion' in conjunction with biomedicine. They contend that 'any attempt to reconnect historic knowledge with modern science in Africa must be part of a universal science in order to be credible' (Feierman and Janzen 2011: 244). While this notion appears commendable, inherent tendencies of mistrust and scepticism towards various treatment modalities obstruct a universally accepted foundation for cooperation and collaboration. This was evident in the subsequent conflicts and tensions that arose within the field of practice, as identified in several studies, which highlight the obstacles to effective collaboration between biomedical professionals and TFH.

Feierman and Janzen (2011) have noted that the Ghanaian philosopher Gyekye, who has critically examined the historical interplay of thought, technology and religion in pre-colonial and post-colonial Africa, offers a comprehensive framework for reconciling African science with Western scientific paradigms. They highlight Gyekye's identification, through his analysis of pre-colonial history, of how the extensive and innovative advancements in African medicine and technology are deeply rooted in empirical innovations and adaptations. However, Feierman and Janzen, reflecting Gyekye's insights, assert that a significant deficiency within the pre-colonial tradition of African science, when analysed through the lens of Western science, is the absence of scientific theories that generate knowledge for its own sake and accommodate the diverse abstract reasoning characteristic of modern science.

From Gyekye's (2013) perspective, the pervasive secrecy surrounding African traditional knowledge represents a considerable obstacle to scientific advancement. Feierman and Janzen observe that while Gyekye acknowledges 'the rich empirical observations and practical techniques of African arts', he maintains that 'the tendency to ascribe knowledge to spiritual agents must be addressed in order to reconcile this knowledge with the hallmarks of modern science, namely experimentation and sustained investigation' (2013: 245). In other words, Gyekye argues that beliefs in the supernatural or the reliance on spiritual mediums for the diagnosis and treatment of ailments are detrimental and carry negative implications. Gyekye's perspective aligns with that of Candy Gunther Brown in her introduction to the edited volume on *Global Pentecostal and Charismatic Healing*, in which she emphasizes that 'spiritual causes and cures for human suffering do not always produce unequivocally healthful results. Supernaturalism can obscure the pathogenic impact of political and economic globalisation and deflect attention from engaging in constructive reforms of a more material nature' (Brown 2011: 10). Furthermore, Brown contends that 'at its worst, a supernaturalised model of sickness and healing encourages already-suffering individuals to internalise blame for failures that could instead be traced to systemic oppression of those very individuals by more powerful individuals, groups, and impersonal material forces, many of which are external to but act upon their local situations' (2011: 10).

While I find the concerns raised by Gyekye and Brown (2011) to be pertinent in the context of certain reported practices of healing rituals that are deemed injurious and diminish any potential for restoration and hope in religious healing (Edwards 2014), I also disagree, particularly with Gyekye's argument. This is because Gyekye's perspective does not appear to align seamlessly with distinctive African methods of diagnosing and proposing solutions to illness and medical conditions. For many Africans, and more specifically Ghanaians, the attribution of diseases and the utilization of spirit mediums have always been prevalent. This aspect seems to be central to healing practices, most of which have faced criticism from Western perspectives. Konadu (2007), in his study of Akan medicine in Ghana, posits that the understanding and interpretation of cosmology informs or almost determines the conception and understanding of therapy and disease causation.

A substantial body of literature has described traditional healing as a form of African psychotherapy (Field 1960; Forster 1962), wherein, through the spirit mediums, information is elicited from individuals experiencing illness during the healing process. In Ghana, the practice of *abisa* (meaning divine consultation) at indigenous healing shrines or cults (Field 1960) and, in the case of prayer camps, the practice of *akwankyere* exemplify many of these traditions (Onyinah 2012). Sundberg (2020) explores how spirit medium practices, such as revelation and dreams, play a crucial role in the prescription and application of medicine in the form of leaves or herbs for the treatment of various ailments.

In examining the views expressed by Konadu, Azevedo raises the issue that if the understanding derived from African conceptions of the human being posits that the individual is a spiritual entity, then 'how intellectually suspicious are the theories claiming that Africans always invoke supernatural causes for diseases, when their actual iteration refers to the natural, that is, the man "spirit-encapsulated" and not to a spirit in the skies, in the tomb, or in the realms of the ancestors' (Azevedo 2017: 95). From this perspective, Konadu questions the viewpoints of Western researchers who neglect 'the nature of workings of traditional systems, divorced from their indigenous cultural reality and values, and uncritically accept and identify with Eurocentric conceptualisations of Africa to the extent that they have created African versions of things' (Konadu 2008: 179). It is important to emphasize that most African theories of disease causation do not disregard the natural or biological causes of illness. In fact, as already mentioned, Onyinah (2012) has observed that, among the Akans of Ghana, individuals only resort to supernatural means of cure when all attempts to seek medical care, including biomedicine, have failed, and the consequences of the disease have become severe.

The relationship between African indigenous knowledge systems of healthcare or traditional medicine and biomedicine has been characterized by antagonism, mistrust and suspicion (Anyinam 1997). Nonetheless, an examination of the two reveals various converging points that could be harnessed, integrated and implemented to provide much-needed universal and holistic healthcare. In some parts of Africa, traditional medicine has, for instance, been incorporated into the general healthcare system and reformulated as a new system of scientific knowledge to augment the development of biomedicine and healthcare, as well as to support the advancement of modern scientific expertise (Meincke 2015).

This integration allows for 'culturally sensitive' approaches, mediation and negotiation rather than an opposing and intolerable stance that sometimes produces negative consequences for patients' health (Taylor 2003). Understanding one's cultural past and history, as well as methods of healing, is an important starting point that could shape discussion and provide a platform for cross-cultural negotiation and dialogue necessary for the incorporation and integration of TFH with biomedicine for effective and holistic healthcare. This should form the basis of the post-colonial approaches to mental healthcare which the prayer camps under study presents both the physical and spiritual infrastructure as well as rich variety of cosmologies and healing practices that can help decontextualize universal frameworks.

Summary

There is no doubt that the significance of religion and faith exerts a persistent influence on the lives of many Ghanaians, particularly regarding health and healing. The prominence of religion and faith in healthcare, especially among individuals seeking solutions for mental health conditions, has prompted various state and non-state actors to investigate the role of religion in the provision of mental healthcare in Ghana. The necessity for such intersectoral partnerships between biomedicine and faith healing has also attracted the attention of numerous scholars examining the intersection between TFH and mental healthcare in Ghana.

Previous studies, along with the findings of this study, indicate that culture and traditional world-views continue to exert a significant influence on individuals' lives, as religion is an integral part of the cultural fabric. Cultural world-views and practices shape healing systems grounded in local ontologies, which manifest in the operations of local institutions, such as prayer camps. To a large extent, the healing practices at prayer camps reflect the cultural and religious world-views of Ghanaian societies and derive their values and efficacy from the entrenched cultural knowledge of health and healing. To effectively operate within such a cultural context, it is crucial to mobilize these institutional mechanisms to adequately address the healthcare needs of the populace. Nonetheless, questions regarding institutional authority, safety and efficacy will persist as concerns. These issues can, however, be addressed through a system of dialogue and effective communication, conducted in a respectful and interactive process that eschews displays of power, authority and hierarchical differences that are formalized through established institutions of power.

What remains essential is finding ways to understand the cosmologies, ontologies and metaphoric frameworks of disease aetiologies that hold meaning for the respective communities or audiences within Ghanaian society and collaboratively adopting models that will address those world-views. In some instances, this may necessitate a decolonial approach or methodologies, as discussed in this chapter, to effectively translate and meet the needs of the population; otherwise, they may remain underserved. In terms of decolonizing approaches to mental healthcare, areas of concern include ontological considerations focusing on the beliefs and world-views that form the aetiological theories of the people, as well as the therapeutic pathways deemed meaningful and influential in shaping behaviours and therapeutic choices.

In the final chapter, I provide concluding remarks and recommendations based on the findings of the study.

CONCLUSION

The analysis and findings presented in this book confirm or reaffirm the conclusions of previous studies, particularly those related to the role of religion in health and healing across sub-Saharan Africa (Olsen and Sargent 2017; Janzen 1978). Significantly, the findings substantiate the beliefs individuals hold regarding religion as a source of therapeutic intervention when they are unwell. The beliefs and diagnoses attributed to illness influence the help-seeking behaviours of patients and their relatives. In this book, patients and caregivers at the selected prayer camps expressed a positive perspective on the role of religion in managing and coping with mental illness. Resources such as prayers, Bible studies, counselling and communal relationships within the camp between caregivers and patients assisted individuals in managing anxieties, fears, recurrent behaviours and fostering hope in the treatment and healing of their ailments.

The favourable attitude towards belief in religious and spiritual resources for addressing mental illness did not deter participants from utilizing other methods, such as biomedicine. Leaders of selected prayer camps exhibited a collaborative spirit with health professionals, permitting the intervention of alternative healing options when necessary. This effort to integrate other healing modalities into the activities of prayer camps provided a platform to augment scientific interventions with spirituality as a means of complementing and satisfying individuals' notions and ideas about healing. Such efforts were crucial in delivering a holistic approach to healing that resonated with the beliefs of the community. As a progressive society, these initiatives contribute profitably to the efforts made by government institutions such as Mental Health Authority (MHA) and medical professionals in promoting holistic well-being in the face of limited resources, particularly in the realm of mental healthcare.

The discussion underscores the fact that the overall understanding of how the Akan perceive the concept of the person and its ontological relationship with the cosmos has implications for mental health. While good health is contingent upon the harmony of the mind, body and soul within the individual, there is also a necessity for a relationship with society to be considered healthy. Moreover, the general understanding of, and belief in, the existence of supernatural beings in the cosmos renders individuals particularly susceptible to their environment. On one hand, individuals may fear the afflictions that might befall them if they contravene society's sanctioned moral codes or established norms. Conversely, there exists a strong belief in the ability of certain individuals to manipulate cosmic powers for malevolent purposes, resulting in the affliction of various ailments, including mental illness. Collectively, these factors influence how individuals relate to their environment, to one another within society, and how illness – specifically mental illness – is constructed. The conceptualization of mental illness by participants at prayer camps must be understood within this framework, as it is inherently linked to Akan traditional interpretations and world-views concerning the causes of illness and healing. In seeking solutions to the issue of mental illness, the Akan do not solely rely on biomedical treatment but also on other therapeutic interventions, such as religious healing, which align with their cultural and belief systems.

In Ghana, belief systems are sustained by cosmological views, which continue to guide individuals' attitudes and approaches to the treatment of mental illness and other health issues more broadly. Post-colonial authors addressing African psychiatry have sought to decolonize the discourses surrounding mental health in Africa and facilitate the integration of perspectives that resonate with psychiatric practices in post-colonial societies (Pringle 2019). Prayer camps in Ghana represent institutions from which one can conceivably learn about the integration of traditional or indigenous belief systems in the care of the mentally ill.

Another inference drawn from the discussion is the imperative of understanding the cultural context and its significance to health and healing. It is essential to appreciate the way of life of individuals without prejudicing what is deemed important in alternative settings. In Ghana, the navigation of different healing modalities in the pursuit of a cure by individuals living with mental illness and their families not only reveals the urgency of reconciling with their conditions but also highlights the endemic and enduring nature of cultural meanings associated with illness. It is critical to comprehend that the varied interpretations of health and healing found in different parts of the world will ultimately lead to the emergence of different medical taxonomies that may not be universally applicable.

Although the prospects of any medical or healing system, whether scientific or otherwise, cannot be dismissed, such prospects are largely contingent upon the value placed on them by the individuals who benefit from those systems. In other words, what is deemed positive in terms of medical care depends on the outcomes experienced by the patients receiving those services. Despite advancements in medical science and healthcare treatment, there are still individuals who utilize traditional, religious or alternative forms of medicine for health purposes. Even in so-called developed nations with sophisticated medical systems, people continue to resort to alternative medicines, including forms of religious healing (Brown 2013; McGuire 2008). Largely, these practices, as demonstrated by the discussion, arise from cultural and traditional notions and conceptions of health and healing. While scientific methods exist for treating illnesses, religious approaches to healing employ various divinatory and ritualistic practices that are meaningful and provide participants with the emotional and transformative experiences they seek.

While it may be challenging to measure or quantify the outcomes of healing experienced by individuals following prayer or religious rituals, it is feasible to assess the curative value derived from such ritual practices. The crux of the matter lies in the perceived conflict between biomedicine and religious healing. However, there is no irrationality in integrating diagnostic processes that blend scientific and religious healing if they yield the desired outcomes. After all, individuals navigate between different healing spaces in Ghana in their quest for a cure for illness, illustrating how they can maintain parallel orientations towards diverse medical systems and remain receptive to both.

Despite the fact that scientific advancements in medicine have yielded unequivocal results, certain regions of the world continue to lack access to sophisticated medical technologies. In resource-limited countries, for instance, there remain opportunities for improvement in enhancing the delivery of medical care and practice. In such contexts, it is imprudent to entirely dismiss practices that have historically provided necessary solutions to medical conditions. To dismiss such practices amount to what could be described as throwing away the baby with the bathwater in psychiatric practices, for example (Leff 1990). The marginalization of religious and indigenous cultural practices as backward, primitive or archaic in the face of contemporary technological and scientific advancements can result in potentially detrimental consequences for healthcare. The World Health Organization has acknowledged this need and has made several efforts to integrate cultural knowledge and experience into the treatment of mental illness as part of primary healthcare requirements.

While culture has emerged as a salient and unique category warranting exploration in mental healthcare, it has also generated an empire of nosological hegemony, wherein various conceptions of mental disorders become central to academic inquiry and clinical practice. At times, this has resulted in the production of disparate epistemic frameworks that highlight positionalities in the categorization, understanding and interpretation of mental illness, as well as in the competing relationships between biomedical service providers and faith healers in Ghana and throughout the African continent. This scenario presents both a challenge and a resource. It is a challenge because such approaches introduce a competing system within an already heightened medically pluralistic environment. As a resource, the diverse frameworks provide an opportunity for researchers and practitioners to reassess their own positions and potentially seek appropriate channels that can serve as common ground in the treatment and assessment of mental illnesses.

*

Textbooks and literature on religion and mental health, particularly those pertaining to Africa, seldom address methodological issues or the ways in which past studies have been conducted using approaches that are contextually appropriate. Research in mental health has predominantly employed a top-down approach. It is evident in much of the literature that there is a pressing need to adopt innovative methodologies that recognize cultural contexts and individuals' perceptions of their environment when interpreting illness. The implementation of a universalist-relativist approach, or, preferably, endogenous techniques, could be beneficial in expanding the scope of mental healthcare.

Cosmologies of Mental Health has highlighted how the experience of illness is shaped by cultural understandings and interpretations. This has been corroborated by previous studies on health and healing in Africa and globally. A critical aspect of illness interpretation is the philosophical framework that underlies theories of causation and the methods employed to address them. This underscores the significant role that indigenous knowledge systems play in the interpretation of illness, particularly in the domain of mental health (see e.g. Danto and Zangeneh 2022; Wambebe 2018; Stewart et al. 2017).

According to UNESCO (2021), indigenous knowledge refers to the ways in which a society develops its own understanding, skills and ideologies over time through interaction with its environment. These knowledge systems form the basis upon which decisions are made in everyday life. In other words, they serve as the fulcrum around which life and societal issues are addressed and resolved. This knowledge is central to the cultural complexities that encompass areas such as language, systems of classification, ritual and spirituality. The ritual and spiritual dimensions may include world-views, various religious practices, spirit mediums and other intermediaries that influence economic, political, social and health matters. UNESCO (2021) argues that these fundamental aspects of knowledge formation and systems of knowing are part of 'cultural diversity and provide a foundation for locally appropriate sustainable development' across all domains of life.

This book has demonstrated that indigenous perceptions and world-views of illness play a crucial role in healthcare systems, the communication of health matters and the resolution mechanisms employed. Thus, an understanding of indigenous knowledge systems related to illness is essential for conveying illness experiences and serves as a foundation for a broader exploration of issues pertaining to mental illness.

The implication of this is that research studies and projects aimed at addressing health-related matters, whether within the field of psychiatry or otherwise, must take significant measures to comprehend local knowledge systems and how these shape understandings of health and healing within the health economy of the populations involved in such studies. A particular example is the concept of the person, which relates to the understanding of health and healing, and how this concept informs individuals' perspectives on health and the healing approaches that they utilize.

Despite the mounting evidence that the concept of the person is gradually gaining traction in discourses surrounding culture, religion and mental health, current studies in Ghana indicate that such concepts have generally been subordinated to broader ethnographic and clinical objectives in mental health research conducted in the country. While individuals occupy a central and integrative role in mental healthcare, the question remains as to how well those who seek to engage or treat individuals with mental illnesses understand the people they serve, including their perceptions or interpretations of illness and the perceived causes of their suffering.

Methodologically, there is a need to develop approaches that can adapt to local contexts and understandings of illness. The concept of the person, as elucidated in Akan thought, for example, provides insight into how health, well-being and the causes of diseases are derived from or articulated through the construction of personhood. The pertinent question is, how can we adopt definitions and methodological tools that will help elicit individuals' own understandings and meanings of health and healing? Any methodology or approach that is divorced from indigenous cultural realities and values risks uncritically imposing external views and conceptualizations of illness that may be alien to specific contexts and could undermine potential outcomes that address existential challenges in mental healthcare and healthcare in general. In this sense, developing indigenous knowledge frameworks or systems as models for research in religion, mental health and culture may serve as schemas and provide alternative approaches for understanding mental health and healing in diverse cultural settings.

The development of indigenous models will be crucial not only for highlighting the significance of the cosmologies of health and healing but also for elucidating the knowledge and philosophical underpinnings that seek to describe the meanings, root causes or explanations of diseases. This is imperative as the existential meanings of illness vary across cultures. For instance, within the traditional Ghanaian context, and specifically among the Akan, a disease condition is perceived as more than a mere physical ailment. This necessitates a broader examination of the range of factors within individuals' cultural and cosmological views that elucidate the causes and meanings of diseases, including mental illness. Furthermore, illnesses such as HIV/AIDS have narratives that are also embedded within religious and cultural contexts (Crentsil 2007). For biomedical health professionals, psychiatrists or psychologists, it is essential to cultivate cultural and religious competence to understand community cosmological world-views regarding health, illness and treatment. This is vital for fostering collaborative engagement.

*

Technological advancement has significantly contributed to modern innovations in the field of biomedicine, providing substantial benefits to the well-being and welfare of numerous individuals globally. While these innovations are essential in addressing human health needs, it is also true that technology has not provided solutions to all healthcare requirements. There is a growing concern that contemporary biomedical treatments do not adequately meet the healthcare needs of populations, culminating in a rising interest in non-conventional therapies worldwide. However, the inclination of individuals to seek non-conventional therapies cannot be entirely attributed to the failures or ineffectiveness of scientific technologies; rather, it corresponds with their cultural beliefs, interpretations and practices regarding illness. I have argued that the drive for individuals in regions such as Ghana and elsewhere in Africa to seek religious and spiritual solutions to their health issues does not necessarily indicate a lack of medical infrastructure, as some have suggested (Benyah 2024). Instead, this inclination arises from beliefs associated with the interpretation of their illnesses. Notably, individuals in so-called Western developed countries also explore alternative forms of medicine, including spiritual healing.

As discussed in this book, every society has developed its healing institutions and practices based on a shared understanding of human nature and the causes of suffering. Despite the challenges posed by colonial ideologies and systems of medical governance, local systems and knowledge of medicine and healing have evolved, enduring the test of time and continuing to thrive with popular support. In Ghana, as discussed, institutions such as prayer camps have emerged as 'informal healthcare' centres that offer healing services that are culturally and religiously meaningful to their constituents. Although not recognized as psychiatric centres led by trained professionals, the inclusion of biomedical care at prayer camps through collaboration with health professionals renders these camps similar to Aro Village, established by Lambo in Nigeria, and the Fann Psychiatric Clinic in Senegal, led by Henri Collomb (Antic 2024). While these institutions were staffed by trained psychiatrists, they incorporated culturally meaningful symbolic healing elements into their patient care.

As Christian institutions, prayer camps may be viewed as part of colonial legacies; however, they simultaneously offer religious healing rituals that blend Christian and indigenous or traditional forms of spirituality while appearing modern and global by integrating biomedical care through their engagement with health professionals. These collaborations present significant opportunities for decolonizing mental healthcare and psychiatric practice in Ghana and beyond. The recourse to institutions such as prayer camps should not be perceived as a backward or primitive approach to healthcare but rather as integral to the beliefs and practices of local communities. In the field of psychiatric practices, prayer camps could be engaged as 'local healing practices in productive and efficient ways', particularly in terms of how 'local conceptualisations of psychological suffering could shape mainstream clinical research' (Antic 2024: 158; see also Pringle 2019).

In addressing medical conditions such as mental illness, which are deeply rooted in cultural nosology, it is imperative that we draw from institutions grounded in specific socio-cultural contexts that provide meaning to local communities. The prayer camps in Ghana exemplify such institutions, offering avenues for cultural negotiation and transformation and serving as sites for training health professionals in psychiatry to gain cultural competence, thereby contributing to the decolonization of mental health practices.

*

Like any other form of healing therapy, prayer camps exhibit specific excesses, particularly concerning individuals living with mental illness who go there to seek healing. Reported claims include forced fasting, chaining, abuse of power and authority by prayer camp staff and other practices that detract from the potential for restoration. While it has been established that prayer camps do not always attribute mental illness to supernatural evil forces, it is crucial to note that when malevolent causes are invoked, the treatment process can be delayed, ultimately exacerbating the patient's condition and potentially leading to untimely death. Although some studies have indicated positive health implications of practices such as fasting, other research has demonstrated that excessive forms of fasting can have deleterious effects on the health of chronically ill individuals (Fitchett et al. 2004; Krause and Wulff 2004). For instance, a study conducted in Ghana revealed that excessive fasting deteriorated the health condition of individuals with diabetes and breast cancer who sought healing from prayer camps (Korsah and Domfeh 2020; Atobrah 2012).

Some of these practices stem from the abuse of power by prayer camp leaders. Additional factors, such as chaining, can also be attributed to inadequate resources and a lack of control mechanisms within the prayer camps. As previously highlighted, most prayer camps are self-regulated and do not report to any religious body or organization. Consequently, their leaders wield considerable power, which they occasionally misuse in their duties. A particularly troubling aspect is the assertion by some prayer camp leaders that their injurious practices are divinely sanctioned. It is essential that questions regarding claims of supernatural power and authority are not dismissively ignored, as they are intertwined with hierarchies of trust and authority that, if not properly managed, can have devastating consequences for the individuals they seek to treat. In this context, there is a need for both state and non-state actors in the field of mental healthcare to build trust through engagement with faith-based healers to enhance regulatory oversight, supervision and mentorship, with the aim of improving mental healthcare at prayer camps.

Thus, these challenges necessitate modification through educational campaigns and needs assessment programmes designed to provide appropriate responses to such issues. For improved treatment and healthcare practices, mental health professionals have initiated measures aimed at collaborating with prayer camps through the decentralization programme of the MHA, to address some of the existing challenges encountered at these camps. Collaboration occurs through visits to the camps, administering medication to patients and organizing workshops and educational training sessions for prayer camp staff. Reports indicate that these activities have yielded positive results (see e.g. Yaro et al. 2020). This collaborative effort helps to alleviate the tensions and conflicts that often characterize the resolution of human rights issues at some of these prayer camps. Simultaneously, it presents opportunities to address some of the entrenched religious positions. Notably, the ethical dimension of this collaboration poses challenges for both faith-based healers and health professionals in resolving healthcare obstacles (Read 2019).

To mitigate some of the disadvantages associated with prayer camps, the government must establish a robust health information system that acknowledges the role and contributions of religious leaders in mental healthcare, particularly within prayer camps. In doing so, both state and non-state actors in the fields of psychiatry and global mental health must develop policies and strategies that seek to regulate the activities of prayer camps in the realm of mental healthcare. Furthermore, there is a pressing need for sustained and integrative collaboration and/or intersectoral partnerships between community health units and caregivers, healers or prophets serving in prayer camps. In this vein, I concur with Arias et al. (2016) regarding the recommendation to assist prayer camps in providing interventions and fostering intersectoral healthcare collaboration that will enhance the quality of life for patients at these facilities. Specifically, the establishment of intersectoral partnerships, cooperation, open discussion and engagement between medical staff and spiritual care workers would be beneficial in addressing some of the harmful practices observed in certain prayer camps. Such collaborations or partnerships are likely to ensure training and proper care, enhancing mutual understanding and respect among healthcare professionals, thereby increasing support and wellness for individuals living with mental illness and their families in Ghana.

NOTES

Introduction

1 For a detailed description of the roles of these practitioners, please refer to Appiah-Kubi (1981) and Ayim-Aboagye (2006).
2 See Chapter 4 for detailed discussion on the cultural historicity of prayer camps in Ghana.
3 I use the term 'patient' to refer to those receiving treatment for mental illness at prayer camps. The Akan word for patient is *yarefo*, which translates as 'sick person'. At prayer camps, some caregivers and health professionals use the same term when referring to mentally ill individuals seeking treatment.
4 The Akan constitute more than half of Ghana's population and are arguably the largest ethnic group in Ghana, comprising the Asantes, Fantes, Nzema, Ahanta, Akuapem, Bono and so on (Buah 1998).

Chapter 1

1 These categorizations have also been divided into two analytical categories of 'normative' and 'ontological' or descriptive categories with each having theoretical and empirical implications with the ways the human being is understood and expected to live within the society or community (again, see Wiredu 1992; Gyekye 1995). It is important to note that the introduction of religions such as Christianity and Islam has had an influence on such beliefs and so the expressions of such beliefs are often mixed with those of Judeo-Christian traditions.
2 Ayim-Aboagye (1997: 34) offers an extensive discussion on the psychological implications of the soul concept and its relation to Freud's theory of human personality. The author posits that the Akan concept of personality possesses both theological and scientific validity, particularly when examined within the framework of Freud and Jung's scientific theories.
3 For an in-depth exploration of this topic, refer to chapter 3 titled 'The Spirit Incarnate' in Ephirim-Donkor's (2015) book, *African Personality and Spirituality: The Role of Abossom and Human Essence*.
4 See the Parrinder's (1951) chapter on 'Injury to the Soul' in *West African Psychology* for more details.
5 For a deeper understanding of the distinctions between *kra* and *sunsum*, refer to Akesson (1965).

6 The Yorubas of Nigeria have a similar concept. In Yoruba thought, a person is comprised of the union of the *ara* (body), emi (mind/soul) and *ori* (inner head), all of which are believed to be brought into being by specific gods. An individual's unique qualities and destiny come from *ori*, which is viewed as a deity (see Adeofe 2004).
7 For further explanation on the Akan concept of the soul and how Akesson attempts to distinguish between the soul and the *kra*, as well as its implications for human life in Akan communities, refer to Akesson (1965).
8 Pra is one of the river deities in Ghana.
9 For further reading, see the Atiemo's (1998) MPhil thesis titled 'Mmusuyi and Deliverance'.
10 Debrunner (1961) presents a similar viewpoint, suggesting that when an individual falls ill, their *kra*, or life force, is conceptualized as a separate entity existing behind them.
11 For further information, see the article 'WPA Position Statement of Spirituality and Religion in Psychiatry' by Moreira-Almeida et al. (2016), in which the World Psychiatric Association recommends that mental health practitioners seriously consider the spiritual history of patients when providing care for mental health issues.
12 Please refer to Shantha Rau Barriga's blog post entitled 'The (In)human Dimension of Ghana's Prayer Camps', which is available at https://www.hrw.org/news/2014/10/10/inhuman-dimension-ghanas-prayer-camps. Additionally, you may access the response to Barriga's post authored by a Ghanaian scholar specializing in religion and human rights at https://www.opendemocracy.net/en/openglobalrights-openpage/filling-gap-why-prayer-camps-in-ghana-are-sometimes-only-option/ (accessed on 10 October 2022).

Chapter 2

1 Descartes's assertion, translated as 'I think, therefore I am', has been argued to inform the foundation of Cartesian dualism within Western medical practice. Cartesian dualism denotes the separation of the mind from the body. This philosophy has been regarded as non-holistic in healthcare, failing to consider the social, environmental and spiritual dimensions of disease and health. Consequently, biomedicine has faced criticism for its inability 'to adequately incorporate (and synthesize) the connections between a patient's thoughts and feelings and physical symptoms and the physiological aspects of disease' which prompted 'emphasis on the demand for more "holistic" therapies connecting mental, physical, spiritual, and environmental aspects of disease and health' (Cohen 2006: 10).
2 See also the explanation of *sunsum* by Akesson (1965) and Debrunner (1961) for similar views.
3 The social aspect of the care for the mentally ill by family members was central to the treatment of mentally ill patients at Lambo's psychiatric village in Aro, Nigeria, in the 1950s, and later seen in the Fann Hospital established by a French military psychiatrist, Henri Collomb, in Dakar, Senegal. Families were involved in the treatment process by accompanying their relatives to seek healthcare, a practice believed to have therapeutic effects on patients and minimize their sense of alienation (see Collignon 2015; Akyeampong 2015).
4 For further reading, see Jablensky et al.'s (1992) article on 'Schizophrenia: Manifestations, Incidence and Course in Different Cultures. A World

Health Organization Ten-Country Study' and Cooper and Sartorius's (1977) 'Cultural and Temporal Variations in Schizophrenia: A Speculation on the Importance of Industrialisation'. Hopper's (2004) 'Interrogating the Meaning of "Culture"' is also relevant here.

Chapter 3

1 In the book titled *Voices of Affliction: Aspects of Traditional Healing Practices and Their Impact on Akan Families in Ghana*, Obeng (2004) examines how the Akan people categorize diseases and how these classifications shape their approaches to seeking remedies. A key insight lies in their dual understanding of illness, whereby ailments are attributed to both physical and spiritual factors. Obeng provides detailed insights into this bipartite concept of disease within Ghana's Akan community.

Chapter 4

1 The term 'healing camps' is also used interchangeably to refer to these entities. The term 'healing' is employed due to its central role in the activities and primary purpose of these camps.
2 Camp leaders exude great authority and power, commanding considerable respect from supplicants. Their statements are regarded as directive messages from God, leading their followers and supplicants to obey. For further insights into the authority of prophets at prayer camps in Ghana, refer to chapter 3 of Daswani's book, *Looking Back, Moving Forward*.
3 For an in-depth examination of the calling and ministry of Prophet Mintah, as well as the proliferation of prayer camps in Ghana, consult Larbi (2015: 384–6).
4 Larbi (2015) and Onyinah (2012) may have overlooked the account of Prophet Appiah's group as it unfolded within the context of a historic mission church (Methodist Church), rather than a Pentecostal tradition. The studies conducted by Larbi and Onyinah focused on emergence of prayer camps within Pentecostal denominations.
5 Samuel Nyankson, a prophet and Methodist catechist, spent numerous active years in the Ashanti town of Gyakobu, near Dunkwa Offin in Ghana. He later crossed paths with Prophet Appiah, and Nyankson's activities had a significant impact on Appiah (see Baëta 1962).
6 Appiah and his group's activities date back to the early 1920s. After being dismissed from the Methodist Church, Appiah and his followers severed ties and subsequently established the Musama Disco Christo Church (MDCC), which was one of the earlier variants of African Independent Churches in Ghana, commonly referred to as *Sunsum sorè*. Baëta designates them as 'spiritual churches' due to their emphasis on pneumatic or spirit-led experiences.
7 This report was submitted by the Mental Health Authority of Ghana (MHA), which is the governmental agency responsible for overseeing the provision of mental healthcare services in Ghana. As part of its decentralization agenda for mental healthcare, the MHA is collaborating with certain prayer camps to deliver healthcare services to individuals seeking treatment at these camps. It is worth noting that the

accuracy of the reported number of prayer camps may be subject to debate. The full report can be accessed at the following link: https://www.graphic.com.gh/daily-graphic-editorials/prayer-camps-not-hospitals.html (accessed on 20 May 2024). See also WHO's (2022) Mental Health Atlas report. This is reported as non-hospital facilities in mental healthcare.

8 Prior to the introduction and implementation of the 'cash-and-carry scheme', the Ministry of Finance and Economic Planning, on behalf of the government of Ghana, provided initial seed funding in the form of free drugs to government health facilities through the Central Medical Store. The intention was for these facilities to sell the drugs to patients and utilize the proceeds to sustain the drug supply through a revolving fund scheme. However, the cash-and-carry scheme was subsequently introduced, resulting in the government ceasing to allocate funds for the purchase of drugs, with the exception of specific cases. As a consequence, the burden of these costs shifted directly to consumers or patients (Asenso-Okyere et al. 1999).

9 These particular challenges prompted the introduction of Ghana's National Health Insurance Scheme (NHIS) in 2003 by President John Agyekum Kufour, with the aim of eliminating the 'cash-and-carry' system prevalent at the time. Despite the relief afforded by the NHIS, the scheme reportedly faces various obstacles, including delayed fee payments by the government, leading some healthcare centres and providers to demand upfront cash payments from clients prior to treatment or medication administration.

10 This was revealed to me by a prayer camps staff during a fieldwork in January 2020. I also encountered another individual at one of the camps I visited who had been brought to the camp by relatives to seek support for a mental health problem. This person was living overseas when the problem arose.

11 'I wish Ghana were a prayer camp', available at https://www.modernghana.com/news/206247/i-wish-ghana-were-a-prayer-camp-mills.html#google_vignette (accessed on 30 June 2024).

12 Larbi (2015) also mentions the visitation of former president Rawlings to the Bethel Prayer Camp in Sunyani, Ghana. There are other reports of visitation to these centres by different heads of states. These visits are very common during the periods when they are seeking to win political power.

13 The Twelve Apostles Church, commonly referred to as Nackabah in the Western province of Ghana, has gained considerable popularity. John Nackabah, a devoted follower of Prophet Harris, played a vital role in the formation of the Twelve Apostles Church, and his name has become closely associated with the church.

14 For a comprehensive analysis of the factors contributing to the waning influence of spiritual churches in Ghana, refer to Asamoah-Gyadu's study in 2005.

15 I do not extensively focus on the criticism of prayer camps in this study. Some of the issues have been addressed elsewhere (refer to Benyah 2022).

16 Onyinah (2012) also acknowledges that the terms 'prayer camp' and 'prayer centre' are used synonymously to designate the same entity.

17 Examples of such churches includes Alive Chapel International in Accra led by Bishop Salifu Amoako and Prayer Palace in Spintex Road Accra led by Prophet Emmanual Adjei. There is some kind of fluidity and/or hybridity between neo-Prophetic churches and charismatic churches which blurs their conceptualizations.

18 Regarding the treatment of individuals with mental illness in Ghana's prayer camps, the inadequate infrastructure and limited resources often result in the use of restraints, namely chaining, especially for those with severe forms of mental illness

who tends to be aggressive during treatment. Unfortunately, the protracted exposure to chains or shackles can cause significant injuries, particularly impacting those individuals.

19 While I acknowledge the financial prosperity some prayer camp leaders attain through their healing activities, it is important to note that this study does not focus on their affluence.

20 Field survey in the central region of Ghana in February 2021 and April 2024.

21 See Onyinah (2012) for detailed discussion of the reasons CoP severed relationship with some prayer camp leaders in Ghana.

22 Email communication with Opoku Onyinah, 10 April 2024 (see also Onyinah 2012: 188).

23 The number was revealed in a WhatsApp communication with the Moderator of the Presbyterian Church of Ghana (PCG), 10 May 2024, Accra.

24 Scandals involving religious leaders in Ghana often revolve around leaders of healing centres, which frequently prompts the public to question their credibility as men of God or religious figures. The absence of adequate supervision in certain prayer centres or camps has also resulted in the excessive exercise of power and the violation of the rights of individuals seeking treatment or support at these facilities.

25 Onyinah (2012: 188) asserts that a likely reason for the limited promotion of residential camps in charismatic churches is their emphasis on deliverance ministry. Nonetheless, this does not imply that church members do not participate in camp visits, as evidenced by his research findings.

26 See https://potterscity.com/meet-our-founder-2/ for further details about the prayer centre (accessed on 9 April 2024).

27 Email correspondence with the former chairman of the CoP on 12 April 2024. For more information, see https://thecophq.org/goka-prayer-centre-gets-new-leadership/ (accessed on 12 April 2024).

28 See revised guidelines for operating prayer centres in the Church of Pentecost, 2016. I assume these directives are implemented to prevent the inappropriate use and abuse of titles within the church, as well as to maintain a certain level of control and orderliness.

29 Revised guidelines for operating prayer centres in the Church of Pentecost, 2016: 2.

30 See discussion of 'salvation as healing and deliverance' in *African Charismatics* by Asamoah-Gyadu (2005: 164–200).

31 For further exploration of this topic, one can refer to the discussion initiated by C. H. Dodd in his work *The Parables of the Kingdom*. Dodd is recognized for introducing the concept of 'realized eschatology' to discussions regarding the kingdom of God. According to Dodd, this term encapsulates the notion of 'the manifest and effective assertion of the divine sovereignty against all the evil of the world'. This includes the healing of sicknesses as well as the impact of the 'powers of the world to come' on the present world through a series of unparalleled and unreproducible events (Dodd 1953: 50–1).

32 Among the Akan people of Ghana, the deities, known as *abosom*, are believed to be offspring of the Supreme Being, God (*Onyame*). Consequently, the deities are regarded as intermediaries between God and humanity.

33 This later influenced the emergence of spiritual renewal movements in the historic mission churches to address these spiritual needs and also provide a solution to the attrition rate of their members to the Pentecostal churches. These issues are fully addressed by Omenyo (2002) in Pentecost outside Pentecostalism.

34 The Twelve Apostles Church, commonly referred to as *Nackabah* in the Western Region of Ghana, was established due to the ministry of William Wade Warris, a Liberian Grebo Prophet, in early-twentieth-century Ghana. For further information, please refer to Baëta's work, *Prophetism in Ghana*, 9–27.

Chapter 5

1 For further reading, Exline's (2002) article on 'stumbling blocks on the religious road: Fractured relationships, nagging vices, and the inner struggle to believe' is recommended.

2 Some scholars, such as Twumasi (2005), categorize both indigenous and faith healers under the umbrella term of *traditional healers*. Appiah-Kubi employs the umbrella term *priest-healer* in reference to various types of healers in the Akan community (see Appiah-Kubi 1989). In Ghana, however, traditional healers are often specifically associated with indigenous medical practitioners whose services align with traditional belief systems. They have long been advocated as important resources for mental healthcare in sub-Saharan Africa (Patel 2011; Ayim-Aboagye 2006).

3 The term 'theoretical closure' is borrowed from Jean Comaroff (1981: 367) to denote the supposition that 'medical systems' form a natural and discrete domain and the view that such 'medical systems' exist as parts of ahistorical and closed systems. In simple terms, Comaroff employs the term to describe a situation where the aetiological explanation and therapy of a particular medical system is prioritized over others. She argues that such an aetiological hegemony among medical systems hinders opportunities for knowledge sharing across different medical domains, which ultimately has implications for the patients who seek these medical practices to resolve their issues.

4 I use the term 'Western psychiatry' to refer to forms of psychiatric practices developed and practiced in America or Europe.

5 The project was funded by a group known as the Friends of Bawku in the Netherlands and PCG Ghana. The hospital is a specialized psychiatric facility with a capacity of ten beds and is expected to provide services in adult psychiatry, forensic psychiatry, drug and alcohol detoxification, geriatric psychiatry and psychotherapy services (PCG Ghana, 2024). For more information, see https://pcgonline.org/2022/10/14/presbyterian-church-of-ghana-opens-psychiatric-hospital-at-bolgatanga/ (accessed on 2 August 2024).

6 This makes a total figure of 2,896 which represents 9.52 per cent per 100,000 population.

7 Draichhio (2020) refers to the MHA documents on the Procurement and Sale of Psychotropic Drugs. For further information, refer to the policy brief compiled by Mental Health Authority of Ghana, Ghana Somubi Dwumadie and UKAid titled 'Access to psychotropic medicines in Ghana: Issues, strategies, and recommendations'. Available at https://options.co.uk/wp-content/uploads/2023/09/Ghana-Somubi-Dwumadie-Policy-Brief-Psychotropic-Supply-21072023.pdf (accessed on 10 August 2024).

8 Mental Health Authority (2018), State of Mental Health in Ghana, a YouTube documentary available at https://www.youtube.com/watch?v=Dfn0mRNqGb4 (accessed on 24 March 2022).

Chapter 6

1 This can be example of *aduto* as described by Konadu (2007: 68). See also Chapter 4 for discussion on Akan disease classification.
2 An informant indicated during a conversation that his decision to cease his involvement in sakawa was prompted by the mental deterioration of three friends who were also engaged in the practice. Several stories such this, https://www.ghanaweb.com/GhanaHomePage/NewsArchive/Sakawa-boy-goes-mad-after-refusing-to-sleep-with-mad-woman-433332, circulate in the Ghanaian media occasionally (accessed on 23 January 2025).
3 The belief that mental illness can be influenced by supernatural malevolent forces is also prevalent in Western contexts, as evidenced by multiple studies conducted in countries such as the UK, New Zealand and Australia, among others (cf. Mehta and Thornicroft 2013). Thielman (1998: 3) asserts that 'historically, Western medical writers have held a variety of views on the relationship between religion, spirituality, and madness'.

Chapter 7

1 See Benyah (2022) for discussion on the issues of human rights concerns at prayer camps in Ghana.
2 See this link for a full seminar discussion: https://www.youtube.com/watch?v=dgyDaZ4Oy3I&t=11s.

Chapter 8

1 Letter titled 'Application for educational visit' was dated 14 November 2002 and shared by a General Secretary interviewed at one of the prayer camps selected for the study.
2 See Chapter 4 for background of clients at prayer camps.
3 I have addressed some of these concerns elsewhere. See Benyah (2022).
4 For further details, see 'Filling the gap: why prayer camps in Ghana are sometimes the only option', available at https://www.opendemocracy.net/en/openglobalrights-openpage/filling-gap-why-prayer-camps-in-ghana-are-sometimes-only-option/ (accessed on 7 November 2022).

Chapter 9

1 See the link https://www.sightsavers.org/programmes/ghana-participation-programme/ for the activities and work done by the group.
2 A classification of the various forms of sickness is known as nosology (derived from the ancient Greek, *-logy*, meaning 'discourse on' and 'disease'). Hahn (1996: 32) elucidates that 'nosologies group events of sickness on the basis of criteria that are detectable and deemed significant. A nosology is useful if it helps us understand sicknesses, if it allows prediction of their course, if it facilitates communication of our

experiences of sickness, if it enables a more effective response, preventing, curing, or palliating sickness.' He argues further that 'a universal cross-cultural nosology is possible, but only if it takes cultural setting into account' (Hahn 1996: 32).

3 A similar case can be observed in the establishment of the Fann Hospital, which aimed to bridge the gap between culturally bound symptoms or interpretations of mental illness and Western conceptions of mental illness (see Kilroy-Marac 2019 for further reading).

REFERENCES

Abel, C., and K. Busia (2005), 'An Explanatory Ethnobotanical Study of the Practice of Herbal Medicine by the Akan People of Ghana', *Alternative Medicine Review*, 10 (2): 112–22.

Adeofe, L. (2004), 'Personal Identity in African Metaphysics', in L. M. Brown (ed.), *African Philosophy: New and Traditional Perspectives*, 69–83, New York: Oxford University Press.

Adinkrah, M. (2015), *Witchcraft, Witches, and Violence in Ghana*, New York: Berghahn Books.

Adjei, S. B. (2019), 'Conceptualising Personhood, Agency, and Morality for African Psychology', *Theory & Psychology*, 29 (4), 484–505.

Adogame, A. (2022), *Indigeneity in African Religions: Oza Worldviews, Cosmologies and Religious Cultures*, London: Bloomsbury.

Adu-Gyamfi, S., and E. Anderson (2022), 'African Traditional Healing and Biomedicine: A Reconstruction of Colonial and Post-Independence Health-Care History under Kwame Nkrumah, 1951–66', *Journal of West African History*, 8 (1): 87–118.

Adubofuor, S. B. (1987), *Akan Cosmology and Akan Christianity in Contemporary Ghana*, MTh thesis, Aberdeen University.

Ae-Ngibise, K., S. Cooper, E. Adiibokah, B. Akpalu, C. Lund, V. Doku and The MHaPP Research Programme Consortium (2010), '"Whether You Like It or Not People with Mental Problems Are Going to Go to Them": A Qualitative Exploration into the Widespread Use of Traditional and Faith Healers in the Provision of Mental Health Care in Ghana', *International Review of Psychiatry*, 22 (6): 558–67.

Agyekum, K. (2020), 'Akan Cultural Concepts and Expressions for "Stress", "Distress", "Sorrow", and "Depression', *Nordic Journal of African Studies*, 29 (3): 1–21.

Ahyi G. R. (1997), 'Traditional Models of Mental Health and Illness in Benin', in P. Hountondji (ed.), *Endogenous Knowledge Research Trails*, 217–46, Senegal: CODESRIA.

Aka, P. C., Y. M. Alex-Assensoh and H. Wahab (2022), *The Political Economy of Universal Healthcare in Africa: Evidence from Ghana*, London: Routledge.

Akesson, S. K. (1965), 'The Akan Concept of the Soul', *African Affairs*, 64 (252): 280–91.

Akin, John S., Nancy Birdsall and D. M. De Ferranti (1987), *Financing Health Services in Developing Countries: An Agenda for Reform*, Washington, DC: World Bank.

Akrong, Abraham (2006), 'Jesus with the Face of an Ancestor', *Ghana Bulletin of Theology*, 1 (1): 20–36.

Akyeampong, Emmanuel (2015), 'A Historical Overview of Psychiatry in Africa', in Emmanuel Akyeampong, Allan G. Hill and Arthur Kleinman (eds), *The Culture of Mental Illness and Psychiatric Practice in Africa*, 24–49, Bloomington: Indiana University Press.

Alexander, F. G., and S. T. Selesnick (1966), *The History of Psychiatry: An Evaluation of Psychiatric Thought and Practice from Prehistoric Times to the Present*, New York: American Library.

Alhassan, A. R. K., and A. Ridwan (2023), 'Identity Expression – the Case of "Sakawa" Boys in Ghana', *Human Arenas*, 6 (2): 242–63.
Amfo, N. A. A., E. E. Houphouet, E. K. Dordoye and R. Thompson (2018), '"Insanity Is from Home": The Expression of Mental Health Challenges in Akan', *International Journal of Language and Culture*, 5 (1): 1–28.
Ammerman, N. (2013), *Sacred Stories, Spiritual Tribes: Finding Religion in Everyday Life*, New York: Oxford University Press.
Amoah, E. (2014), '"Poverty Is Madness": Some Insights from Traditional African Spirituality and Mental Health', in D. N. Hopkins and M. Lewis (eds), *Another World Is Possible: Spiritualities and Religions of Global Darker Peoples*, 207–18, London: Taylor and Francis.
Anane, Opoku J. (2018), *Advanced Akan Dictionary*, Kumasi: Centre for National Culture.
Andary, L., S. Yvonne and K. Steven (2003), *Assessing Mental Health across Cultures*, Bowen Hills: Australian Academic Press.
Anderson, Allan (2010), 'Varieties, Taxonomies and Definitions', in A. Anderson, M. Bergunder, A. F. Droogers and C. Van der Laan (eds), *Studying Global Pentecostalism: Theories and Methods*, 13–29, Berkeley: University of California Press.
Anderson, Allan Heaton (2018), *Spirit-Filled World: Religious Dis/Continuity in African Pentecostalism*, Cham: Palgrave Macmillan.
Aning, K. (2019), *Rehabilitation of Alcohol and Substance Abuse Persons: The Case Study of Compassion Rehabilitation Centre*, unpublished MPhil thesis, University of Ghana.
Antić, A. (2021), 'Transcultural Psychiatry: Cultural Difference, Universalism and Social Psychiatry in the Age of Decolonisation', *Culture Medicine and Psychiatry*, 45: 359–84.
Antić, A. (2024), 'Psychiatry and Decolonization: Histories of Transcultural Psychiatry in the Twentieth Century', *Journal of the History of Ideas*, 85 (1): 149–77.
Anyinam, C. (1997), 'Medicine in Africa', in H. Selin (ed.), *Encyclopaedia of the History of Science, Technology, and Medicine in Non-Western Cultures*, 679–83, Dordrecht: Kluwer Academic.
Appiah-Kubi, K. (1981), *Man Cures God Heals: Religion and Medical Practice among the Akan of Ghana*, New York: Friendship Press.
Appiah-Kubi, K. (1989), 'Religion and Healing in an African Community: The Akan of Ghana', in L. E. Sullivan (ed.), *Healing and Restoring: Health and Medicine in the World's Religious Tradition*, 203–24, New York: Macmillan.
Arias, Daniel, LaurenTaylor, Angela Ofori-Atta and Elizabeth H. Bradley (2016), 'Prayer Camps and Biomedical Care in Ghana: Is Collaboration in Mental Health Care Possible?', *PloS One*, 11 (9): 1–16.
Armstrong, A. (2016), '"Sakawa" Rumours: Occult Internet Fraud and Ghanaian Identity', in R. Littlewood and R. Lynch (eds), *Cosmos, Gods and Madmen: Frameworks in the Anthropologies of Medicine*, 67–92, New York: Berghahn Books.
Asamoah-Gyadu, J. K. (2004), 'Of "Sour Grapes" and "Children's Teeth": Inherited Guilt, Human Rights and Processes of Restoration in Ghanaian Pentecostalism', *Exchange*, 33 (4): 334–53.
Asamoah-Gyadu, J. K. (2005), '"Christ Is the Answer: What Is the Question?" A Ghana Airways Prayer Vigil and its Implications for Religion, Evil and Public Space', *Journal of Religion in Africa*, 35 (1): 93–117.
Asamoah-Gyadu, J. K. (2007), 'On the "Mountain" of the Lord: Healing Pilgrimages in Ghanaian Christianity', *Exchange*, 36 (1): 65–86.
Asamoah-Gyadu, J. K. (2013), *Contemporary Pentecostal Christianity: Interpretations from an African Context*, Oxford: Regnum Books.

Asamoah-Gyadu, J. K. (2015a), *Sighs and Signs of the Spirit: Ghanaian Perspectives on Pentecostalism and Renewal in Africa*, Akropong-Akuapem: Regnum Africa.
Asamoah-Gyadu, J. K. (2015b), 'Witchcraft Accusations and Christianity in Africa', *International Bulletin of Missionary Research*, 39 (1): 23–7.
Asamoah-Gyadu, J. K. (2005a), *African Charismatics: Currents Developments within Independent Indigenous Pentecostalism in Ghana*, Leiden: Brill.
Asamoah, M. K., J. Osafo and J. Agyapong (2014), 'The Role of Pentecostal Clergy in Mental Health-Care Delivery in Ghana', *Mental Health, Religion and Culture*, 17 (6): 601–14.
Asante, Emmanuel (2017), *Issues in African Traditional Religion, Humanities, Ethnicity and Development: Impact on African Christianity*, Accra: SonLife Press.
Asem, Kafui, E. (2005), *A History of the Church of Pentecost, Volume One*, Accra: Pentecost Press.
Asenso-Okyere, Kwadwo, Isaac Osei-Akoto W., Adote Anum and Augustina Adukonu (1999), 'The Behaviour of Health Workers in an Era of Cost Sharing: Ghana's Drug Cash and Carry System', *Tropical Medicine and International Health*, 4 (8): 586–93.
Asenso-Okyere, W. K. (1995), 'Financing Health Care in Ghana', *World Health Forum*, 16 (1): 86–91.
Assimeng, M. (1995), *Salvation, Social Crisis and the Human Condition*, Accra: Ghana University Press.
Atiemo, A. O. (1994), 'Deliverance in the Charismatic Churches in Ghana', *Trinity Journal of Church and Theology*, 4 (2): 39–49.
Atiemo, A. O. (1998), *Mmusuyi and Deliverance: A Study of Conflict and Consensus in the Encounter between African Traditional Religion and Christianity*, MPhil thesis, University of Ghana, Legon.
Atiemo, A. O. (2006), 'Singing with Understanding: The Story of Gospel Music in Ghana', *Studies in World Christianity*, 12 (2): 142–63.
Atiemo, A. O. (2013), *Religion and the Inculturation of Human Rights in Ghana*, London: Bloomsbury Academic
Atiemo, A. O. (2014), 'Filling the Gap: Why Prayer Camps in Ghana Are Sometimes the Only Option', accessed 15 November 2022, https://www.opendemocracy.net/en/openglobalrights-openpage/filling-gap-why-prayer-camps-in-ghana-are-sometimes-only-option/.
Atiemo, A. O. (2017), 'In Need of a New Lens: An African Christian Scholar's Religious Critique of Western European Attitudes toward Religion and Development in Africa', *Religion and Theology*, 24 (3–4): 250–73.
Atobrah, Deborah (2012), 'When Darkness Falls at Did-Day: Young Patients' Perceptions and Meanings of Chronic Illness and Their Implications for Medical Care', *Ghana Medical Journal*, 46 (2): 46–53.
Awedoba, A. L. (2002), *Culture and Development in Africa with Special References to Ghana: Some Basic Issues Volume 1*, Accra: Institute of African Studies.
Ayegboyin, D. (2006), '"Dressed in Borrowed Robes": The Experience of the New Pentecostal Movements in Nigeria', *Ghana Bulletin of Theology*, 1 (1): 37–54.
Ayim-Aboagye, D. (1997), *The Psychology of Akan Religious Healing*, Turku: Abo Akademi Press.
Ayim-Aboagye, D. (2006), *Indigenous Psychiatry: Transcultural Study of Traditional Practitioners in West African Healing Communities with Focus on Ghana*, Turku: Abo Akademi University.
Ayinde, O., A. Ojagbemi, V. Makanjuola and O. Gureje (2021), 'African Religions, Spirituality and Mental Health Healing Practices', in Alexander Moreira-Almeida,

Bruno Paz Mosqueiro and Dinesh Bhugra (eds), *Spirituality and Mental Health across Cultures*, 277–92, Oxford: Oxford University Press.

Azevedo, M. J. (2017), *Historical Perspective on the State of Health and Health Systems in Africa: The Pre-Colonial and Colonial Eras*, Switzerland: Palgrave Macmillan.

Baëta, C. G. (1962), *Prophetism in Ghana: A Study of Some Spiritual Churches*, London: SCM Press.

Banda, C. (2020), 'Regenerated without Being Recreated? A Soteriological Analysis of the African Neo-Pentecostal Teaching on Generational Curses', *Hervormde Teologiese Studies*, 76 (3): 1–12.

Barnard, D. (1995), 'Chronic Illness and the Dynamics of hoping', in S. Kay Toombs, David Barnard and Ronald A. Carson (eds), *Chronic Illness: From Experience to Policy*, 38–57, Bloomington: Indiana University Press.

Bartels, Francis L. (1965), *The Roots of Ghana Methodism*, Accra: Methodist Book Depot.

Bartle, P. F. W. (1983), 'The Universe Has Three Souls', *Journal of Religion in Africa*, 14 (2): 85–114.

BBC (2018), 'Caged while Seeking Mental Health Help', available: https://www.youtube.com/watch?v=p9Pl0MGu2YQ&t=68s (accessed 14 July 2024).

Ben-Zeev, D. (2018), 'Mobile Health for Mental Health in West Africa: The Case for Ghana', *Psychiatric Services*, 69 (7): 741–3.

Ben-Zeev, D., A. Larsen, D. A. Attah, K. Obeng, et al. (2024), 'Combining mHealth Technology and Pharmacotherapy to Improve Mental Health Outcomes and Reduce Human Rights Abuses in West Africa: Intervention Field Trial', *JMIR Mental Health*, 11: e53096.

Bennet, J. F., and J. Rohde (2008), '"Hospitals and Clinics"', in J. Middleton and J. C. Miller (eds), *New Encyclopaedia of Africa*, 535–9, New York: Thompson Gale.

Benyah, F. (2022a), 'Prayer Camps, Healing, and the Management of Chronic Mental Illness in Ghana: A Qualitative Phenomenological Inquiry', in A. R. Hatala and K. Roger (eds), *Spiritual, Religious, and Faith-Based Practices in Chronicity: An Exploration of Mental Wellness in Global Context*, 173–94, London: Routledge.

Benyah, F. (2022b), 'Prayer Camps, Mental Health, and Human Rights Concerns in Ghana', *Journal of Religion in Africa*, 51 (3–4): 283–308.

Benyah, F. E. K. (2024a), 'Healing the Incurable? Pentecostal Prayer Camps and Healing of Chronic Illnesses in Ghana', *Mission Studies*, 41 (2): 173–94.

Benyah, F. E. K. (2024b), 'Appropriation and Contestation of Akan Traditional Healing Approaches in the Healing of Mentally Ill Patients at Prayer Camps in Ghana', *Exchange*, 53 (2): 130–55.

Benyah, F. E. K., and S. Sjö (2024), 'Media Portrayals of Religion, Prayer Camps and Persons with Mental Illness in Ghana: A Discursive and Narrative Analysis', *Journal of Religion, Media and Digital Culture*, 13 (1): 43–64.

Bila, N. J., and C. L. Carbonatto (2022), 'Culture and Help-Seeking Behaviour in the Rural Communities of Limpopo, South Africa: Unearthing Beliefs of Mental Health Care Users and Caregivers', *Mental Health, Religion & Culture*, 25 (6): 543–62.

Biritwum Richard, B. (1994), 'The Cost of Sustaining the Ghana's "Cash and Carry" System of Health Care Financing at a Rural Health Centre', *West African Journal of Medicine*, 13 (2): 124–7.

Blum, Jason. N. (2012), 'Retrieving Phenomenology of Religion as a Method for Religious Studies', *Journal of the American Academy of Religion*, 80 (4): 1025–48.

Boaheng, I. (2024), 'A Theological Reflection on the Akan Doctrine of the Human Soul', *Journal for the Study of Religion*, 37 (1): 1–22.

Bourguignon, E. (1976), 'The Effectiveness of Religious Healing Movements: A Review of Recent Literature', *Transcultural Psychiatric Research Review*, 13 (1): 5–21.
Bowlby, J. (1969), *Attachment and Loss: Vol. 1*. Harmondsworth: Penguin Books.
Braam, A. W. (2017), 'Towards a Multidisciplinary Guideline Religiousness, Spirituality, and Psychiatry: What Do We Need?', *Mental Health, Religion & Culture*, 20 (6): 579–88.
Brockington, I. F. (1996), *Motherhood and Mental Health*, Oxford: Oxford University Press.
Brown, C. G (ed.) (2011), *Global Pentecostal and Charismatic Healing*, Oxford: Oxford University Press.
Brown, C. G. (2013), *The Healing Gods: Complementary and Alternative Medicine in Christian America*, Oxford: Oxford University Press.
Brown, Candy G. (2011), 'Introduction: Pentecostalism and the Globalisation of Illness and Healing', in Candy Gunther Brown (ed.), *Global Pentecostal and Charismatic Healing*, 3–26, Oxford: Oxford University Press.
Buah, F. K. (1998), *A History of Ghana*, London: Macmillan.
Buchanan, Denise, and Ian Warwick (2021), 'First Do No Harm: Using "Ethical Triage" to Minimise Causing Harm When Undertaking Educational Research among Vulnerable Participants', *Journal of Further and Higher Education*, 45 (8): 1090–103.
Buertey, A. A., A. Attiogbe and L. Aziato (2020), 'Stigma by Association: Experiences of Community Psychiatric Nurses in the Accra Metropolis, Ghana', *International Journal of Africa Nursing Sciences*, 13: 100260.
Busia, Kofi A. (1954), 'The Ashanti', in Daryll Forde (ed.), *African Worlds: Studies in the Cosmological Ideas and Social Values of African Peoples*, 190–209, Oxford: Oxford University Press.
Cabo, Rafael, and Mark P. Mattson (2019), 'Effects of Intermittent Fasting on Health, Aging, and Disease', *New England Journal of Medicine*, 381: 2541–51.
Canavan, M. E., H. L. Sipsma, A. Adhvaryu, A. Ofori-Atta, H. Jack, C. Udry, I. Osei-Akoto and E. H. Bradley (2013), 'Psychological Distress in Ghana: Associations with Employment and Lost Productivity', *International Journal of Mental Health Systems*, 7 (1): 1–9.
Carey B. (2015), 'The Chains of Mental Illness in West Africa', *New York Times*, available: https://www.nytimes.com/2015/10/12/health/the-chains-of-mental-illness-in-west-africa.html (accessed on 21 May 2023).
Chavunduka, G. L. (1978), *Traditional Healers and the Shona Patient*, Gwelo: Mambo Press.
Chitando, Ezra (2005), 'The Phenomenology of Religion and the Study of African Traditional Religions', *Method and Theory in the Study of Religion*, 17 (4): 299–316.
Chukwukere, I. (1978), 'Akan Theory of Conception: Are the Fante Really Aberrant?', *Africa*, 48 (2): 135–48.
Clarke, C. R. (2014), 'Jesus in the Theology and Experience of African Pentecostals', in C. R. Clarke (ed.), *Pentecostal Theology in Africa*, 58–76, Eugene, OR: Pickwick.
Cohen, M. H. (2006), *Healing at the Borderland of Medicine and Religion*, Chapel Hill: University of North Carolina Press.
Coleman, A. M. (2019), 'The Ethics of Psychiatric Care and Research in Resource-Poor Settings: The Case of a Research Trial in a Prayer Camp in Ghana', *Indian Journal of Medical Ethics*, 4 (2): 134–9.
Collignon, R. (2015), 'Some Aspects of Mental Illness in French-Speaking West Africa', in Emmanuel Akyeampong, Allan G. Hill and Arthur Kleinman (eds), *The Culture of Mental Illness and Psychiatric Practice in Africa*, 163–85, Bloomington: Indiana University Press.

Comaroff, J. (1981), 'Healing and Cultural Transformation: The Tswana of Southern Africa', *Social Science and Medicine*, 15 (3): 367–78.
Comaroff, J. (1982), 'Medicine, Symbol, and Ideology', in Peter Wright and Andrew Treacher (eds), *The Problem of Medical Knowledge: Examining the Social Construction of Medicine*, 49–68, Edinburgh: Edinburgh University Press.
Cooper, J., and N. Sartorius (1977), 'Cultural and Temporal Variations in Schizophrenia: A Speculation on the Importance of Industrialization', *British Journal of Psychiatry*, 130 (1): 50–5.
Cox, H. (2001), *Fire from Heaven: The Rise of Pentecostal Spirituality and the Reshaping of Religion in the Twenty-First Century*, London: Cassell.
Cox, J. L. (2010), *An Introduction to the Phenomenology of Religion*, London: Continuum.
Cox, J. L. (2018), *Transcultural Psychiatry*, London: Routledge.
Crentsil, P. (2007), *Death, Ancestors, and HIV/AIDS among the Akan of Ghana*, Doctoral dissertation, University of Helsinki, Finland.
Crossley, David (1995), 'Religious Experience Within Mental Illness: Opening the Door on Research', *British Journal Psychiatry*, 166 (3): 284–6.
Crumbley, Deidre Helen (2008), *Spirit, Structure, and Flesh: Gendered Experiences in African Instituted Churches among the Yoruba of Nigeria*, Madison: University of Wisconsin Press.
Csordas, Thomas J. (1997), *The Sacred Self: A Cultural Phenomenology of Charismatic Healing*, Berkeley: University of California Press.
Cunyngham-Brown, R. (1937), *Report on Mission to the British Colonies of the West Coast of Africa on the Care and Treatment of Lunatics: The Gold Coast Colony*, London: Crown Agents.
Danquah, J. B. (1968), *The Akan Doctrine of God*, London: Frank Cass.
Danto, David, and Masood Zangeneh (eds) (2022), *Indigenous Knowledge and Mental Health: A Global Perspective*, Cham: Springer.
Daswani, G. (2015), *Looking Back, Moving Forward: Transformation and Ethical Practice in the Ghanaian Church of Pentecost*, Toronto: University of Toronto Press.
Davis, Duane (2019), 'The Phenomenological Method', in Gail Weiss, Ann V. Murphy and Gayle Salamon (eds), *50 Concepts for a Critical Phenomenology*, 3–10, Evanston, IL: Northwestern University Press.
De Witte, M. (2018), 'Buy the Future: Charismatic Pentecostalism and Liberation in a Neoliberal World', in A. Afolayan, O. Yacob-Haliso and T. Falola (eds), *Pentecostalism and Politics in Africa*, 65–85, Switzerland: Palgrave Macmillan.
Debrunner, H. W. (1961), *Witchcraft in Ghana: A Study on the Belief in Destructive Witches and Its Effect on the Akan Tribes*, 2nd edn, Accra: Presbyterian Book Depot.
Dein, S. (2017), 'Religious Experience and Mental Health: Anthropological and Psychological Approaches', *Mental Health, Religion & Culture*, 20 (6): 558–66.
Dein, S. (2018), 'Against the Stream: Religion and Mental Health – the Case for the Inclusion of Religion and Spirituality into Psychiatric Care', *BJPsych Bulletin*, 42 (3): 127–9.
Dickson, A. K. (1984), *Theology in Africa*, Maryknoll, NY: Orbis Books.
Donovan, Peter (2005), 'Neutrality in Religious Studies', in Russel T. McCutcheon (ed.), *The Insider/Outsider Problem in the Study of Religion: A Reader*, 235–47, New York: Continuum.
Draicchio, C. (2020), '"Extraordinary Conditions" and Experiments with Collaboration in "Zones of Social Abandonment" Mental Health Care between Psychiatry and Prayer Camps in Rural Ghana', *Politique africaine*, 157 (1): 165–82.

Edwards, J. (2014), 'Ghana's Mental Health Patients Confined to Prayer Camps', *The Lancet*, 383 (9911): 15–16.
Ephirim-Donkor, A. (2008), 'Akom: The Ultimate Mediumship Experience among the Akan', *Journal of the American Academy of Religion*, 76 (1): 54–81.
Ephirim-Donkor, A. (2015), *African Personality and Spirituality: The Role of Abosom and Human Essence*, New York: Lexington Books.
Exline, Julie. J. (2002), 'Stumbling Blocks on the Religious Road: Fractured Relationships, Nagging Vices, and the Inner Struggle to Believe', *Psychological Inquiry*, 13 (3): 182–9.
Fabrega, Horacio (1989), 'Cultural Relativism and Psychiatric illness', *Journal of Nervous and Mental Disease*, 177 (7): 415–25.
Fadiman, A. (1997), *The Spirit Catches You and You Fall Down: A Hmong Child, Her American Doctors, and the Collision of Two Cultures*, New York: Farrar, Straus and Girous.
Faleye, O. A. (2023), *Public Health in Postcolonial Africa: The Social and Political Determinants of Health*, London: Routledge.
Falola, T., and Heaton, M. M. (2006), *Traditional and Modern Health Systems in Nigeria*, Trenton, NJ: Africa World Press.
Fancello, S., and A. Gusman (2022), *Charismatic Healers in Contemporary Africa: Deliverance in Muslim and Christian Worlds*, London: Bloomsbury.
Feierman, S. (2000), 'Explanation and Uncertainty in the Medical World of Ghaambo', *Bulletin of the History of Medicine*, 74 (2): 317–44.
Feierman, S., and J. Janzen (1994), *Social Basis of Health and Healing in Africa*, Berkeley: University of California Press.
Feierman, S., and J. Janzen (2011), 'African Religions', in J. Brooke and R. Numbers (eds), *Science and Religion around the World*, 229–51, New York: Oxford University Press.
Fernando, S. (2014), *Mental Health Worldwide: Culture, Globalization and Development*, Basingstoke: Palgrave Macmillan.
Field, M. J. (1960), *Search for Security: An Ethno-Psychiatric Study of Rural Ghana*, London: Faber and Faber.
Field, M. J. (1961), *Religion and Medicine of the Gã People*, reprint/with a new preface, Accra: Presbyterian Book Depot.
Fisher, R. B. (1998), *West African Religious Traditions: Focus on the Akan of Ghana*, New York: Orbis Books.
Fitchett, George, Patricia E. Murphy, Jo Kim, James L. Gibbons, Jacqueline R. Cameron and Judy A. Davis (2004), 'Religious Struggle: Prevalence, Correlates and Mental Health Risks in Diabetic, Congestive Heart Failure, and Oncology Patients', *International Journal of Psychiatry in Medicine*, 34 (2): 179–96.
Forster, E. B. (1962), 'The Theory and Practice of Psychiatry in Ghana', *American Journal of Psychotherapy*, 16 (1): 7–51.
Fortes, M., and D. Y. Mayer (1966), 'Psychosis and Social Change among the Tallensi of Northern Ghana', *Cahier D'Etudes Africaines*, 21: 5–40.
Foster, G. M. (1976), 'Disease Etiologies in Non-Western Medical Systems', *American Anthropologist*, 78 (4): 773–82.
Fosu, G. B. (1981), 'Disease Classification in Rural Ghana: Framework and Implications for Health Behaviour', *Social Science & Medicine*, 15 (4): 471–82.
Gallagher, S. (2023), *The Self and Its Disorders*, Oxford: Oxford University Press.
Gammelin, L. (2018), 'Health-Seeking Nomads and Faith-Healing in a Medically Pluralistic Context in Mbeya, Tanzania', *Mission Studies*, 35 (2): 245–68.

Gammelin, L. (2023), *'We Are in Between': Health-Seeking, Gender and Authority in a Charismatic Church in Mbeya, Tanzania*, Sweden: Media-Tryck, Lund University.

Garrett, C. (2002), 'Spirituality and Healing in the Sociology of Chronic Illness', *Health Sociology Review*, 11 (1): 61–9.

Geschiere, Peter (1997), *The Modernity of Witchcraft: Politics and the Occult in Postcolonial Africa*, Charlottesville: University of Virginia Press.

Geschiere, Peter (2003), 'Witchcraft as the Dark Side of Kinship: Dilemmas of Social Security in New Contexts', *Etnofoor*, 16 (1): 43–61.

Ghana Statistical Service (2021), *2020 Population and Housing Census: Summary Report of Final Results*, Accra: Ghana Statistical Service.

Glover, L., J. Jomeen, T. Urquhart and C. R. Martin (2014), 'Puerperal Psychosis – a Qualitative Study of Women's Experiences', *Journal of Reproductive and Infant Psychology*, 32 (3): 254–69.

Godin, G., and G. Kok (1996), 'The Theory of Planned Behavior: A Review of Its Applications to Health-Related Behaviors', *American Journal of Health Promotion*, 11 (2): 87–98.

Gojer, A., R. Gopalakrishnan and A. Kuruvilla (2018), 'Coping and Spirituality among Caregivers of Patients with Schizophrenia: A Descriptive Study from South India', *International Journal of Culture and Mental Health*, 11 (4): 362–72.

Goldstone, B. (2017), 'A Prayer's Chance: The Scandal of Mental Health in West Africa', available at https://harpers.org/archive/2017/05/a-prayers-chance/ (accessed 13 April 2023).

Golo, B. W. K. (2023), 'Examining Pastor-Prophet Authority in Neo-Pentecostal Deliverance Practices in Ghana', *Journal of Pentecostal and Charismatic Christianity*, 44 (2), 155–75.

Golo, B.-W. K., and F. E. K. Benyah (2025), 'Consented Abuses? Analyzing Perspectives of Christian Young Adults Regarding Human Rights Concerns in Neo-Pentecostal Deliverance Practices in Ghana', *Transformation*, 42 (2): 144–60.

Grant, Paul (2020), *Healing and Power in Ghana: Early Indigenous Expressions of Christianity*, Waco, TX: Baylor University Press.

Gray, A. J. (2017), 'Reflections on the WPA Position Statement on Spirituality and Religion', *Mental Health, Religion & Culture*, 20 (6): 552–7.

Grillo, L. S., A. van Klinken and H. J. Ndzovu (2019), *Religions in Contemporary Africa: An Introduction*, London: Routledge.

Grills, Nathan (2009), 'The Paradox of Multilateral Organizations Engaging with Faith-Based Organizations', *Global governance*, 15 (4): 505–20.

Grimes, R. L. (2000), *Deeply into the Bone: Re-Inventing Rites of Passage*, Berkeley: University of California Press.

Gureje, O., J. Appiah-Poku, T. Bello, et al. (2020), 'Effect of Collaborative Care between Traditional and Faith Healers and Primary Health-Care Workers on Psychosis Outcomes in Nigeria and Ghana (COSIMPO): A Cluster Randomised Controlled Trial', *Lancet* 396 (10251): 612–22.

Gyamfi, N., K. W. Mprah, I. Mensah, C. K. Boye, P. A. Mensah and E. Badu (2022), '"For Me I See MINE to Be a Family Sickness" – Consumers Understanding and Perception of the Etiology of Mental Illness in Community-Based Residential Facilities in Ghana', *Mental Health, Religion & Culture*, 25 (1): 68–84.

Gyekye, K. (1984), 'Akan Concept of a Person', *International Philosophical Quarterly*, reprint in Richard A. Wright (ed.), *African Philosophy: An Introduction*, 277–87, New York: University Press of America.

Gyekye, K. (1987), *An Essay on African Philosophical Thought: The Akan Conceptual Scheme*, Cambridge: Cambridge University Press.

Gyekye, K. (1995), *An Essay on African Philosophical Thought: The Akan Conceptual Scheme, Revised Edition*, Philadelphia, PA: Temple University Press.

Gyekye, K. (1998), 'Person and Community in African Thought', in P. H. Coetzee and A. P. J. Roux (eds), *Philosophy from Africa: A Text with Readings*, 317–36, Johannesburg: International Thompson Publishing.

Gyekye, K. (2013), *Philosophy, Culture and Vision: African Perspectives*, Accra: Sub-Saharan.

Gyimah, L., A. Ofori-Atta, S. Asafo and L. Curry (2023), 'Seeking Healing for a Mental Illness: Understanding the Care Experiences of Service Users at a Prayer Camp in Ghana', *Journal of religion and health*, 62 (3): 1853–71.

Hahn, Robert A. (1996), *Sickness and Healing: An Anthropological Perspective*, New Haven, CT: Yale University Press.

Hammack, P. L. (2008), 'Narrative and the Cultural Psychology of Identity', *Personality and Social Psychology Review*, 12 (3): 222–47.

Hank, K., and B. Schaan (2008), 'Cross-National Variations in the Correlation between Frequency of Prayer and Health among Older Europeans', *Research on Aging*, 30 (1): 36–54.

Hanrieder, Tine (2017a), 'The Public Valuation of Religion in Global Health Governance: Spiritual Health and the Faith Factor', in Uriel Abulof and Markus Kornprobst (eds), *Communication, Legitimation and Morality in Modern Politics*, 81–99, London: Routledge.

Hanrieder, Tine (2017b), 'The Public Valuation of Religion in Global Health Governance: Spiritual Health and the Faith Factor', *Contemporary Politics*, 23 (1): 81–99.

Hatala, A. R., C. Njeze, D. Morton, T. Pearl and K. Bird-Naytowhow (2020), 'Land and Nature as Sources of Health and Resilience among Indigenous Youth in an Urban Canadian Context: A Photovoice Exploration', *BMC Public Health*, 20 (538): 1–14.

Hatala, A. R., and J. B. Waldram (2016), 'The Role of Sensorial Processes in Q'eqchi' Maya Healing: A Case Study of Depression and Bereavement', *Transcultural Psychiatry*, 53 (1): 60–80.

Hatala A. R., J. B. Waldram and T. Caal (2015), Narrative Structures of Maya Mental Disorders, *Culture, Medicine and Psychiatry*, 39 (3): 449–86.

Heaton, M. (2013), *Black Skin, White Coats: Nigerian Psychiatrists, Decolonization, and the Globalization of Psychiatry*, New African Histories Series, Athens, OH: Ohio University Press.

Heaton, M. H. (2020), 'Decolonising, Nationalising, and Globalising the History of Psychiatry: From Colonial to Cross-Cultural Psychiatry in Nigeria', in J. Gaudillière, C. Beaudevin, C. Gradmann, A. Lovell and L. Pordié (eds), *Global Health and the New World Order: Historical and Anthropological Approaches to a Changing Regime of Governance*, 81–102, Manchester: Manchester University Press.

Heaton, M. M. (2018), 'Health and Medicine in Colonial Society', in M. Shanguhyia and T. Falola (eds), *The Palgrave Handbook of African Colonial and Postcolonial History*, 303–18, New York: Palgrave Macmillan.

Heinämaa, Sara (2022),'On the Transcendental and Eidetic Resources of Phenomenology: The Case of Embodiment', in Andrea Smaranda Aldea, David Carr and Sara Heinämaa (eds), *Phenomenology as Critique: Why Methods Matters*, 113–37, New York: Routledge.

Helman, C. (1984), *Culture, Health and Illness*, London: John Wright and Sons.
Heron, J., M. McGuinness, E. R. Blackmore, N. Craddock and I. Jones (2008), 'Early Postpartum Symptoms in Puerperal Psychosis', *BJOG: An International Journal of Obstetrics and Gynaecology*, 115 (3), 348–53.
Heuser, A. (2015), 'Encoding Caesar's Realm – Variants of Spiritual Warfare Politics in Africa', in Lindhardt, Martin (ed.), *Pentecostalism in Africa: Presence and Impact of Pneumatic Christianity in Postcolonial Societies*, 270–90, Leiden: Brill.
Hickling, F. W. (2020), 'Owning Our Madness: Contributions of Jamaican Psychiatry to Decolonizing Global Mental Health', *Transcultural Psychiatry*, 57 (1): 19–31.
Hickling, F. W. (2021), *Decolonization of Psychiatry in Jamaica: Madnificent Irations*, Cham: Palgrave Macmillan.
Hopper, Kim (2004), 'Interrogating the Meaning of "Culture" in the WHO International Studies of Schizophrenia', in Janis H. Jenkins and Robert J. Barrett (eds), *Schizophrenia, Culture and Subjectivity: The Edge of Experience*, 62–86, Cambridge: Cambridge University Press.
Houston, R. A. (2004), 'Clergy and the Care of the Insane in Eighteenth-Century Britain', *Church History*, 73 (1): 114–38.
Hugman, R., E. Pittaway and L. Bartolomei (2011), 'When "Do No Harm" Is Not Enough: The Ethics of Research with Refugees and Other Vulnerable Groups', *British Journal of Social Work*, 41 (7): 1271–87.
Human Rights Watch (2012), 'Like a Death Sentence: Abuses against Persons with Mental Disabilities in Ghana [Internet]', available: https://www.hrw.org/report/2012/10/02/death-sentence/abuses-against-persons-mental-disabilities-ghana (accessed 29 October 2025) .
Idowu, Bolaji, E. (1973), *African Traditional Religion: A Definition*, London: SCM Press.
Idumwonyi, I. M. (2024), *Crashed Realities? Gender Dynamics in Nigerian Pentecostalism*, Leiden: Brill.
Jablensky, A., N. Sartorius, G. Ernberg, M. Anker, A. Korten, J. E. Cooper, R. Dayand A. Bertelsen (1992), 'Schizophrenia: Manifestations, Incidence and Course in Different Cultures. A World Health Organization Ten-Country Study', *Psychological Medicine Monograph Supplement* 20: 1–97.
Jacobson-Widding, A., and D. Westerlund (1989), 'General Introduction', in Anita Jacobson-Widding and David Westerlund (eds.), *Culture, Experience and Pluralism: Essays on African Ideas of Illness and Healing*, 9–12, Uppsala: Acta Universitatis.
Jakob, B., and B. Weyel (eds.) (2020), *Spirituality, Mental Health, and Social Support: A Community Approach*, Berlin: De Gruyter.
Janus, Damian (2019), *Psychopathology and Religion: Structural Convergences between Mental Disorders and Religion*, Lanham, MD: Lexington Books.
Janzen, John M. (1978), *The Quest for Therapy in Lower Zaire*, Berkeley: University of California Press.
Janzen, John M. (1992), 'Ideologies and Institutions in Precolonial Western Equatorial African Therapeutics', in Steve Feierman and Janzen John (eds), *The Social Basis of Health and Healing in Africa*, 195–231, Berkeley: University of California Press.
Kalu, O. (2002), 'Preserving a Worldview: Pentecostalism in the African Maps of the Universe', *Pneuma*, 24 (2): 110–37.
Kalu, O. (2008), *African Pentecostalism: An Introduction*, Oxford: Oxford University Press.
Kao, L., and J. Peteet (2021), 'Spiritually and Culturally Sensitive Evidence-Based Approaches to Taking a Spiritual History', in Alexander Moreira-Almeida, Bruno Paz

Mosqueiro and Dinesh Bhugra (eds), *Spirituality and Mental Health across Cultures*, 325–37, Oxford: Oxford University Press.
Keller, R. (2001), 'Madness and Colonization: Psychiatry in the British and French Empires, 1800–1962', *Journal of Social History*, 35 (2): 295–326.
Kilde, J. H. (2008), *Sacred Power, Sacred Space: An Introduction to Christian Architecture and Worship*, New York: Oxford University Press.
Kilroy-Marac, K. (2019), *An Impossible Inheritance: Postcolonial Psychiatry and the Work of Memory in a West African Clinic*, Berkeley: University of California Press.
Kirkpatrick, L. A. (1992), 'An Attachment-Theory Approach Psychology of Religion', *International Journal for the Psychology of Religion*, 2 (1): 3–28.
Kirmayer, L. (2025), *Healing and the Invention of Metaphor: Toward a Poetics of Illness Experience*, Cambridge: Cambridge University Press.
Kirmayer, L. J. (2004), 'The Cultural Diversity of Healing: Meaning, Metaphor and Mechanism', *British Medical Bulletin*, 69 (1): 33–48.
Kirmayer, L. J. (2007), 'Psychotherapy and the Cultural Concept of the Person', *Transcultural Psychiatry*, 44 (2): 232–57.
Kirmayer, L. J. (2012), 'Cultural Competence and Evidence-Based Practice in Mental Health: Epistemic Communities and the Politics of Pluralism', *Social Science & Medicine*, 75 (2): 249–56.
Kirmayer, L. J., D. Groleau, J. Guzder, C. Blake and E. Jarvis (2003), 'Cultural Consultation: A Model of Mental Health Service for Multicultural Societies', *Canadian Journal of Psychiatry*, 48 (3): 145–53.
Kirmayer, L. J., J. Guzder and C. Rousseau (2013), *Cultural Consultation: Encountering the Other in Mental Health Care*, 2014th edn, New York: Springer Nature.
Kirmayer, L. J., and Leslie Swartz (2013), 'Culture and Global Mental Health', in V. Patel, H. Minas, A. Cohen and M. J. Prince (eds), *Global Mental Health: Principles and Practice*, 41–62, Oxford: Oxford University Press.
Kirmayer, L. J., R. Lemelson and C. A. Cummings (eds) (2015), *Re-visioning Psychiatry: Cultural Phenomenology, Critical Neuroscience, and Global Mental Health*, Cambridge: Cambridge University Press.
Kleinman, A. (1980), *Patients and Healers in the Context of Culture: An Exploration of the Borderland between Anthropology, Medicine, and Psychiatry*, Berkeley: University of California Press.
Kleinman, A. (1988), *The Illness Narratives: Suffering, Healing and the Human Condition*, New York: Basic Books.
Kleinman, A., and B. J. Good (eds) (1986), *Culture and Depression: Studies in the Anthropology and Cross-Cultural Psychiatry of Affect and Disorder*, Berkeley: University of California Press.
Kleinman, A., L. Eisenberg and B. Good (1978), 'Culture, Illness, and Care: Clinical Lessons from Anthropologic and Cross-Cultural Research', *Annals of Internal Medicine*, 88 (2): 251–8.
Koenig, H. G. (2005), *Faith & Mental Health: Religious Resources for Healing*, Philadelphia, PA: Templeton Foundation Press.
Koenig, H. G. (2007), *Spirituality in Patient Care: Why, How, When and What*, Philadelphia, PA: Templeton Foundation Press.
Koenig, H. G. (2018), *Religion and Mental Health: Research and Clinical Applications*, London: Academic Press.
Kohn, R., S. Saxena, I. Levav and B. Saraceno (2004), 'The Treatment Gap in Mental Health Care, *Bulletin of the World health Organization*, 82 (11), 858–66.

Konadu, K. (2007), *Indigenous Medicine and Knowledge in African Society*, London: Routledge.

Konadu, K. (2008), 'Medicine and Anthropology in Twentieth Century Africa: Akan Medicine and Encounters with Medical Anthropology', *African Studies Quarterly*, 10 (2–3): 45–69.

Konadu, K. (2019), *Our Own Way in This Part of the World: Biography of an African Community, Culture and Nation*, Durham, NC: Duke University Press.

Korsah, K. A., and K. A. Domfeh (2020), 'The Realities of Religious Coping Experiences of Patients with Diabetes Mellitus: Implications for Policy Formulation in Ghana', *International Journal of Africa Nursing Sciences* 13. Article ID 100245

Kpanake, L. (2018), 'Cultural Concepts of the Person and Mental Health in Africa', *Transcultural Psychiatry*, 55 (2): 198–218.

Kpobi, L., and L. Swartz (2018a), 'Explanatory Models of Mental Disorders among Traditional and Faith Healers in Ghana', *International Journal of Culture and Mental Health*, 11 (4): 605–15.

Kpobi, L., and L. Swartz (2018b), 'Implications of Healing Power and Positioning for Collaboration between Formal Mental Health Services and Traditional/Alternative Medicine: The Case of Ghana', *Global Health Action*, 11 (1): 1445333.

Kpobi, L., and L. Swartz (2019a), 'Indigenous and Faith Healing for Mental Health in Ghana: An Examination of the Literature on Reported Beliefs, Practices and Use of Alternative Mental Health Care in Ghana', *African Journal of Primary Health Care & Family Medicine*, 11 (1): 1–5.

Kpobi, L., and L. Swartz (2019b), 'Indigenous and Faith Healing in Ghana: A Brief Examination of the Formalising Process and Collaborative Efforts with the Biomedical Health System', *African Journal of Primary Health Care & Family Medicine*, 11 (1): 1–5.

Kpobi, L., U. M. Read, R. K. Selormey and E. Colucci (2024), '"We Are All Working toward One Goal. We Want People to Become Well": A Visual Exploration of What Promotes Successful Collaboration between Community Mental Health Workers and Healers in Ghana', *Transcultural Psychiatry*, 61 (1): 30–46.

Kpobi, L. N. A., and L. Swartz (2018), '"The Threads in His Mind Have Torn": Conceptualization and Treatment of Mental Disorders by Neo-Prophetic Christian Healers in Accra, Ghana', *International Journal of Mental Health System*, 12: 1–12.

Krause, K. (2012), 'Pharmaceutical Potentials: Prayer over Medicines in Pentecostal Healing', *Ghana Studies*, 15 (16): 223–50.

Krause, N. (2015), 'Religious Doubt, Helping Others, and Psychological Well-Being', *Journal of Religion and Health*, 54 (2): 745–58.

Krause, Neal, and Keith M. Wulff (2004), 'Religious Doubt and Health: Exploring the Potential Dark Side of Religion', *Sociology of Religion*, 65 (1): 35–56.

Kucharski, A. J., and P. Piot (2014), 'Containing Ebola Virus Infection in West Africa', *Euro Surveill*, 19 (36): 20899.

Kudadjie, J., and J. Osei (1998), 'Understanding African Cosmology: Its Content and Contribution to Worldview, Community, and the Development of Science', in C. W. Du Toit (ed.), *Faith, Science and African Culture: African Cosmology and Africa's Contribution to Science*, 33–64, Pretoria: Research Institute for Theology and Religion.

Kyei, J. J., A. Dueck, M. J. Indart and N. Y. Nyarko (2014), 'Supernatural Belief Systems, Mental Health and Perceptions of Mental Disorders in Ghana', *International Journal of Culture and Mental Health*, 7 (2): 137–51.

Larbi, Emmanuel K. (2002), 'The Nature of Continuity and Discontinuity of Ghanaian Pentecostal Concept of Salvation in African Cosmology', *Asian Journal of Pentecostal Studies*, 5 (1): 87–106.

Larbi, Emmanuel K. (2015), *Pentecostalism: The Eddies of Ghanaian Christianity*, 2nd edn, Accra: Blessed.

Lartey, E. Y. (1986), 'Healing: Tradition and Pentecostalism in Africa Today', *International Review of Mission*, 75 (297): 75–81.

Laugharne R., and T. Burns (1999), 'Mental Health Services in Kumasi, Ghana', *Psychiatric Bulletin*, 23 (6): 361–3.

LeBeau, D. (2003), *Dealing with Disorder: Traditional and Western Medicine in Katutura, Namibia*, Cologne: Rüdiger Köppe Verlag.

Lee, H.-S., T. Griffith and S. Park (2021), 'Bodily Self-Disturbances in Schizophrenia: A Comparative Study of South Korea and the USA', *Psychopathology*, 54 (5): 262–74.

Leff, J. (1990), 'The "New Cross-Cultural Psychiatry": A Case of the Baby and the Bathwater', *British Journal of Psychiatry*, 156 (3): 305–7.

Lewin, J. (2006), 'Acute and Transient Psychotic Disorders and Puerperal Psychosis', *British Journal of Psychiatry*, 189 (5): 468.

Lewis-Fernandez, R., N. K. Aggarwal, P. C. Lam, H. Galfalvy, M. G. Weiss, L. J. Kirmayer, V. Paralikar, S. N. Deshpande, E. Diaz, A. V. Nicasio, M. Boiler, R. D. Alarcon, H. Rohlof,S. Groen, R. C. J. van Dijk, S. Jadhav, S. Sarmukaddam, D. Ndetei, M. Z. Scalco, … J. M. Vega-Dienstmaier (2017), 'Feasibility, Acceptability and Clinical Utility of the Cultural Formulation Interview: Mixed-Methods Results from the DSM-5 International Field Trial, *British Journal of Psychiatry*, 210 (4): 290–7.

Liamputtong, Pranee (2007), *Researching the Vulnerable*, London: Sage.

Lindlof, T. R., and Bryan C. Taylor (2017), *Qualitative Communication Research Methods*, London: Sage.

Linstrum, E. (2016), *Ruling Minds: Psychology in the British Empire*, Cambridge, MA: Harvard University Press.

Lloyd, C. E. M., J. Cathcart, M. C. Panagopoulos and G. Reid (2024), 'The Experiences of Faith and Church Community among Christian Adults with Mental Illness: A Qualitative Metasynthesis', *Psychology of Religion and Spirituality*, 16 (4): 352–66.

Luhrmann, T. M. (2020), *How God Becomes Real: Kindling the Presence of Invisible Others*, Princeton, NJ: Princeton University Press.

Luhrmann, T. M., R. Padmavati, H. Tharoor and A. Osei (2015), 'Hearing Voices in Different Cultures: A Social Kindling Hypothesis', *Topics in Cognitive Science*, 7 (4), 646–63.

Lynch, E., and D. Medin (2006), 'Explanatory Models of Illness: A Study of Within-Culture Variation', *Cognitive Psychology*, 53 (4): 285–309.

Maercker, A., E. Heim and L. J. Kirmayer (2019), *Cultural Clinical Psychology and PTSD*, 1st edn, Göttingen: Hogrefe.

Marcel M. (1972), *A General Theory of Magic*, trans. Robert Brain, London: Routledge and Kegan Paul.

Mathews, M. (2008), 'Explanatory Models for Mental Illness Endorsed by Christian Clergymen: The Development and Use of an Instrument in Singapore', *Mental Health, Religion & Culture*, 11 (3): 287–300.

Mattingly, C., L. Grøn and L. Meinert (2011), 'Chronic Homework in Emerging Borderlands of Healthcare', *Culture, Medicine, and Psychiatry*, 35: 347–75.

Mayo, K. R. (2016), *Creativity, Spirituality, and Mental Health: Exploring Connections*, London: Routledge.

Mbembé, J., and S. Rendall (2002), 'African Modes of Self-Writing', *Public Culture*, 14 (1): 239–73.
Mbiti, J. S. (1970), *African Religions and Philosophy*, New York: Doubleday.
McCaskie, T. C. (2000), *Asante Identities: History and Modernity in an African Village, 1850–1950*, London: Edinburgh University.
McCutcheon, Russell T. (2001), *Critics Not Caretakers: Redescribing the Public Study of Religion*, Albany, NY: SUNY Press.
McCutcheon, Russell T. (2005), *The Insider/Outsider Problem in the Study of Religion: A Reader*, New York: Continuum.
McGuire, M. B. (1985), 'Religion and Healing', in P. E. Hammond (ed.), *The Sacred in a Secular Age*, 268–84, Berkeley: University of California Press.
McGuire, M. B. (2008), *Lived Religion: Faith and Practice in Everyday Life*, Oxford: Oxford University Press.
McNally, Richard J. (2011), *What Is Mental Illness?*, 1st edn, Cambridge, MA: Belknap Press of Harvard University Press.
McPake, B., K. Hanson and A. Mills (1993), 'Community Financing of Health Care in Africa: An Evaluation of the Bamako Initiative', *Social Science and Medicine*, 36 (11): 1383–95.
Mehta, N., and G. Thornicroft (2013), 'Stigma, Discrimination, and Promoting Human Rights', in V. Patel, H. Minas, A. Cohen and M. J. Prince (eds), *Global Mental Health: Principles and Practice*, 401–24, Oxford: Oxford University Press.
Meincke, M. (2015), *Public Health, Science and the Economy: The Onto-Politics of Traditional Medicine in Namibia*, Doctoral dissertation, University of Helsinki.
Mental Health Authority (2018), *Mental Health Policy 2019–30*, Accra: Ministry of Health.
Merry, S. E. (2006), 'Transnational Human Rights and Local Activism: Mapping the Middle', *American Anthropologist*, 108 (1): 38–51.
Meyer, B. (1998), '"Make a Complete Break with the Past": Memory and Post-Colonial Modernity in Ghanaian Pentecostalist Discourse', *Journal of Religion in Africa*, 28 (3): 316–49.
Meyer, B. (1999), *Translating the Devil: Religion and Modernity among the Ewe in Ghana*, Trenton, NJ: African World Press.
Meyerowitz, Eva L. R. (1951), 'Concepts of the Soul among the Akan of Gold Coast', *Africa*, 21 (1): 24–31.
Mfoafo-M'Carthy, M., and J. D. Grischow (2021), 'Social Exclusion and Marginalization of Mental Illness in Ghana', in P. Liamputtong (ed.), *Handbook of Social Inclusion: Research and Practices in Health and Social Sciences*, 1–15, Cham: Springer International.
Michael, M., N. Chiroma and H. E. Yusuf (2021), 'Health and Integrative Wellness: Mapping Wellness and Its Cultural Psychology in Contemporary Africa', *International Bulletin of Mission Research*, 45 (2): 157–66.
Miller, J. F. (1992), *Coping with Chronic Illness: Overcoming Powerlessness*, 2nd edn, Philadelphia, PA: Davis.
Mills, C. (2014), *Decolonizing Global Mental Health: The Psychiatrization of the Majority World*, London: Routledge.
Mohr, Adam (2009), 'Missionary Medicine and Akan Therapeutics: Illness, Health and Healing in Southern Ghana's Basel Mission, 1828–1918', *Journal of Religion in Africa*, 39 (4): 429–61.
Mohr, Adam (2013), *Enchanted Calvinism: Labor Migration, Afflicting Spirits, and Christian Therapy in the Presbyterian Church of Ghana*, Rochester, NY: University of Rochester Press.

Moltmann, J. (1975), *The Experiment Hope*, trans. M.D. Meeks, Philadelphia, PA: Fortress.
Moreira-Almeida, A., A. Sharma, B. J. Van Rensburg, P. J. Verhagen and C. C. Cook (2016), 'WPA Position Statement on Spirituality and Religion in Psychiatry', *World Psychiatry*, 15 (1): 87–8.
Moreira-Almeida, A., Bruno Paz Mosqueiro and Dinesh Bhugra (eds) (2021), *Spirituality and Mental Health across Cultures*, Oxford: Oxford University Press.
Morley, P. (1978), 'Culture and the Cognitive World of Traditional Medical Beliefs: Some Preliminary Considerations', in Peter Morley and Roy Williams (eds), *Culture and Curing: Anthropological Perspectives on Traditional Medical Beliefs and Practices*, London: Peter Owen.
Mullings, L. (1984), *Therapy, Ideology, and Social Change: Mental Healing in Urban Ghana*, Berkeley: University of California Press.
Munson, R. (1981), 'Why medicine Cannot Be a Science', *Journal of Medicine and Philosophy*, 6 (2): 183–208.
Mustain, M. R., and D. A. Helminiak (2015), 'Understanding Spirituality in Recovery from Addiction: Reintegrating the Psyche to Release the Human Spirit', *Addiction Research & Theory*, 23 (5): 364–71.
Mwaura, P. N. (2014), 'Spirituality and Healing in African Indigenous Cultures and Contemporary Society', in Gillian Mary Bediako, Benhardt Y. Quarshie, J. K. Asamoah-Gyadu (eds), *Seeing New Facets of the Diamond: Christianity as a Universal Faith: Essays in Honour of Kwame Bediako*, 325–35, Akropong: Regnum Africa.
Myers, N., R. Meeker and V. Odeng (2024), 'Pastors as Partners in Care: African Immigrant Pastors' on Mental Health Care Referral Processes for Young Congregants Experiencing Symptoms of Psychosis in the US', *Community Mental Health Journal*, 61: 138–46.
Naeem, F., S. Naz and P. Phiri (2023), 'Culturally Adapted CBT for Psychosis', in *Psychological Interventions for Psychosis*, 125–39, Cham: Springer.
Nager, A., L. M. Johansson and K. Sundquist (2005), 'Are Socio-Demographic Factors and Year of Delivery Associated with Hospital Admission for Postpartum Psychosis? A Study of 500,000 First-Time Mothers, *Acta Psychiatrica Scandinavica*, 112: 47–53.
Nel, Marius (2019), *African Pentecostalism and Eschatological Expectations: He Is Coming Back Again!*, Newcastle: Cambridge Scholars.
Nkrumah, P. K. (1992), *The Interaction between Christianity and Ashanti Religion*, PhD dissertation, Drew University, Madison, New Jersey.
Obeng, Cecilia Sem (2004), *Voices of Affliction: Aspects of Traditional Healing Practices and Their Impact on Akan Families in Ghana*, Cologne: Rudiger Koeppe Verlag.
Ocran, D. S. (2004), *Prophetism in Ghana: A Case Study of Some Charismatic Churches*, MPhil Thesis, University of Ghana, Legon, Accra.
Oduro-Frimpong, J. (2014), 'Sakawa Rituals and Cyberfraud in Ghanaian Popular Video Movies', *African Studies Review*, 57 (2): 131–47.
Oduyoye, Mercy (1986), *Hearing and Knowing*, Maryknoll: Orbis.
Ofori-Atta, A., J. Attafuah, H. Jack, F. Baning and R. Rosenheck (2018), 'Joining Psychiatric Care and Faith Healing in a Prayer Camp in Ghana: Randomised Trial', *British Journal of Psychiatry*, 212 (1): 34–41.
Ofori-Atta, A., U. M. Read and C. A. Lund (2010), 'Situation Analysis of Mental Health Services and Legislation in Ghana: Challenges for Transformation', *African Journal of Psychiatry*, 13 (2): 99–108.
Olsen, William C. (2017), 'Body and Sunsum: Stroke in Asante', in William C. Olsen and Carolyn Sargent (eds), *African Medical Pluralism*, 50–68, Bloomington: Indiana University Press.

Olsen, William C., and Carolyn Sargent (2017), *African Medical Pluralism*, Bloomington: Indiana University Press.

Omenyo, C. N. (2002), *Pentecost Outside Pentecostalism: A Study of the Development of Charismatic Renewal in the Mainline Churches in Ghana*, Uitgeverij: Boekencentrum.

Omenyo, C. N. (2011), 'Man of God Prophesy unto Me: The Prophetic Phenomenon in African Christianity', *Studies in World Christianity*, 17 (1), 30–49.

Omenyo, C. N. (2014), 'African Pentecostalism', in Cecil M. Robeck and Amos Yong (eds), *The Cambridge Companion to Pentecostalism*, 132–51, Cambridge: Cambridge University Press.

Omenyo, C. N., and A. O. Atiemo (2006), 'Claiming Religious Space: The Case of Neo-Prophetism in Ghana', *Ghana Bulletin of Theology*, 1 (1): 55–68.

Onyinah, Opoku (2002), 'Deliverance as a Way of Confronting Witchcraft in Modern Africa: Ghana as a Case History', *Asian Journal of Pentecostal Studies*, 5 (1): 107–34.

Onyinah, Opoku (2012), *Pentecostal Exorcism: Witchcraft and Demonology in Ghana*, Blandford Forum: Deo.

Onyinah, Opoku (2020), 'Spiritual Warfare: The Cosmic Conflict between Good and Evil', in Wolfgang Vondey (ed.), *The Routledge Handbook of Pentecostal Theology*, 321–31, London: Routledge.

Opare-Henaku, A. (2013), *Notions of Spirits as Agents of Mental Illness among the Akan of Ghana: A Cultural-Psychological Exploration*, PhD dissertation, Virginia Commonwealth University, http://scholarscompass.vcu.edu/etd/3302/ (accessed 20 May 2019).

Opare-Henaku, A., and S. O. Utsey (2017), 'Culturally Prescribed Beliefs about Mental Illness among the Akan of Ghana', *Transcultural Psychiatry*, 54 (4), 502–22.

Oppong, S., I. A. Kretchy, E. P. Imbeah and B. A. Afrane (2016), 'Managing Mental Illness in Ghana: The State of Commonly Prescribed Psychotropic Medicines', *International Journal of Mental Health Systems*, 10: 1–10.

Orsi, Robert (1997), 'Everyday Miracles: The Study of Lived Religion', in David D. Hall (ed.), *Lived Religion in America: Toward a History of Practice*, 3–21, Princeton, NJ: Princeton University Press.

Osafo, J. (2012), *Attitudes towards Suicide: Exploring the Cultural Meanings of Suicide in Ghana*, unpublished doctoral dissertation, Norwegian University of Science and Technology, Trondheim, Norway.

Osafo, J., I. Agyapong and M. K. Asamoah (2015), 'Exploring the Nature of Treatment Regimen for Mentally Ill Persons by Neo-Prophetic Ministers in Ghana', *International Journal of Culture and Mental Health*, 8 (3): 325–39.

Osei, Akwasi O., Joseph B. Asare and Mark A. Roberts (2021), *History of Mental Health Care in Ghana*, Accra: Sedco.

Owoahene-Acheampong, S. (1998), *Inculturation and African Religion: Indigenous and Western Approaches to Medical Practice*, New York: Peter Lang.

Park, C. J. (2016), 'Chronic Shame: A Perspective Integrating Religion and Spirituality', *Journal of Religion & Spirituality in Social Work: Social Thought*, 35 (4): 354–76.

Parker, John (2004), 'Witchcraft, Anti-Witchcraft and Trans-Regional Ritual Innovation in Early Colonial Ghana: Sakrabundi and Aberewa, 1889–1910', *Journal of African History*, 45 (3): 393–420.

Parrinder, G. E. (1980), *Sex in the World Religions*, London: Oxford University Press.

Parrinder, Geoffrey (1951), *West African Psychology: A Comparative Study of Psychological and Religious Thought*, London: Lutterworth Press.

Patel, N., E. Bennett, M. Dennis, N. Dosanjh, A. Mahtani, A. Miller and Z. Nadirshaw (2000), *Clinical Psychology, 'Race' and Culture: A Training Manual*, Leicester: BPS Books.

Patel, V. (2011), 'Traditional Healers for Mental Health Care in Africa', *Global Health Action* 4 (1): 7956.

Patel, V., and P. Martin (2010), 'Global Mental Health. A New Global Health Field Comes of Age', *Journal of the American Medical Association*, 303 (19): 1976–7.

Patel, Vikram, Jane Mutambirwa and Sekai Nhiwatiwa (1995), 'Stressed, Depressed, or Bewitched? A Perspective on Mental Health, Culture and Religion', *Development in Practice*, 5 (3): 216–24.

Peprah, P., R. M. Gyasi, P. O.W. Adjei, W. Agyemang-Duah, E. M. Abalo and J. N. A. Kotei (2018), 'Religion and Health: Exploration of Attitudes and Health Perceptions of Faith Healing Users in Urban Ghana', *BMC Public Health*, 18 (1358): 1–12.

Piot, C. (2010), *Nostalgia for the Future: West Africa after the Cold War*, Chicago, IL: University of Chicago Press.

Pobee, John S. (2001), 'Health, Healing and Religion: An African View', *International Review of Mission*, 90 (356–7): 55–64.

Porterfield, Amanda (2005), *Healing in the History of Christianity*, Oxford: Oxford University Press.

Premawardhana, D. (2018), *Faith in Flux: Pentecostalism and Mobility in Rural Mozambique*, Philadelphia: University of Pennsylvania Press.

Pringle, Y. (2019), *Psychiatry and Decolonisation in Uganda*, Basingstoke: Palgrave Macmillan.

Prosén, Martina (2020), 'Abundant Life – Holistic Soteriology as Motivation for Socio-Political Engagement: A Pentecostal and Missional Perspective', in Elias Kifon Bongmba (ed.), *The Routledge Handbook of African Theology*, 361–79, New York: Routledge.

Quarcoopome, T. N. (1987), *West African Traditional Religion*, Ibadan: African Universities Press.

Quayesi-Amakye, J. (2011), 'Localizing the Therapeutic Use of Natural Elements in Jesus' Ministry: The Prophetic Functionality of Nyame Ahyiraso in Pentecostal Prayer Centres in Ghana', *Ogbomoso Journal of Theology*, 16 (3): 2–14.

Quayesi-Amakye, J. (2013), *Christology and Evil in Ghana: Towards a Pentecostal Public Theology*, Amsterdam: Rodopi.

Ratele, K. (2019), *The World Looks Like This from Here: Thoughts on African Psychology*, 1st edn, Johannesburg: Wits University Press.

Rattray, R. S. (1923), *Ashanti*, Oxford: Clarendon press.

Rattray, R. S. (1927), *Religion and Art in Ashanti*, Oxford: Clarendon Press.

Rattray, R. S. (1929), *Ashanti Law and Constitution*, Oxford: Clarendon Press.

Read, U. M. (2016), 'Madness and Miracles: Hoping for Healing in Rural Ghana', in Littlewood Roland and Lynch Rebecca (eds), *Cosmos, Gods and Madmen: Frameworks in the Anthropologies of Medicine*, 45–66, New York: Berghahn Books.

Read, U. M. (2017), '"Doctor Sickness" or "Pastor Sickness"? Contested Domains of Healing Power in the Treatment of Mental Illness in Kintampo, Ghana', in Helene Basu, Roland Littlewood and Arne S. Steinforth (eds), *Spirit & Mind: Mental Health at the Intersection of Religion & Psychiatry*, 167–88, Berlin: Lit Verlag.

Read, U. M. (2019), 'Rights as Relationships: Collaborating with Faith Healers in Community Mental Health in Ghana', *Culture Medicine and Psychiatry*, 43 (4): 613–35.

Read, U. M. (2020), '"Clearing the Streets": Enacting Human Rights in Mental Health Care in Ghana', in J.-P. Gaudilliére, C. Beaudevin, C. Gradmann, A. M. Lovell and L. Pordié (eds), *Global Health and the New World Order: Historical and Anthropological Approaches to a Changing Regime of Governance*, 103–29, Manchester: Manchester University Press.

Read, U. M., and C. Doku Victor (2013), 'Mental Health Research in Ghana: A Literature Review', in A. de-Graft Aikins, S. Agyei-Mensah and C. Agyemang (eds), *Chronic Non-Communicable Diseases in Ghana: Multidisciplinary Perspectives*, 88–108, Accra: Sub-Saharan.

Read, U. M., E. Adiibokah and S. Nyame (2009), 'Local Suffering and the Global Discourse of Mental Health and Human Rights: An Ethnographic Study of Responses to Mental Illness in Rural Ghana', *Globalization and Health* 5 (1): 1–16.

Read, U. M., S. Jilka and S. P. Singh (2023), 'Collaborating with Traditional and Faith Healers in Mental Health: A Public Health Approach', *World Social Psychiatry*, 5 (2): 144–8.

Read, U. M., and S. Nyame (2019), '"It Is Left to Me and My God": Precarity, Responsibility, and Social Change in Family Care for People with Mental Illness in Ghana', *Africa Today*, 65 (3): 3–28.

Reynolds, Rodney J. (2016), 'Spreading the Gospel of the Miracle Cure: Panama's Black Christ', in Roland Littlewood and Rebecca Lynch (eds), *Cosmos, Gods and Madmen: Frameworks in the Anthropologies of Medicine*, 25–44, Oxford: Berghahn Books.

Riandey, B., and M. Quaglia (2009), 'Surveying Hard to Reach Groups', in P. Bonnel, M. Lee-Gosselin, J. Zmud and J-L. Madre (eds), *Transport Survey Methods: Keeping Up with a Changing World*, 127–44, Bingley: Emerald.

Robbins, Joel (2003), 'On the Paradoxes of Global Pentecostalism and the Perils of Continuity Thinking', *Religion*, 33 (3): 221–31.

Roberts, Jonathan (2021), *Sharing the Burden of Sickness: A History of Healing and Medicine in Accra*, Bloomington: Indiana University Press.

Roger, K., and A. Hatala (2017), 'Religion, Spirituality & Chronic Illness: A Scoping Review and Implications for Health Care Practitioners', *Journal of Religion & Spirituality in Social Work: Social Thought*, 37 (1): 24–44.

Rosmarin D., S. Pirutinsky and K. Pargament (2011), 'A Brief Measure of Core Religious Beliefs for Use in Psychiatric Settings', *International Journal of Psychiatry in Medicine*, 41 (3): 253–61.

Rozin, P., L. Millman and C. Nemeroff (1986), 'Operation of the Laws of Sympathetic Magic in Disgust and Other Domains', *Journal of Personality and Social Psychology*, 50 (4): 703–12.

Sadowsky, J. (1999), *Imperial Bedlam: Institutions of Madness in Colonial Southwest Nigeria*, Berkeley: University of California Press.

Sarpong, P. K. (2019), *Aspects of Ghanaian Ethos: A Compendium of Articles, Lectures, and Talks on Various Socio-Cultural and Religious Topics*, Accra: Digibooks.

Sarpong, P. K. (2020), *Peoples Differ: An Approach to Inculturation in Evangelisation*, rev edn, Accra: Sub-Saharan.

Schmidt, B. (2017), *Spirits and Trance in Brazil: An Anthropology of Religious Experience*, London: Bloomsbury.

Schmidt, B. E., and L. Huskinson (eds) (2010), *Spirit Possession and Trance: New Interdisciplinary Perspectives*, vol. 7, London: Bloomsbury.

Schneider, D. M., and K. Gough (eds) (1961), *Matrilineal Kinship*, Berkeley: University of California Press.

Schreurs, A. (2001), *Psychotherapy and Spirituality: Integrating the Spiritual Dimension into Therapeutic Practice*, London: Jessica Kingsley.

Scrutton, A. (2021), 'Mental Illness and Demon Possession: Reading the New Testament', in Blyth Caroline (ed.), *Spirit Possession and Communication in Religious and Cultural Contexts*, 32–56, London: Routledge.

Sefa-Dedeh, A. (2014), 'Religion and Psychotherapy', in Angela Ofori-Atta and Sammy Ohene (eds), *Changing Trends in Mental Health Care and Research in Ghana*, 60–8, Accra: Sub-Saharan Africa.

Selby, H. (2011), 'Prayer Camps and Mental Illness', *Ghanaian Chronicle*, https://allafrica.com/stories/201105110583.html.

Senah, K. A., J. K. Adusei and S. A. Akor (2001), *A Baseline Study into Traditional Medicine Practice in Ghana*, Accra: Ministry of Health, DANIDA Project.

Seymour V. (2016), 'The Human–Nature Relationship and Its Impact on Health: A Critical Review', *Front Public Health*, 4 (260): 1–12.

Smith, Jonathan A. (1996), 'Beyond the Divide between Cognition and Discourse: Using Interpretative Phenomenological Analysis in Health Psychology', *Psychology and Health*, 11 (2): 261–71.

Smith, Jonathan A., and Mike Osborn (2015), 'Interpretative Phenomenological Analysis', in Jonathan A. Smith (ed.), *Qualitative Psychology: A Practical Guide to Research Methods*, 3rd edn, 25–52, London: Sage.

Sommer, Andreas (2021), 'Conflicts and Complexities: Medical Science, Exceptional Experiences, and the Perils of Simplistic History', in Alexander Moreira-Almeida, Bruno P. Mosqueiro and Dinesh Bhugra (eds), *Spirituality and Mental Health across Cultures*, 47–59. Oxford: Oxford University Press.

Stanford, M. S., and K. R. McAlister (2008), 'Perceptions of Serious Mental Illness in the Local Church', *Journal of Religion, Disability & Health*, 12 (2): 144–53.

Stanley, B., M. Stanley, A. Lautin, J. Kane and N. Schwartz (1981), 'Preliminary Findings on Psychiatric Patients as Research Participants: A Population as Risk?', *American Journal of Psychiatry*, 138 (5): 669–71.

Stewart, G. H., L. A. Gadama and V. Kerry (2019), 'Puerperal Psychosis: A Brief Review and Unusual Case Report', *Malawi Medical Journal*, 31 (2): 161–3.

Stewart, Suzanne, Roy Moodley and Ashley Hyatt (eds) (2017), *Indigenous Cultures and Mental Health Counselling: Four Directions for Integration with Counselling Psychology*, New York: Routledge.

Sulemana, I., L. Doabil and E. B. Anarfo (2021), 'Psychological Distress in Ghana: Are Unemployed People More Afflicted?', *Journal of Health Psychology*, 26 (10), 1587–96.

Sullivan, Lawrence E. (1989), 'Introduction: The Quest for Well-Being and the Questioning of Medicine', in Lawrence E. Sullivan (ed.), *Healing and Restoring: Health and Medicine in the World's Religious Tradition*, 1–8, New York: Macmillan.

Sundberg, C. (2020), 'Revealed Medicine as an Expression of an African Christian Lived Spirituality', in K. Lauterbach and M. Vähäkangas (eds), *Faith in African Lived Christianity: Bridging Anthropological and Theological Perspectives*, 335–54. Leiden: Brill.

Tade, O. (2013), 'A Spiritual Dimension to Cybercrime in Nigeria: The "Yahoo Plus" Phenomenon', *Human Affairs*, 23 (4): 689–705.

Taussig, M. T. (1980), 'Reification and the Consciousness of the Patient', *Social Science & Medicine. Part B: Medical Anthropology*, 14 (1): 3–13.

Taylor, Janelle S. (2003), 'The Story Catches You and You Fall down: Tragedy, Ethnography and "Cultural Competence"', *Medical Anthropology Quarterly*, 17 (2): 159–81.

Taylor, L. A. (2019), 'Prevention in Prayer Camps? The Ethics of Government Engagement in Ghana's 2012 Mental Health Legislation', in Kelso Cratsley and Jennifer Radden (eds), *Developments in Neuroethics and Bioethics*, vol. 2, 265–87, London: Academic Press.

Thielman, S. B. (1998), 'Reflections on the Role of Religion in the History of Psychiatry', in H. G. Koenig (ed.), *The Handbook of Religion and Mental Health*, 3–20, San Diego, CA: Academic Press.

Thiessen, J., and B. McAlpine (2013), 'Sacred Space: Function and Mission from a Sociological and Theological Perspective', *International Journal for the Study of the Christian Church*, 13 (2): 133–46.

Thornton, Timothy (2022), *Mental Illness*, Cambridge: Cambridge University Press.

Tooth, G. (1950), *Studies in Mental Illness in the Gold Coast*, London: HMSO.

Turner, V. (1969), *The Ritual Process: Structure and Anti-Structure*, Ithaca, NY: Cornell University Press.

Turner, W. H. (1967), 'A Typology for African Religious Movements', *Journal of Religion in Africa* 1 (1): 1–34.

Twumasi, Patrick A. (2005), *Medical Systems in Ghana: A Study in Medical Sociology*, Accra: Ghana Publishing Corporation.

Udelhoven, B. (2015), *Unseen Worlds: Dealing with Spirits, Witchcraft, and Satanism*, Lusaka: FENZA.

Ukah, A. (2016), 'Building God's City: The Political Economy of Prayer Camps in Nigeria', *International Journal of Urban and Regional Studies* 40 (3): 524–40.

UNESCO (2021), 'Local and Indigenous Knowledge Systems (LINKS)'. Available at https://en.unesco.org/links (accessed 20 February 2023).

Usher, K., and C. Holmes (1997), 'Ethical Aspects of Phenomenological Research with Mentally Ill People', *Nursing Ethics*, 4 (1): 49–56.

Vähäkangas, A. (2012), 'Contextual Pastoral Counselling among Terminally Ill AIDS Patients in Tanzania', *Journal of Pastoral Theology*, 22 (1): 6–14.

Vähäkangas, M. (2015), 'Babu wa Loliondo – Healing the tensions between Tanzanian Worlds', *Journal of Religion in Africa*, 45 (1): 3–36.

van der Watt, A. S. J., G. Nortje, L. Kola, J. Appiah-Poku, C. Othieno, B. Harris, B. D. Oladeji, O. Esan, V. Makanjuola, L. N. Price, S. Seedat and O. Gureje (2017), 'Collaboration between Biomedical and Complementary and Alternative Care Providers: Barriers and Pathways', *Qualitative Health Research*, 27 (14): 2177–88.

Van Dijk, R. A. (1997), 'From Camp to Encompassment: Discourses of Transsubjectivity in the Ghanaian Pentecostal Diaspora', *Journal of Religion in Africa*, 27 (2): 135–59.

Van Dijk, R. A, H. Dilger, M. Burchardt and T. Rasing (2014), *Religion and Aids Treatment in Africa: Saving Souls, Prolonging Lives*, London: Ashgate.

Ventevogel, P. (1996), *Whiteman's Things: Training and Detraining Healers in Ghana*, Amsterdam: Het Spinus.

Verhagen, P. J. (2017a), 'Psychiatry and Religion: Consensus Reached!', *Mental Health, Religion & Culture*, 20 (6): 516–27.

Verhagen, P. J. (2017b), 'Spirituality and Religion in Psychiatry: In Dialogue with the World Psychiatric Association Position Statement', *Mental Health, Religion & Culture*, 20 (6): 513–15.

Walach, Harald (2021), 'Can Spirituality Be a Scientific Topic and How?: A Religious but Open-Minded Scientific Approach of Studies on Religion, Spirituality, and Mental Health', in Alexander Moreira-Almeida, Bruno P. Mosqueiro and Dinesh Bhugra (eds), *Spirituality and Mental Health across Cultures*, 61–77, Oxford: Oxford University Press.

Walker, B. B. (2022), *Religion in Global Health and Development: The Case of Twentieth-Century Ghana*, 1st edn, Montreal: McGill-Queen's University Press.

Wambebe, Charles (ed.) (2018), *African Indigenous Medical Knowledge and Human Health*, London: CRC Press.

Warren, D. M. (1975), 'The Role of Emic Analyses in Medical Anthropology: The Case of the Bono of Ghana', *Anthropological Linguistics* 17 (3): 117–26.

Warren, Dennis, M., G. M. Bova, M. A. Tregoning and M. Kliewer (1982), 'Ghanaian National Policy towards Indigenous Healers: The Case of the Primary Health Training for Indigenous Healers' (PRHETIH) Program', *Social Science and Medicine* 16: 1873–81.

Westerlund, D. (2006), *African Indigenous Religions and Disease Causation: From Spiritual Beings to Living Humans*, Leiden: Brill.

White, G. M., and J. A. Marsella (1982), 'Introduction: Cultural Conceptions in Mental Health Research and Practice', in Anthony J. Marsella and Geoffrey M. White (eds), *Cultural Conceptions of Mental Health and Therapy*, 3–38. Dordrecht: D. Reidel.

Whitty, M. T. (2018), '419-It's Just a Game: Pathways to Cyber-Fraud Criminality Emanating from West Africa', *International Journal of Cyber Criminology*, 12 (1): 97–114.

WHO (2002), *Traditional Medicine Strategy 2002–2005*, Geneva: WHO Press.

WHO (2006), *The World Health Report 2006: Working Together for Health*, Geneva: WHO Press.

WHO (2007a), 'Ghana Country Summary', in *Mental Health Improvement for Nations Development (MIND)*, Geneva: Department of Mental Health and Substance Abuse.

WHO (2007b), *Taking Stock: Task Shifting to Tackle Health Worker Shortages*, Geneva: WHO Press.

WHO (2022), *Mental Health Atlas 2020*, Ghana: Country Profile.

Whyte, S. R. (2018), 'Health', in Gaurav Desai and Adeline Masquelier (eds), *Critical Terms for the Study of Africa*, 164–78. Chicago: Chicago University Press.

Wiebe, Donald (1999), *The Politics of Religious Studies: The Continuing Conflict with Theology in the Academy*, New York: St. Martin's Place.

Wiredu, K. (1992), 'The African Concept of Personhood', in Harley E. Flack and Edmund D. Pellegrino (eds), *African-American Perspectives on Biomedical Ethics*, Washington, DC: Georgetown University Press.

Wood, L., P. Hooper, S. Forster and F. Bull (2017), 'Public Green Spaces and Positive Mental Health – Investigating the Relationship between Access, Quantity and Types of Parks and Mental Wellbeing', *Health Place*, 48: 63–71.

World Health Organization (2005), *Preventing Chronic Diseases: A Vital Investment*, Geneva: World Health Organization.

Wyllie, R. W. (1983), 'Ghanaian Spiritual and Traditional Healers' Explanations of Illness: A Preliminary Survey', *Journal of Religion in Africa*, 14 (1): 46–57.

Yaro, P. B., E. Asampong, P. T. N. Tabong, S. A. Anaba, S. S. Azuure, A. Y. Dokurugu and F. A. Nantogmah (2020), 'Stakeholders' Perspectives about the Impact of Training and Sensitization of Traditional and Spiritual Healers on Mental Health and Illness: A Qualitative Evaluation in Ghana', *International Journal of Social Psychiatry*, 66 (5): 476–84.

Yates, Rob (2009), 'Universal Health Care and the Removal of User Fees', *Lancet*, 373: 2078–81.

Yendork, J. S., G. B. Brew, E. A. Sarfo and L. Kpobi (2019), 'Mental Illness Has Multiple Causes: Beliefs on Causes of Mental Illness by Congregants of Selected Neo-Prophetic Churches in Ghana', *Mental Health, Religion & Culture*, 21 (7): 647–66.

Yendork, J. S., L. Kpobi and Elizabeth A. Sarfo (2017), '"It's Only Madness That I Know": An Analysis of How Mental Illness Is Conceptualized by Congregants of Selected Charismatic Churches in Ghana', *Mental Health, Religion & Culture*, 19 (9): 984–99.

Yong, A. (2011), *The Spirit of Creation: Modern Science and Divine Action in the Pentecostal-Charismatic Imagination*, Grand Rapids, MI: Eerdmans.

Young, A. (1976), 'Internalizing and Externalizing Medical Belief Systems: An Ethiopian Example', *Social Science and Medicine*, 10 (3–4): 147–56.

Zhang, Y., C. Liu, Y. Zhao, X. Zhang, B. Li and R. Cui (2015), 'The Effects of Calorie Restriction in Depression and Potential Mechanisms', *Current Neuropharmacology*, 13 (4): 536–42.

INDEX

www.ingramcontent.com/pod-product-compliance
Ingram Content Group UK Ltd.
Pitfield, Milton Keynes, MK11 3LW, UK
UKHW020808290926
15470UKWH00003B/1029

9 781350 463479